FREE PRESS vs. FAIR TRIALS

Examining Publicity's Role
in Trial Outcomes

LEA's COMMUNICATION SERIES
Jennings Bryant / Dolf Zillmann, General Editors

Selected Titles in the Communication Series include:

Dennis/Wartella • *American Communication Research: The Remembered History*

Ellis • *Crafting Society: Ethnicity, Class, and Communication Theory*

Reese/Gandy/Grant • *Framing Public Life: Perspectives on Media and Our Understanding of the Social World*

Riffe/Lacy/Fico • *Analyzing Media Messages: Using Quantitative Content Analysis in Research*

Salwen/Stacks • *An Integrated Approach to Communication Theory and Research*

For a complete list of titles in LEA's Communication Series,
please contact Lawrence Erlbaum Associates, Publishers,
at www.erlbaum.com

FREE PRESS vs. FAIR TRIALS

Examining Publicity's Role
in Trial Outcomes

Jon Bruschke
California State University, Fullerton

William E. Loges
Oregon State University

LAWRENCE ERLBAUM ASSOCIATES, PUBLISHERS

2004   Mahwah, New Jersey   London

Lawrence Erlbaum Associates, Inc., Publishers
10 Industrial Avenue
Mahwah, NJ 07430

Cover design by Sean Trane Sciarrone

Library of Congress Cataloging-in-Publication Data

Bruschke, Jon.
Free press vs. fair trials : examining publicity's role in trial outcomes / Jon Bruschke, William E. Loges.
   p. cm.
   Includes bibliographical references and index.
ISBN 0-8058-4325-6 (cloth : alk. paper)
1. Free press and fair trial—United States.   I. Title: Free press versus fair trials.   II. Loges, William E.   III. Title.
KF9223.5.B78   2003
345.73'07—dc21   2003046231
                                                        CIP

Books published by Lawrence Erlbaum Associates are printed on acid-free paper, and their bindings are chosen for strength and durability.

Printed in the United States of America
10 9 8 7 6 5 4 3 2 1

Contents

Foreword   vii

Preface   xi

1   Introduction   1

The Basic Issues   3

Current Legal Doctrine   5

Social Science   7

Theoretical Orientation   12

Conclusion   16

2   What We Think We Know   19

Laboratory Studies That Did Not Include Trial Evidence   29

Studies That Included Trial Evidence and Found a Pretrial
Publicity Effect   32

Laboratory Studies That Partially Support the Existence
of a Pretrial Publicity Effect   47

Laboratory Studies That Did Not Find a Pretrial Publicity
Effect   58

Putting It All Together: Issues Raised and Answered
in These Studies   65

3   Field Research   76

Literature Review   76

New Research   77

The State of Knowledge After Considering Field Research   88

Forging an Appropriate Remedy   92

4   Pretrial Publicity and Media Theory: "General" Publicity   99
        Revisited
        Media Theory: The Invisible Elephant   99
        In Search of a Cultivation Effect   113
        Conclusion: Pretrial Publicity in the Wake of Media
            Theory   132

5   Conclusions   134
        In Summary: What Do We Know Now?   134
        Adding Theory: What Does it All Mean?   138
        Psychological Theories   139
        Economic-Legal Theory   143
        Looking Forward: What Do We Still Need to Know?   150

        Appendix: Detailed Discussion of City-Level Data   157

        References   165

        Author Index   175

        Subject Index   181

Foreword

It seemed that everything had gone off without a glitch. We had very quietly taken our client through the basement of the Brooklyn Federal Court House. The FBI had very kindly and professionally led us through a puzzle of corridors until we finally entered the court room through a side door.

Within ten minutes we had pled not guilty, the case was provisionally dismissed, and my client had given autographs to Court personnel. The Courtroom was, by design, otherwise empty. The Federal Prosecutor had cooperated fully in maintaining the privacy of the hearing.

As our team, made up of my client, his wife, his public relations expert, and myself began to climb into two cars to take us quickly to LaGuardia Airport, we were convinced we had pulled it off—in and out of court with no publicity circus erupting. But as I placed my client and his wife in his vehicle, I was approached by a "trailer" from a local weekly Brooklyn paper. Not even a real reporter, this young lady was just hanging around the Courthouse checking for any filings that might lead to a story. She recognized my client at the curb outside and ran to us to ask questions. I closed the rear door of my client's car, signaled the driver to take off, and double clutched the "trailer" with the fact nothing was happening. Renowned publicity specialist Mike Nason and I then ducked into the next car and we were off to the airport still confident of our coup.

The drive, mid-day with professional drivers, from the Brooklyn Federal Court House to La Guardia is not more than fifteen minutes. As we pulled into the unloading zone at our terminal, Mike called back to my client's headquarters in Orange County, otherwise known as the Crystal Cathedral. The news trucks for ABC, NBC, and CBS were already pulling into the parking lot. Larry King had called to see if he could do an interview that evening. In fifteen minutes the world news was aware of everything that had happened in the Courtroom. On the flight home, the pilot came out and greeted myself and my client, Dr. Robert Schuller. He wanted us to know that a media juggernaut had already formed at our gate at LAX.

News now moves at the speed of the NET. If you are unprepared you are at its mercy.

In Dr. Schuller's case he had been wrongfully accused of attacking a United flight attendant. Because of his status, any news surrounding the event (even the good news of a dismissal) cost the ministry millions of dollars in donations. Part of my job was to get the dismissal (the easy part), and the rest was to avoid any publicity (the impossible part).

Publicity is a multi-edged word which, of course, can impact a trial. But it can also grind the subject into fine powder, destroying reputations, relationships, and careers as it rolls over everything in its path.

Just two months before the Schuller case, Mike Nason and I witnessed first hand the effects of publicity on ordinary lives. President Clinton had just been rumored to have had an affair with an intern named Monica Lewinsky. One week into the story a Portland man by the name of Andy Bleiler was identified by the New York Post to have had an earlier affair with Monica. Mike called for help from Portland where he had arrived at the bequest of Andy's wife, Kathy. I flew in to Portland and arrived at their home as it was just turning dark. It was a scene out of a Francis Ford Coppola war film.

I never knew there were so many television station crews (23 of them), and they were all camped on the lawn and street in front of the Bleiler's 1,500 square foot home. Light stands had been erected, bathing the house in white light. As I fought my way into the house, it was full of people (neighbors offering support) and crying children. The adults were nailing blankets over the windows to block out the blinding lights and staring eyes of the camera lenses pushed against the window panes. Andy couldn't get out of the house to go to work, the children couldn't go to school, and the world—literally—was watching.

It turns out Ms. Lewinsky had sent souvenirs of her time at the White House to the Bleilers and they had had many conversations. In three days the Bleilers would be interviewed by Ken Starr's top two investigators. All evidence in their possession was delivered as well. In the mean time Mike and I hosted the world press in Portland. Finally, we got the press conference organized and off the Bleiler lawn, but I will never forget the feeling of knowing that everything you said would flash live around the world. When I checked into my hotel room thirty minutes later, my message light was flashing. I was shocked when the voice message machine announced that I had sixty-five messages. They were from Diane Sawyer, Maria Shriver, Geraldo Rivera and Wolf Blitzer, just to name a few. I had represented Angelo Buono (the Hillside Strangler) and William Bonin (The Freeway Killer), but never had I seen publicity like that which had descended on Portland.

The point is that the publicity game has shifted into warp speed and it would be absolute incompetence for an attorney to not be as prepared for handling his client's case in the courtroom of public opinion as he or she would at trial. There is no choice. Answering "no comment" just won't get it done any longer. If your client is public fodder you have to get aboard, or the train will leave without you. The speed of cascading events can easily overwhelm even the most prepared and talented.

As a result, the work of Drs. Bruschke and Loges is both timely and relevant. In this new era of flashpoint media it is key to recognize that which is impacting your case and how it is being influenced. Information is power. Most lawyers do not take the time or energy to understand the significance of the data before them. For those who do, the press can be a cleaver cutting into the morals and psychological base of the opponent.

I represented Jerry Tarkanian, then coach of the University of Nevada Las Vegas (UNLV), against the National Collegiate Athletic Association (NCAA) for fraud. At the time the NCAA was the 800 lb. gorilla. They had never lost a case and employed the nation's best lawyers. In Las Vegas, Coach Tarkanian was king and the NCAA knew it. They wanted to try the case anywhere else and we kept the publicity fires burning in the real city that does not sleep. The NCAA's abuses of Coach Tarkanian's program were outrageous and I was determined to let our jury pool (the citizens of Las Vegas) know about it.

In reality, as Drs. Bruschke and Loges brilliantly map out, the pretrial publicity would not have been that harmful to our opponents. Coach Tarkanian was only the king with basketball fans and he had many critics and detractors. But it didn't matter, the publicity caused the NCAA to become more and more convinced that they would get "slaughtered on the strip." When all their motions to change venue failed, they melted. They asked for Federal Mediations and made an offer Coach and his wife, Lois, couldn't refuse.

Make no mistake about it, publicity is a game. To master it one must understand the beast. But it continues to evolve and morph at lightening speed. To keep up is unbelievably difficult, but to voluntarily remain behind the curve is professionally suicidal.

In quantum physics we are learning that our physical universe is not what it seems. In fact, it is physically made up of very non-physical elements. Drs. Bruschke and Loges introduce a form of "quantum civics,"[1] wherein the damage which we initially perceive from pre-trial publicity is more sham than substance. Their conditions, which must be met before publicity damage is inflicted, are brilliant in their clarity and simplicity. More importantly, they are almost always ignored or overlooked.

This important work also touches on key aspects of legal reform. Proper training of trial lawyers is obvious but needs to be repeated on a regular basis. However, we hear much less about the need to improve jury instructions. In this area, Drs. Bruschke and Loges's advice is a bull's eye as we struggle to modernize a sometimes archaic system.

To understand anything we must first cease to be afraid of it. Then, when reanalyzed with the intent to embrace and understand, we begin to see the wheels of publicity for what they really are. We can begin to discern the damaging from the helpful. We can begin to recognize the tools which can counter the negative. We can begin to see a friend and not an enemy.

With this important body of work by Dr. Bruschke and Dr. Loges, the journey can begin for many who would otherwise continue to be caught whirling and confused in the spin cycle of our modern day media machine.

—*Terry Giles*

---

[1]A term coined by Richard Cheshire in the book titled *Leading By Heart*.

Preface

What qualifies a person to be a juror? We discussed this once over lunch. Jon suggested that a juror should be rational, impartial, intelligent, and capable of suspending judgment until all testimony and argument is presented at trial. Bill suggested that a juror should be of legal age, not insane, not personally related to the victim or defendant, and not obviously biased for or against the defendant.

It could be that an ideal juror is a combination of all those traits, but in fact few people could meet all of those qualifications. In fact, shortly after we ate lunch, actress Winona Ryder was convicted by a jury that included her former employer, studio chief Jon Peters. Far be it from us to claim that Mr. Peters was not an ideal juror. It could be that our wished-for careers as rock-and-roll stars might depend on the good judgment of people just like him. But would you, dear reader, want to be held in judgment for a criminal offense by your ex-boss?

The point of this book is that many things can cross a person's mind in the jury room, but that the odds of information provided solely from the mass media making the difference in a single juror's decision of guilt or innocence are very small. We also noted an irony in the very nomenclature of what is often called the free press versus fair trail debate: The adjectives describing each component give the false sense that the only important concern is for the press to be free and the trials to be fair. A free press is an unarguably laudable goal, but a major problem with the press is that it is not often fair. Fair trails are the cornerstone of justice, but if they are expensive rather than free they are available only to the wealthy. Switching the adjectives offered the dual benefits of providing valuable new insights into the processes involved and also giving us a title for the book. Thus, a productive way to address the free press and fair trial issue is to think of ways to make the press fair and the trials free as the logical counterpart of keeping the press free and the trials fair.

We found ourselves in agreement on these points, but we realized at lunch that we had strikingly different perspectives on the data and arguments presented here. Jon concluded that a juror needed the qualities of a good debater. Bill decided that a juror needed the qualities of a sober craps player. Somewhere between us lies American justice. We'll present our slightly differing vantage points at the outset and let you decide exactly where between them the ideal system resides.

Introductory Comments by Bill Loges

If you spend enough time lazing around on your sofa with a remote control, you'll learn a lot about crime, especially if you get such cable channels as Court TV, A&E, or The Discovery Channel. You'll see fantastic forensics, persistent policemen, determined district attorneys, and an infallible justice system. I have yet to see a regularly scheduled series based on The Innocence Project, through which Peter Neufeld, Barry Scheck, and their colleagues have freed more than 100 wrongly imprisoned Americans. Then there's the efforts of Professor David Protess at Northwestern University, whose students helped him free more than a dozen prisoners from Illinois' death row after revealing innumerable flaws in the state's justice system, from investigation to arrest to prosecution to sentencing. Eventually, their efforts led Governor George Ryan of Illinois to commute the sentences of every inmate on Illinois' death row—over 150 inmates—to life sentences without parole on the basis of flaws in the system that convicted and sentenced these prisoners.

Why wouldn't a series based on the documented flaws in the American justice system succeed? In his book *Demographic Vistas*, David Marc observes that television cop shows virtually always favor the cops. He suggests that it would be intolerable to TV viewers for the bad guys to win week after week, unlike in the genre of gangster films (from the 1930s version of *Scarface* to *The Godfather* films) in which one can root for the gangster safe in the knowledge that the story will end—often at the expense of the criminal. Even though the TV cop show has evolved, such that *NYPD Blue*'s Andy Sipowicz is an open criminal and *The Shield*'s Vic Mackey is a borderline psychotic, Marc's argument is best supported by true crime shows.

In a way, shows such as *Forensic Files* and *American Justice* might prepare viewers to be the kind of juror Jon longs for. Steady viewers of these shows might become savvy about scientific methods for criminal investigation, hip to criminal procedure and defense tactics, and not easily fooled by weak prosecutions. But to me, these shows are a relentless lesson in the wisdom and trustworthiness of the law enforcement and judicial systems. In these programs, cops, prosecutors, and forensic scientists fail only temporarily and the outcome is never in doubt. The crime is solved—in the sense that a perp is arrested and convicted. Defense attorneys are sometimes consulted, but they rarely actually rebut the premise that the procedure that led to their clients' conviction and sentence is sound.

At the risk of giving away the ending, I'll reveal here that this book argues that defendants in criminal trials enter a system that is so fundamentally skewed against them that the added influence of pretrial publicity is negligible in all but a few exceptional cases. It is likely that the sort of bias evident in the evening news and in true crime shows is a reproduction of the situation confronting defendants, not a unique element that adds new bias.

I believe that the presumption of innocence in our legal tradition represents our collective awareness of our bias against defendants. In other words, the presumption of innocence is not an attribute of the defendant. It only exists if the other parties involved in the prosecution recognize it. The defendant's height and weight don't depend on the attitude of the jury, but the defendant's presumption of innocence does. We put this presumption in our legal code to remind ourselves, as jurors and even as victims, that we must withhold judgment until evidence is presented because we are tempted to indulge a bias against people accused of crimes. We know ourselves too well.

In dramatic presentations, including (perhaps especially including) presentations based on actual events, presumptions of innocence are often inconvenient. They make foreshadowing, through ominous music and incriminating wardrobes, difficult. Often, drama works best when we know who the villain is. In some crime drama the pleasure comes from a surprise villain, but that twist is more rare than one might think. The drama works by appealing to our bias against the accused, and by taking our side. But such constant pandering to our biases may have made it more difficult for us to remember the presumption of innocence when we join juries. Just as advertising panders to our weakness for fatty foods and has contributed to the creation of a population of alarmingly overweight Americans, the consistent message of crime drama may contribute to the creation of a population of jurors who place more faith in the performance of police, prosecutors, and criminalists than they deserve. This is part of the cultivation theory we review in this book.

The introduction of DVDs was accompanied by the realization that the medium that delivered Hollywood movies could accommodate much more information than just the movie itself. It thus became common to add commentary by directors, actors, and others involved with the making of the film to DVD releases. I believe a similar second audio track might be advisable in TV shows about crime. Let the program's producers deliver the show they want, but let the principal characters comment on that show. Defendants, defense attorneys, defense witnesses (including expert witnesses), and the defendant's family could comment on the presentation of the producers—almost like a defendant can respond to the prosecutor's case at trial!

Or maybe that wouldn't work. If I had some special talent for designing TV shows that people wanted to watch, I'd probably be doing that for a living instead of writing this sort of thing.

I want to acknowledge with gratitude the help of all the graduate assistants at Baylor University and California State University, Fullerton who helped Jon and me gather and process the data we report in this book. Linda Bathgate at Erlbaum has been extremely patient with us too, and very encouraging when that was necessary. Mostly I think it's important here for me to acknowledge how much this book is Jon's brainchild, and it has been a treat to be able to take part in its construction (usually by writing the bad bits). Finally, I want to acknowledge Mary's Garage Band as the best possible diversion from meeting a publisher's deadline.

Introductory Comments by Jon Bruschke

One of the great but largely unknown literary theories of our new century has been proposed by my wife, and it holds that the most interesting part of any book is almost unvaryingly the preface. The more popular, pedestrian, and prurient theory, practiced more than articulated by an army of undergraduates, is that the best way to read a book is to scan the introduction and conclusion. For reasons noble and academic (and not the *least* political), I like my wife's theory better. Since I've taken up the practice of reading the preface carefully I've discovered that a host of incredibly telling information can be gleaned by the intrepid reader willing to commit the extra 10 minutes to the task. Mostly, it's possible to tell whether the writer is unbelievably pompous (trying to locate their new book against, say, the works of Aristotle), interpersonally insecure (they feel a compelling need to thank every person in their date book for fear of offending even one), or utterly unable to write in a digestible way even when given the license to compose with a little more flair. Pretty much, you can be sure that if you have to read the paragraphs in the preface two or three times to figure out what the author is trying to say it's a good bet you'll default to the Undergraduate Literary Theory and find yourself plausibly considering the Lifetime Movie Network horror flick as a better use of your time. Occasionally, the preface will be a dead giveaway that you're going to love the book; I forget the title and author, but the most lucid instance of this phenomenon I can recall was one where the author ended the preface by dedicating the book to her dog. I will not dedicate this book to my cat, but only because (a) I dedicate a serious chunk of my discretionary income to her already, and (b) she is actively frustrating the completion of this work, swatting at my fingers even as I type this sentence. For some reason, she hates the sight of human digits typing. What I will do is utilize these preface pages for observations I take to be totally random, or at least without predictable pattern.

My first aside, and I offer it with considerable despondency, is that probably nobody will read this book for fun. I will repress the nearly overpowering academic urge to lecture about how exciting data analysis can be. There is a sentence to that effect somewhere in nearly every introductory statistics textbook, and those sentences are cause for undergraduate laughter upon first glance and serious hatred not long after when it is discovered that skimming the conclusion chapter of the book will garner virtually no useful information at all. I harbor no illusions that people will pick this book up for a good read; I actually count my hours spent with SPSS as "quality time" and yet still find it difficult to wade through the methodological homilies that others write. The introductory textbooks don't quite lie; statistical analysis *is* fun if you are doing it, but it is rarely fun to read. Similarly, neither has the "literature review" caught on in the same way as, say, the "detective novel" as a formula for mass appeal. I can't make the reading of this book entirely fun, but I can sneak the occasional joke past our editor. Given that the audience for these pages is likely to be of the sober and serious variety, I've tried to make the writing lively enough that the hearty soul stolid enough to work through the pages of review and analysis will find the occasional well-written sentence to make the road to the conclusion a little more scenic.

Secondly, I'd like to address some of the typical barriers those in our audience are likely to face when reading our work. Those who have read our work who are lawyers often have a difficult time believing that most crimes aren't covered by the media at all, that most people don't see or can't remember even front-page stories, and that there is almost no pro-defendant coverage. Media scholars will take these conclusions as commonplace. Our media friends will believe we have flipped a lid when we mention that getting trial transcripts is nigh-on impossible, that there is no easy-to-find summary of trials, and they gasp at the horrifyingly high prices that are charged for trial transcripts ($1 a page if you're lucky, and these things run into the thousands of pages). Our legal system creates "public documents" in a way that is designed for those litigating the cases to have reasonable access to, and is especially not designed for nosy scholars to photocopy economically. It is also a little difficult to convince media folk how widely court rules can vary across jurisdictions. It is nearly impossible to convince media people that legal cases almost never go to trial and are plea-bargained the vast, vast majority of the time or that a judge can, by and large, conduct a jury selection however they damn well please. We'll start by asking, right here in the preface, for the indulgence (in some cases, the willful suspension of disbelief) of our varied audiences. If we make a factual claim that strikes you as having virtually no chance of actually being true, we'll ask you to at least look up our footnotes before you dismiss us out of hand.

The final point to make here has to do with habits of thinking. Lawyers think and act in case law linguistics and take it as self-evident that what really matters is the case law behind a given question. This seems extraordinarily wrong to those trained in empirical methods of inquiry. If Galileo's inquisition offered us nothing beyond a really good Indigo Girls song it taught us that there's an empirical reality which has a beautifully stubborn way of resisting, and ultimately refuting, whatever set of legal strictures exist at a given time.

Thus, what seems to legal practitioners as self-evident truth—that the way to handle a difficult legal question is to sort carefully through the case law—seems to other thinkers as being the problem in the first place. Similarly, lawyers rightly point out that social science has a lazy habit of basing its conclusions on the combined experience of a small battalion of sophomores majoring in Psychology, which often is little more than a collection of strong opinions about MTV programming and a working knowledge about which states sell beer to 18-year-olds. The methods of social science often seem so different from actual legal practice that they are completely irrelevant to it, and the methods that would be most ecologically valid would be so intrusive and time-intensive that researchers would perish in both tenure and actual terms before the studies could be finished.

There is an arrogance on both sides, stemming no doubt from the cognitive dissonance generated by having accumulated massive student loan debt while pursuing advanced degrees (as well as normal human pride), that often results in each side deciding that its approach alone is the right one. We plead for open mindedness. There is more than one way to answer any question, and opinions from all sides can shed new light on an issue. Those in the legal community who conclude that all that is necessary is to determine whether, based on case law and abstract legal thinking, a constitutional right exists or not miss many larger issues about resource allocation and juror decision-making. In short, if case law leads to the conclusion that jurors will not be biased by pretrial publicity, but empirical observation proves that jurors are, elegant reasoning will not be enough to stop the legal conclusion from being judged rather poorly by history. If, on the other hand, case law points to the conclusion that a constitutional right does exist but empirical observation shows that jurors are quite capable of ignoring or simply forgetting pretrial information, we could easily have a system pouring resources into expensive remedies for a problem that doesn't exist while neglecting the important legal work that does need to be done. (The most important function of a preface is to suggest other good books out there; anyone who doubts that there are plenty of important areas of jurisprudence that are badly under-funded should immediately stop reading this book and buy *No Matter How Loud I Shout* by Edward Humes for a frightening glimpse into the administration of juvenile justice.) Scholars who are sure that research alone would lead to better practice do well to reflect on how nice it is to spend your summer thinking about writing projects and vacations rather than 6-month backlogs of cases, recall the study of Phrenology, and remember how many lives were ruined by the academic belief in the racial neutrality of IQ scores. No part of this diatribe is meant to equate any current work with the worst abuses of the past (some lawyers have even been known to take Galileo's side in the historical dispute), but these lessons should remind us all that knowledge is ephemeral enough that it is difficult to see, navigate, and triangulate when viewed from many angles, much less a single one. If you are sporting enough to be reading a book outside of your field, you are probably already the sort of noble and good-looking scholar who doesn't discount the ideas that are foreign to their mind and training. Don't blow it now.

The best part of the preface is the thank-you part. I'd like to thank Sylvia, who brings me pieces of paper to sign without reading, because of her beautiful heart and despite her beautiful dogs. Thanks go to Jeanine, for letting me know when I've gone too far and always letting me know when an afternoon ice cream break is in order. To Cameron, Toni, and Josh I owe a debt of thanks for their hard work coding and their patience awaiting payment. Josh Gregory has a serviceable outside jump shot and did most of the legwork for chapter 3. I dedicate the Appendix to Josh Clark, who no longer has an appendix of his own, but handled the operation very well. I'm going to thank Laura Heider, even though she got a book published before I did, even though her picture on her book makes her look like a model and the sight of Bill and I will undoubtedly convince our publisher to use clip art on the back cover, and even though I already gave her a husband. It may be that no one is more responsible for this book being written than Occie Evans, my high school football coach who made it clear that my future lay in academics and not athletics. Edna Rogers is the best dissertation advisor ever, one of the most life-changing people I've met, and someone patient enough to let me research all this legal stuff even though she was herself a Home Economics undergraduate major and an Interpersonal Communication scholar specializing in marriages. Above all, she is the only professor in the history of the University of Utah to ever flip her eyelids inside-out during a PhD seminar. I would like to thank the 1969 Mets for proving that anything is possible, no matter how far behind you get, a lesson of special importance to the completion of this book. Linda is an editor of unparalleled humor and perspective, and is imbued with a wisdom rare and uncanny enough to know that most good ideas are hatched while watching baseball games. I consider myself truly fortunate to work with her. Milo and his grandparents, the model matriarch Nancy and the trudungent Wilfred, have provided welcomed inspiration. Finally and ultimately, I'd like to thank Fred (that under-appreciated progenitor of literary theory), who does an excellent job of not letting my own arrogance run away with me, who reminds me by example that I'm not really that smart after all, and who gives more meaning to my life than any other person, activity, or cat. To her, I owe everything.

I'd like to close by insisting that, the preceding pages notwithstanding, this is a serious academic work. Fortunately, the quantitative methods aren't too specialized and if you can read a table with percentages in it you are more than halfway there. This simplicity will strike some, no doubt, as a limitation. I prefer to think of it as taking on a fairly straightforward question with a fairly straightforward method. At any rate, the questions are important ones, and we hope to address them in a meaningful way. A point we will beat to death later is that the question is best handled from a multitude of perspectives, and we hope we have something in here for everyone.

CHAPTER ONE

Introduction

> The media circus that appears at so many trials these days needs a ringmaster to balance the rights of the media and the accused. It does not need more clowns. (Walton, 1998, p. 588)

There are many aspects to pretrial publicity that make it fun to think about, not the least of which is the maze of overlapping attentions and interwoven interests that it seems to conjure. Lawyers decry pretrial publicity while simultaneously raising their own career stock (and hourly fee) by accumulating more if it. As much as they complain, lawyers sometimes have an interest in cultivating publicity (Imrich, Mullin, & Linz, 1995; Shapiro, 1994). The media both perpetrate and comment on the frenzy—newspapers and television stations generate the publicity in the first place and then actively comment on the likely effect that the coverage will have on the trial. Litigants endure more and more egregious privacy intrusions and indignities and then cash royalty checks from what are increasingly lucrative book contracts that tell their story. Many litigants have, ironically enough, taken the route of appearing on televised talk shows to lament media interest in their legal cases. The landscape is bizarre indeed.

But at least it is not new. Concerns that pretrial publicity might interfere with the verdicts of judicial proceedings extend back to the earliest days of this country. In Aaron Burr's 1807 treason trial the Federalist *Gazette and Daily Advertiser* staunchly and voluminously supported the defense, while the Jeffersonian *National Intelligencer* defended the prosecution with equal vigor. When in 1850 dismembered parts of George Parkman showed up in the laboratory of Harvard professor John W. Webster the "penny papers" gave elaborate coverage which "probably set the record for the period" (Lofton, 1966). In 1801 Fisher Ames was openly decrying the "sort of rivalship among printers, who shall have the most wonders, and the strangest and most wonderful crimes" (cited in Lofton, 1966). Our own century has witnessed the Sacco–Vanzetti trial, the Scopes case, Hauptmann's defense in the Lindberg prosecution, Leopold and Loeb's conviction, and the Hiss trial. Events seemed to culminate in the Sam Sheppard case; the U.S. Supreme Court remanded the Sheppard conviction on the grounds that pretrial publicity had precluded the possibility of a fair trial (*Sheppard v. Maxwell*, 1966). A Special Committee of the Association of the Bar of the City of New York issued a special study published in two parts that was "intended for use in all parts of the United States" and whose materials demonstrated a "need of prompt remedial action" (Medina, 1967, pp. vii–viii). The Special Committee concluded that after Sheppard "there is steady progress in the right direction, with occasional setbacks" (p. x).

Whatever journalistic restraint the Special Committee was able to find in 1966 must have completely evaporated by O. J. Simpson's trial in 1994. Not only was the Simpson trial the most heavily covered legal case of all time, it may have been the most widely covered media event ever. And Simpson distinguished himself with an accomplishment that Hauptmann, Scopes, Eugene Debs, Sheppard, and even Socrates could not attain: He was acquitted. Other notable figures who earned key legal victories in the 1990s were Lorena Bobbitt, the Los Angeles Police Department officers accused of beating Rodney King, Puffy Combs (later remonikered "P. Diddy"), and even the Menendez brothers (at least at their first trial). High-profile acquittals in the 1970s included Angela Davis, John Connally, and John Mitchell (Simon, 1977). There is almost an impression that some press agent declared to these new (and newly made) celebrities that "there is no such thing as bad publicity" and they collectively discovered that the best way to get free press was to stage an enormous media trial. Against this backdrop and amidst the din of popular commentary, it is safe to say that academic research has its own role, which, if not quite as popular, sexy, and entertaining, is at least really important.

Pretrial publicity spurs interest in many different parts of the academy but is mastered by none. Those in the law school have an obvious concern about the topic, and books on matters concerning free speech and fair trials cover rows and rows of the law library. Also with an obvious stake in the issue are the scholars of media, who fill an equal number of shelves with books talking about media effects. Social scientists of all stripes have conducted studies trying to isolate and define a pretrial publicity effect, and those who have conducted empirical research cover the range from psychologists to sociologists to communication scholars who would distinguish their work from that of their media colleagues. The field that has taken to the study of pretrial publicity most prominently seems to be psychology—21 of the 23 laboratory studies reviewed later have either been published in psychology journals or written by psychologists—and that fact has undoubtedly contributed to a tendency for research to focus on how messages might be processed. One can easily imagine other fields focusing on other areas, such as how media are attended to (as communication scholars might explore) or how media interact with the broader body politic (as sociologists might be interested in). There is certainly an advantage to bringing so many different perspectives to bear on a topic. Insights common to one field but rare to another are likely to be overlooked simply due to unfamiliarity with the concepts common to a different set of journals and organizations. But there are also difficulties associated with attention from so diverse a group of intellectuals. Often, the research can be based on assumptions so different that conclusions are difficult to compare, and the depth that is usually associated with a single field's focus on a topic (think of the work psychologists have done on intelligence) is not evident for pretrial publicity. This book tries to bring together the research conducted in different fields with different theories with the hope that it is possible to make some consistent conclusions. The strengths of some research efforts fill in the blind spots of others, and the space afforded by journal articles rarely allows a comprehensive integration of all that is out there.

The list of questions raised by pretrial publicity is a long one. Does pretrial publicity bias the outcomes of trials? It does seem like the answer to this question would have to be "yes" to justify all the fuss, but it turns out that the answer is anything but straightforward. If pretrial publicity does bias the outcome of trials, what sort of pretrial publicity is damaging? Is it all bad, or are some sorts worse than others? Anyone trying to come up with a remedy would obviously benefit from knowing whether there are particular types of publicity that should be protected against. Nonetheless, it will take a lot of sorting through the research to try to find a pattern to publicity effects that has much to do with content. If there is a pretrial publicity effect, what should be done about it? Will juries simply ignore publicity if they are asked to do so? Is it enough to look for jurors who haven't heard anything about the trial? Finally, there are some basic issues raised about what a fair trial means. What is to be done if pretrial publicity actually helps defendants? If remedies are expensive (it's no leap to say that changing venue costs a pile of money) and pretrial publicity only makes a difference in certain instances, can we apply remedies only in the close cases, or should all defendants have all remedies available to them?

This chapter gives a basic overview of these issues and sacrifices depth for perspective. It reviews some basic facts and the issues typically raised in a trial with pretrial publicity. Taking a big step back, it reviews broad patterns found in academic research, and quickly glances at extant legal doctrine. Finally, it gives an overview of the theoretical orientation of the book. This quick review ought to provide a sense of the breadth of the issues invoked and an orientation to the work done to date; the simple questions raised turn out to have complicated answers.

THE BASIC ISSUES

The importance of pretrial publicity can be measured in both its meaning and its frequency. Some have described pretrial publicity as "one of the most pressing problems facing society" (Sue, Smith, & Pedroza, 1975), and base the claim on both its legal importance and the manner in which this particular legal issue relates to the broader public. It is well established that Sixth Amendment rights to a fair trial can come into conflict with First Amendment rights of a free press (Jones, 1991; Kerr, 1994; Kramer, Kerr, & Carroll, 1990; Rollings & Blascovich, 1977), and those conflicts are certainly evident in highly publicized trials. On the one hand, there is the danger that courts will overcorrect for defendant rights at the expense of legitimate First Amendment interests (Constantini & King, 1980–1981; Kramer et al., 1990; Newsom, 2000) and the body politic will suffer from the absence of a free flow of information. On the other hand, courts may fail to protect defendant rights and innocent defendants may be convicted due to unfair publicity rather than evidence at trial. Naturally occurring coverage is almost universally antidefendant (Carroll et al., 1986; Imrich et al., 1995; Kramer et al., 1990; Kovera, 2002; Moran & Cutler, 1991; Nietzel & Dillehay, 1983; Ogloff & Vidmar, 1994; Riley, 1973; Studebaker, Robbennolt, Pathak-Sharma, & Penrod, 2000; Tankard, Middleton, & Rimmer, 1979). Prodefendant coverage, to such an extent that the concept can be said to exist at all (see Bruschke & Loges, 1999; Strauss 1998), occurs in less than 6% of coverage (Nietzel & Dillehay, 1983) or less than 0.1% of all criminal trials. Based only on what is being said about them, criminal defendants have good reason to dislike excessive pretrial publicity. Regardless of whether First Amendment or Sixth Amendment rights are the more threatened, publicized cases involve a number of complexities and perils. These range from "protracted selection of jurors, to various motions which in turn create more delays, to greater costs, to mistrials with additional burdens in the already congested court calendars, and possibly to public loss of confidence and alienation from the legal system" (Padawer-Singer & Barton, 1975, p. 126). The issue of pretrial publicity is a deserving one if only because of the weight of the issues at stake.

This need to balance interests has resulted in attempts to regulate publicity outside the courtroom and to correct for it once it works its way inside the courtroom. Outside the courtroom, there have been attempts by professional organizations to regulate publicity. The American Bar Association developed "Standards" in 1968 and "Model Rules" in 1983 that were intended to regulate the behavior of the bar and the press (Imrich et al., 1995), but they are rarely enforced (Kramer et al., 1990) and routinely violated (Frasca, 1998; Imrich et al., 1995; Tankard et al., 1979). Inside the courtroom walls there is an identifiable number of cases where courts have thrown out convictions due to extensive pretrial publicity (Constantini & King, 1980–1981; Imrich et al., 1995; Kline & Jess, 1966; Simon, 1966), although one survey found that fewer than 100 of 250,000 criminal convictions get overturned due to coverage concerns (Spencer, 1982).

Pretrial publicity is also important because of the simple frequency of its occurrence. From the tabloid shows like *LA Cops* and *America's Most Dangerous Car Chases* to the more erudite *American Justice* and the omnipresent *Court TV,* broadcasters are finding that crime coverage is one way to stay afloat in a competitive viewing market. Despite the seeming prevalence of media focus, pretrial publicity does not occur in a large proportion of cases (Hough, 1970), and one review concludes that only 5% of felony arrests receive coverage (Frasca, 1988). Relying on Frasca's work, one estimate has calculated that 12,000 defendants a year face extensive pretrial publicity (Kerr, 1994). Two caveats are in order. First, there is some difficulty in defining what constitutes "extensive" publicity (a point developed in later chapters), and this factor may make it difficult to place full confidence in this estimate. Second, coverage is not distributed equally across those cases that receive it and there can be little doubt that some cases attract more attention than others. One study of felony murder cases, for example, found coverage in only 18.6% of federal murder and robbery trials (Bruschke & Loges, 1999). Surette (1992) contends that when media coverage of a trial hits a certain saturation point the trial becomes a media event unto itself and takes on a dramatic quality akin to a miniseries. The line between information and entertainment blurs, even more than it does in whatever counts for normal coverage. Those trials that, for whatever reason, become the focus of media attention take on an importance simply because of how they can hold popular interest and possibly shape public opinion.

In the end, two things about the frequency of pretrial publicity are striking. First, pretrial publicity occurs in a proportionately tiny number of cases, and thus concerns over the incidence of publicity derive from the total number of cases affected (a respectable 12,000 a year) rather than the percentage of cases involved (no more than 20% and probably somewhere between 1% and 5%). Second, media attention is not distributed evenly across publicized cases, and even among the cases that the media do cover a few cases get a disproportionate amount of attention.

CURRENT LEGAL DOCTRINE

Courts are charged with balancing the interests of the defendant and the state, and have held that excessive publicity can be grounds for appeal based on the assumption that publicity can create an unfair situation for the defendant that the courts have an obligation to remedy effectively. Judicial concern over the Sam Sheppard case produced a ruling in the Supreme Court's landmark *Sheppard v. Maxwell* decision (1966). The case served as a starting place for legal doctrine to sort out when pretrial publicity is sufficiently onerous to justify a remedy and what the remedy ought to be. Roughly three decades after *Sheppard* the progress has been halting, and at least one review characterized the case law as "conflicting" (Kramer et al., 1990). Some commentators have simply listed cases where publicity has been found to be damaging next to cases where it has not (Nietzel & Dillehay, 1983), whereas others have concluded that case law conflicts (Kramer et al., 1990; Surette, 1992). Judicial definitions of what constitutes prejudice are based on "vague" notions of bias (Rollings & Blascovich, 1977) that are "circular" and slippery (Moran & Cutler, 1991). Others have called the case law inconsistent over time and liken its application to a "shell game" (Walton, 1998).

By and large, judicial standards have been developed outside of social science understandings of human behavior or have openly rejected social science findings (Moran & Cutler, 1991; Ogloff, 2002; Rollings & Blascovich, 1977). In part, this may be due simply to judicial ignorance of social science research or open judicial hostility to introducing social science into legal proceedings at all. Indeed, the way that social science research interfaces with legal practice is a complicated issue that has caught the attention of other scholars as an area of study in its own right (Lindman, 1989; Melton, 1987). Apart from judicial ignorance, however, questions about the realism of current pretrial publicity studies (reviewed below) have caused the legal community to turn away from social science research as a source of information on which to base decisions (Bornstein, 1999; Carroll et al., 1986; Davis, 1986; Jones, 1991; Padawer-Singer & Barton, 1975; Padawer-Singer, Singer, & Singer, 1977; Pember, 1990; Studebaker et al., 2002). Some commentators conclude that there is a fundamental incompatibility between the methods, goals, and terms used in social science and those used in jurisprudence, taking the view that "from a legal perspective, it is impossible to operationalize a uniform methodology for the determination of prejudice" (Moran & Cutler, 1991, p. 346). Others take a gentler view: "Change of venue surveys allow for the delicate intersection of two worlds: Social science research and the legal system. Each world has its own traditions and standards, and attempts to merge them lead to a somewhat imperfect fit" (Posey & Dahl, 2002, p. 124). For whatever reason, there is little correspondence between current legal definitions and rules about the problem and current social science findings. To the extent that courts rely on social science at all, they will examine specific opinion surveys in particular cases to determine community bias (e.g., McConahay, Mullin, & Frederick, 1977; Nietzel & Dillehay, 1983; Posey & Dahl, 2002; Vidmar & Melnitzer, 1984), even though a number of scholars have made a strong case for linking empirical findings to judicial practice (Carroll et al., 1986; Lindman, 1989; Ogloff, 2002; Riley, 1973; Studebaker & Penrod, 1997; Vidmar & Judson, 1981).

It may seem strange for a book devoted to pretrial publicity to jump so swiftly past the extant case law, and the maneuver requires some explanation. The perspective this book takes is that legal doctrine should follow from empirical knowledge (see Ogloff, 2002), and its purpose is normative and not descriptive. Although there can be much discussion about the appropriate role of social science in the courtroom, there is little doubt that pretrial publicity questions turn on empirical knowledge. Whether or not pretrial publicity can create a state of mind for jurors that can't be overcome by judicial instructions and trial evidence is not a legal question, but an empirical one (Simon, 1977).

Thus, a review of case law is in large measure a digression into the absurd: Case law can only develop validly if it is based on a sound understanding of empirical relationships identified by social science. Because social science hasn't produced much clear knowledge about the crucial empirical relationships (a point developed at length a little later on), it is more or less impossible for case law to do its job. At present, it seems that case law is not precise or well developed, and that may simply be an accurate reflection of the knowledge available to legal decision makers. Whether or not judges should be paying more attention to social science research is at this juncture a moot point: Social science hasn't had much to offer. The ideal situation, of course, is one where social science has produced a clear set of findings and judicial officers incorporate those findings into a coherent set of rules.

SOCIAL SCIENCE

Subsequent chapters develop in depth the findings of social science research. At this point, one overarching pattern bears mention. In a nutshell, laboratory studies have found that pretrial publicity (PTP) has an effect, but those results do not replicate in field research. This is a new viewpoint and one not shared by current reviews and one that may be due to the relative paucity of field research (Studebaker et al., 2000; Vidmar, 2002). In 1997, Studebaker and Penrod synthesized the research findings this way: "In sum, it appears that the effects of pretrial publicity can find their way into the courtroom, can survive the jury selection process, can survive the presentation of trial evidence, can endure the limiting effects of judicial instructions, and cannot only persevere through deliberations, but may actually intensify" (p. 445). Steblay, Besirevic, Fulero, and Jiminez-Lorente (1999) came to a very similar conclusion 2 years later at the conclusion of a meta-analysis:

> The data support the hypothesis that negative pretrial publicity significantly affects jurors' decisions about the culpability of the defendant. Jurors exposed to publicity which presents negative information about the defendant and crime are more likely to judge the defendant as guilty than are jurors exposed to limited PTP.... Initial observation of the dataset showed mixed results as to the effect of PTP. It appears now with closer analysis that some of the nonsupportive results may simply have been due to lack of statistical power. (p. 229)

Both sets of reviewers believed that their conclusions extend from the laboratory to the field. Steblay et al. wrote: "From a legal and policy perspective, the important question now is what might be done to safeguard the rights of a defendant in a case where documented negative PTP appears to be a significant problem" (p. 230). This appears to be the advice that social scientists are giving the legal system. Fulero (2002) published an affidavit that he submitted to the court in a local murder case, and noted that it was similar to the affidavit Penrod submitted in *McVeigh*. The affidavit began with the conclusion that pretrial publicity can bias the outcome of a trial, noted that voir dire, jury instructions, and continuance all failed as remedies, and concluded that a change of venue or change of jurors was the only remedy likely to be effective.

These conclusions are hasty. Although the work of Steblay et al. in particular is a rigorous summary of laboratory research, the discovery of a consistent pattern of findings hidden beneath low power and small sample sizes is not the same as demonstrating that laboratory research replicates in actual practice. No study reviewed by either Steblay et al. or Studebaker and Penrod observed actual trials and compared highly publicized and less publicized cases, which is the data necessary to demonstrate the point. Kerr wrote in 1994:

> The empirical question is whether such prejudice survives the remedies the court applies. The most direct way to examine this question would be to associate the occurrence of pretrial publicity with actual jury verdicts—is the conviction rate higher in cases receiving prejudicial pretrial publicity? There have been a few isolated attempts to do this. The problem with such investigations is that they fail to examine a matched sample of cases without pretrial publicity. Without such data it is not possible to establish whether there is an association between the amount or type of pretrial publicity and the jury verdict. Apparently, no one has yet collected the appropriate data to answer this question. (p. 121)

The data Kerr asked for have since been collected and published in 1999, after either Steblay et al. or Studebaker and Penrod had the opportunity to review the work. Bruschke and Loges (1999) found identical conviction rates between highly publicized federal first-degree murder cases and those receiving no coverage at all, and replicated the finding when reviewing a separate dataset that included both federal first-degree murder cases and federal robbery cases along with other variables (included here in chap. 3).

How is it possible that the conclusions of the reviewers could be so firm and yet the results fail to replicate in the field? Three explanations are possible. They are not exclusive, all may add insight into the mystery, and sorting them out will in large measure be the bulk of the work of the remainder of this book. First, there is the possibility that the laboratory research simply failed to adequately simulate the conditions of actual courtrooms, and the findings they obtained were thus irrelevant to actual practice. Although there is a virtually universal agreement that studies should strive to maximize realism (Jones, 1991; Kovera, 2002; Moran & Cutler, 1991; Padawer-Singer & Barton, 1975; Padawer-Singer et al., 1977; Studebaker & Penrod, 1997; Studebaker et al., 2002; Vidmar, 2002), and most agree that there are inherent limitations in laboratory studies that will always make generalizability difficult (Freedman, Martin, & Mota, 1998; Hans & Doob, 1976; Otto, Penrod, & Dexter, 1994; Rollings & Blascovich, 1977; Wilcox

& McCombs, 1967), opinion divides on how research that deviates from actual courtroom experience ought to be evaluated. One camp holds that the research is totally "phony" and should be disregarded altogether (Pember, 1984). Others have expressed concern that current research deviates from realistic settings in ways that have been described as "serious" (Freedman & Burke, 1996) and "critical" (Jones, 1991). A second view holds that the lack of realism means that scholars and legal practitioners should be extremely cautious about extrapolating to actual courtrooms (Freedman & Burke, 1996; Jones, 1991). Middle-of-the-road assessments maintain that realism and control trade off (Carroll et al., 1986; Riley, 1973), suggesting a need for both field and laboratory research (Carroll et al., 1986; Studebaker et al., 2000; Vidmar, 2002), or that careful control is needed to isolate pretrial publicity effects (Otto et al., 1994). Fulero's 1987 review concluded that despite the limitations, the findings to date are sufficiently clear enough to inform legal practice, and Steblay et al. (1999) found that "the strongest effects are obtained in studies which are parallel in many features to the experience of real jurors" (p. 229). A final group is relatively unconcerned about the lack of realism, and they cite evidence that laboratory studies generally match actual practice to reach the conclusion that simulation research is typical of actual trials (Kerr, 1994; Wilson & Bornstein, 1998). Studebaker and Penrod (1997) fall into this camp. The divergences of opinion are sharp; some concluded the lack of realism has underestimated pretrial publicity effects (Studebaker et al., 2002), whereas others concluded the opposite and believed it has overestimated the influence of publicity (Freedman et al., 1998). Of course, all these conclusions were reached before the field research of Bruschke and Loges documented that laboratory results do not replicate in the field. At least one possible reason that laboratory results do not replicate in the field is that the conclusions of those like Pember have merit, and the laboratory results are conducted under conditions sufficiently different from actual practice that their findings cannot speak to courtroom behavior.

A second possible explanation for the divergence between the findings in the laboratory and those in the field is the treatment of remedies. Laboratory findings and commentators generally conclude that extant remedies fail to eliminate bias (Studebaker et al., 2002). Jury instructions are ignored (Freedman et al., 1998; Hans & Doob, 1976; Kramer et al., 1990; Sue, Smith, & Gilbert, 1974). Jury selection has produced more mixed reviews, with some scholars applauding the process for its ability to remove bias (Padawer-Singer & Barton, 1975), some scholars reporting equivocal results or admitting confusion (Carroll et al., 1986; Vidmar & Melnitzer, 1984; Zeisel & Diamond, 1978), but with the strongest opinions decrying its effectiveness (Dexter, Cutler, & Moran, 1992; Kerr, Kramer, Carroll, & Alfini, 1991; Padawer-Singer, Singer, & Singer, 1974). Sequestering is rare (Vidmar, 2002) and the results for deliberation are mixed (Kovera, 2002). Other remedies, such as a continuance, have similarly failed to counteract publicity biasing or actually exacerbated its influence (Kramer et al., 1990; but some view continuance as the best available remedy to date; see Kerr, 1994). Overall, court-imposed remedies are not thought to have had much success at eliminating possible biases, despite the fact that most legal practitioners other than defense attorneys believe that they work (Kerr, 1994). The majority view has been well summarized by Kerr (1994): "pretrial publicity can bias jury opinion, but ... common remedies may not be very effective in preventing or over-coming such bias" (p. 121; see Jones, 1991, and Studebaker & Penrod, 1997, for an identical conclusion). Regardless of the merits of such conclusions, it can be pointed out that very little research thus far has studied remedies in combination with one another. In the laboratory it is easy enough to isolate the effectiveness of any given remedy, but such an approach may miss the fact that in all actual trials remedies always occur in combination with one another and also include a number of natural remedies that are not contemplated in the laboratory.

For example, in actual trials it is difficult to imagine that all jurors have been exposed to the exact same publicity at the exact same time (and usually within a week of the trial). However, deliberation has been discovered to be an ineffective remedy based on studies conducted under exactly those conditions. It is quite possible to imagine that deliberations might go differently if not all jurors had seen the same coverage at the same time, or that the passage of time might make publicity harder to remember. This is an example of a "natural" remedy not present in laboratory research. Another instance of a natural remedy concerns jury instructions. Because of the difficulty of having mock jury deliberations extend over several days, mock jurors are generally instructed at the outset of a relatively short trial (always less than 1 day, usually less than an hour) and instructed again before deliberations. During actual trials, however, trials extend for several days and jurors may be instructed at the beginning and ending of each day to try to remain objective. Thus, a repeated instruction may gain more prominence than a one-time instruction. This repetition naturally occurs as a function of the length of actual trials and is not contemplated in laboratory research.

Most importantly, remedies are rarely considered in combination with one another. Thus, although it may be true that neither voir dire nor jury instructions nor deliberation is effective in isolation (as they are often studied in laboratory settings), it may well be true that they work in combination with one another (as they always occur in actual trials). What limited evidence exists on the point is awfully suggestive. Kerwin and Shaffer (1994) noted a trend in the literature where instructions failed when used without deliberation but succeeded when deliberations were part of the research design. Two studies confirmed the hypothesis that mock jurors could, indeed, discount inadmissible evidence presented at trial when both instructions and deliberations were present, and noted that the bias was evident before deliberation but was eliminated after deliberation had occurred. They conclude with a warning against studies that examine individual opinions rather than group decisions as the dependent variable:

> Will deliberating *juries* base their verdicts on inadmissible information? Four jury simulations ... have addressed this question and, in contrast to the juror simulations, have uncovered little or no suggestion that juries readily base their decisions on information they have been instructed to ignore. The current project ... demonstrates the important role that jury deliberations can have in a study's outcomes. (p. 161)

Subsequent research on deliberations that included admissibility instructions have produced two additional studies that support the success of remedies used in combination with one another (London & Nunez, 2000). This research, of course, speaks only to the interaction of two possible remedies acting in conjunction with one another, but we believe that the point may extend to the situation where a variety of court-imposed and naturally occurring remedies (delay, voir dire, instructions, and deliberation) all come into play.

Third, it may be that the function of law is more of a resource game than it is a search for truth, or, more accurately, the search for truth that the court embarks on may be swamped by the influence of imbalanced access to resources. Political scientists studying appellate court decisions have discovered that richer, more powerful interests tend to prevail (e.g., George & Epstein, 1992; Songer & Kuersten, 1995), that additional defense resources can offset that advantage (Songer, Kuersten, & Kaheny, 2000), and that a private attorney can produce more favorable outcomes for the defendant than a public defender (Daudistel, Hosch, Holmes, & Graves, 1999). At least one study by a communication scholar has found that wealth is the most dominant factor predicting state-level supreme court decisions (Bruschke, 1994). Anecdotally, it is easy to imagine how access to resources might alter the outcome of a trial. It is virtually impossible for the defense to out-spend the state in a criminal case. Even O. J. Simpson spent less than the prosecution. An indigent defendant, relying on an overworked public defender, might minimally have constitutional rights protected with a court-appointed attorney, but is clearly not in as good a position as a wealthy defendant who can afford Johnny Cochrane. In addition, a number of defense costs, ranging from expert witnesses to independent investigators, are easier for wealthy defendants to bear than indigent defendants. Pretrial publicity might, in a strange way, help resource-poor defendants equalize imbalances. One could believe that a public defender might spend more time on a more highly scrutinized case. The high profile nature of a highly publicized case might attract a better lawyer on a pro bono basis. It is hard to imagine F. Lee Bailey taking an interest in Richard Speck but for the publicity surrounding the case. Most defendants plead guilty; across all federal criminal cases in 1995 ($n = 29,036$), 77.3% of the time defendants entered pleas of guilty (Federal Judicial Center, 1997). Of those cases that go to trial, conviction rates are roughly 80% (see the data presented in chap. 3). There is an argument to be made that the worst thing that can happen to a criminal defendant in a conviction-prone system is to be ignored: The normal processes of the legal system tilt toward conviction, and anything that draws attention to criminal defendants and disrupts the typical flow of typical case processing might work in their favor.

In sum, although current reviews of laboratory research have concluded that pretrial publicity biases trials and that these results will generalize to actual trials, field research contrasts with these conclusions. There are at least three reasons that the findings of laboratory and field research might diverge: (a) the laboratory research might simply fail to replicate actual courtroom conditions, (b) the laboratory research might have studied remedies in isolation from one another, when in fact they work in combination with each other (as courts usually apply them), or (c) defendants might receive inadvertent benefits from pretrial publicity that offset any biasing of some jury members.

THEORETICAL ORIENTATION

One of the revelations of the postmodern age is that theories are not the result of divine insight, and all carry their own presuppositions and assumptions that can be summarized and critiqued at a meta-theoretical level. In this age, it is wise to establish meta-theoretical footing (or at least identify what meta-theoretical ground you'd like to stand on) before launching into lists of axioms and hypotheses. This is the final task for the introduction. There are at least two reasons that scholars in adjacent fields might not read each other's work. The first is mundane enough; because time is limited, committee work long and tedious, and pressure to publish intense (with threats of perishing eminent), most of us simply do all we can to keep up with our own fields. Stephen Gould and Jared Diamond are rare and precious aberrations. The second reason is a little more troublesome. Often the theories of different fields are incompatible, and there is a natural tendency to decide that the theories of the field you dedicated 8 years of graduate study and countless thousands of dollars to are probably the correct ones (a point that Thomas Kuhn has made in more extended and erudite terms). But the point of this book is to bring together theories that are not usually discussed in conjunction with one another, and they will at various points be incompatible with one another. The strategy will be to adopt those parts of the theories that can be combined and bracket the points of irreconcilability. Viewed least charitably, this is a cop-out, but viewed through only slightly rose-tinted lenses it accepts the most crucial of what each theory has to offer while pushing aside the extreme stances of each position. Three separate strands of scholarship (what might be called "meta-theories" by other authors) are brought together here, and what is taken (and what is left behind) from each deserves some attention. The review will be brief, and we do not hope to persuade the partisans. Suffice it to say that each of these choices is supported by a larger body of literature than will be reviewed here, and each choice is rejected by an equally substantial amount of scholarship. Our point is not to defend these choices, but to at least identify the directions taken.

The first research tradition is social science. Science itself has been under attack lately (see Rouse, 1987, for a very readable overview of the issues), and the criticisms of science seem to apply to social science in spades. Simplified to its core, most critics do not object to the project of science, but note that science does not occur in isolation from its social context. Although undoubtedly objective in some ways, science is profoundly subjective in others. Scientific directions reflect the sociological context of the day (think of Darwin and why his views were so revolutionary), scientific and technological discoveries profoundly influence social and political life, and privileging scientific methods and the scientists who use them can be pathological and counterproductive. In short, science itself is properly understood as an object of sociological study, not a field apart from and superior to it. These criticisms are accepted here with enthusiasm. On the other hand, science has irrefutable power and the technological progress of the last century was stunning. My grandfather was born in a house without plumbing in a year before Henry Ford built the Model T, and before he died he saw a human being walk on the moon. What science can do and is good at is establishing empirical regularities. Our perspective is that science should be used for what science is good at: Providing answers to empirical questions. In the context of pretrial publicity, social science can and should be used to answer empirical questions about human behavior. How often do people have to see a news story before they remember it? What images might they retain that they can't put out of their heads later? Which of those will make a difference when serving on a jury? Can instructions, voir dire, and deliberations eliminate preexisting biases? These are not questions for philosophers or judges or ethicists, or even postmodern critics. If we read the conclusions of the critics of science correctly, science can and should find its empirical regularities, but scientists should not have special privilege when deciding how those discoveries are best used by society.

The second broad tradition is the law. It is, after all, courts who will ultimately decide the fate of publicized trials, and courts who must select (or design) appropriate remedies. The law is based on some noble premises: That objective (or at least noninvolved) parties should arbitrate disputes, that those proceedings should be as fair as possible, and that to the maximum extent possible the rules that everyone has to live by should be spelled out in advance with as much clarity as is possible and be enforced for the good of all. Somewhere between the ideals and practice, however, the law can run afoul of its principles. The realist movement and its offspring, critical legal studies

(Kelman's 1987 book serves as a useful marker of the core principals and development of ideas), applied the same social criticism to the law that the critics of science apply to science. Legal doctrine and practice can often reflect and impose social prejudices rather than protect minorities from them, the attempt to write and apply clear rules can often result in injustice rather than fairness, and there is a danger in speaking about "the law" as a unified and coherent set of rules that bind all when it is increasingly clear that the law isn't even knowable, much less coherent, and clearly functions differently for those of different races, genders, and classes. In short form, much as the critics of science have taught us that scientists generally make excellent scientists but are bad politicians, the realist movement has taught us that judges can make good arbiters but bad scientists.

Consider the treatment social science research has had in law reviews. Kulish (1998) tackled the question of pretrial publicity and its application to military law, and took the typical legal approach of citing all the case law and not a single social science study. Newsom (2000) launched a criticism of the Florida Supreme Court—that runaway stronghold of liberal activism that leads the nation in death penalty convictions—for its decision to require individual voir dire of potential jurors in highly publicized cases. The concern evidently was that the individual questioning would take too long and that the "impact of these rulings will be more dramatic than the Florida Supreme Court cares to admit" because "if his name is sufficiently publicized in the news media, any criminal defendant will arguably be entitled to conduct individual voir dire" (p. 1071). Setting aside the unexamined question of how long individual voir dire would add to a trial, anyone familiar with plea bargain rates and the social science research on pretrial publicity would immediately recognize what a ludicrously small number of cases would be "sufficiently publicized" for the remedy to affect. Newsom cited no research on the point one way or the other. Strauss (1998) did cite social science research to prove the point that jurors could set aside biases, but oddly cited Simon's (1977) incredibly dated literature review (it reviewed only five studies), despite the fact that three reviews of social science research had been published at the time which were all much more extensive, at least a decade more recent, and much more on-point to the topic Strauss was addressing (Carroll et al., 1986; Fulero, 1987; Studebaker & Penrod, 1997). Strauss cited three other sources to prove the point, all law reviews.

Of course, this is not to suggest that all lawyers are idiots. Undoubtedly, a review of case law written by two social scientists would seem as silly to lawyers as lawyers' reviews of social science seem to social scientists. It is also true that the preceding paragraph selected only a smattering of legal commentary and looked at law reviews rather than case law. We only say that we selected these articles for comment because they are typical of the legal treatment of social science, and there is a strong argument to be made that the courts' treatment of social science research has been even more random than its fate in the law reviews. The limited point we wish to demonstrate is that the law often behaves as a field unto itself, although it is informed by developments in many other areas. It is important that legal practitioners recognize that developments outside the refinement of case law speak to the issues that the courts will address, and that legal training gives one no special ability to evaluate research conducted in other fields.

There is an empirical reality apart from whether a court recognizes that reality or not, and usually the larger the discrepancy between the reality and the court's cognizance of it, the more poorly history remembers the court. Whether or not the courts decided that schools could truly be separate but equal, there was the empirical reality that they weren't. In a similar vein, if publicity biases trials against defendants, it will do so whether or not a court finds that it does. What we take from the legal tradition will be the list of possible remedies imagined thus far and the opinions of legal experts (taken for what they are as opinions and nothing more). In line with the realist criticisms, however, no special deference is given to legal doctrine on empirical questions, and the law must be an object of criticism and not just a hermetically sealed essence, holding the answers to all possible questions for those who study it hard enough.

The third and final research tradition is scholarship that addresses the question of resource equity, and again we rely on research that springs from the realist tradition. Realist scholars have undoubtedly pointed out some significant flaws in current legal theories and practice, and have undoubtedly suffered a backlash from the mainstream that is best described as a knee-jerk defense of privilege. Nonetheless, not all criticisms of the realist approach are without merit, and there are some points where this book will depart from some more radical theories. There are realist scholars who see their role as theorists and not reformers, and more than one author is on record as vigorously claiming that critical theorists should not be in the business of suggesting new rules or policies (see Schlag, 1997). Their job, in this view, is to criticize the law, and the very suggestion that they suggest alternatives to it misses the point and locks in the dominant view. This perspective is rejected here because its rejection of incremental reform seems out of touch with history and because it replaces the privilege of the judge with a higher level of privilege for the philosopher (Richard Rorty has written extensively on both issues). Rather than insisting that no part of "the system" can be salvaged and that the entire thing must be scrapped for any progress to occur, this book takes the perspective that if we understand the forces that the realist movement speaks brilliantly about—the ways bias and structural inequality come into play—it will be possible to understand legal practice (in this case pretrial publicity) better and, perhaps only in small ways, to address those inequalities. Whether or not small reforms legitimate and entrench the system or transform it is beyond the scope of the issues raised here, but this work aligns with Habermas and Rorty, who believe that there is progress to be made in alleviating injustice when we can.

This book develops its theory based on meta-theoretical assumptions drawn from three different scholarly traditions. In each case, the assumptions drawn from each field are extraordinarily mainstream. In each case, the more extreme positions from the traditions are rejected. This is a stance based on the pluralistic assumption that different methods and traditions can be combined, a stance that has both critics and defenders (see Roth, 1987). The theories developed in this book assume that science can establish empirical regularities but ought not to dictate social practice, that the law should strive for fair and better rules but should not substitute legal dogma for empirical knowledge, and that social criticism should address how empirical science and legal rules function in an overall social context but should not exempt itself from offering practical solutions.

CONCLUSION

What is known about pretrial publicity so far? It is not new. It does not happen often in proportional terms, but occurs frequently enough in absolute terms to be of concern. When it does occur, it does not occur the same way for every trial. Sometimes trials are covered modestly whereas at others coverage spirals to absurd levels. Legal practice has identified that in some cases publicity will impede the possibility of a fair trial, but what constitutes too much coverage and what remedies are appropriate in which situations are questions not answered by the current set of legal rules. Academic research has provided no more clarity, with differences between lab and field research and methodological disputes aplenty. By pulling core concepts from three different scholarly traditions—the legal, the social scientific, and the critical—some greater resolution may be gained, and it might be possible to determine whether pretrial publicity has a biasing effect on trials, how that bias might (or might not) occur, and what can be done to correct it.

A good social scientist states hypotheses in advance, but never conclusions. A reviewer has the luxury of setting forth an argument first and offering support for it later. Despite the methodological battles and confusing pattern of results, we believe that there is enough evidence to advance, at least tentatively, three conclusions we call hypotheses, and the rest of this book is dedicated to supplying proof for these claims. The first is the "knowledge–guilt" hypothesis, which states that the more someone knows about a criminal case in advance, the more the person will presume guilt. The hypothesis makes no claim about whether such a bias can be remedied, or whether the presumption of guilt will bias the outcome of the trial. It does maintain that the potential juror who can recall specific information about a crime will come to the trial with a state of mind that presumes more guilt than one who has no information. As reviewed later, there is very strong reason to believe that pretrial judgments do not translate into biased verdicts, although methodologies that rely on predeliberation questioning of mock jurors might produce artificial results that greatly exaggerate the existence of a pretrial publicity effect (Kovera, 2002).

The second hypothesis is called the "cumulative remedy" hypothesis, and it maintains that much of the difference between the lab research and field research can be accounted for by the package of natural and court-imposed remedies that are often isolated in laboratory research but always occur in combination in actual trials. Extant research strongly suggests that remedies working in combination with one another produce results that are much different than when each remedy is studied in isolation.

Finally, the "structural paradox" hypothesis, which does not compete with but stands side-by-side with the cumulative remedy hypothesis, maintains that much of the difference between laboratory research and field research can be explained by a difference in the levels of analysis. The laboratory research has focused on individual-level psychological variables that attempt to measure the "black box" of jurors' minds (probably because so much of the work to date has been done by psychologists). Such research is undoubtedly necessary. However, at the structural level, the system is at least in part one that is based on a resource game, and paradoxically, negative attention equalizes the resource inequities that criminal defendants face at the structural or systemic level of society that is called, after all, the legal system. In the end, two sets of remedies are suggested. The first set of remedies involves improvements in the existing remedies available to a court. Voir dire could be improved with a simple multiple-choice test, a cheap and easy remedy not presently available or contemplated in extant studies of remedies, a test that is designed to eliminate any pretrial biases supposed by the knowledge–guilt hypothesis. Other alterations to the voir dire process and the content of jury instructions might take strides toward eliminating any potential bias from pretrial publicity. The second remedy is a structural-level solution: We must fight for a system where the crucial factors that determine incarceration are guilt and innocence and not access to resources.

This book addresses four basic questions. The first is whether pretrial publicity biases trial outcomes at all. The question is explored in chapter 2, and the answers involve further development of the knowledge–guilt and cumulative remedy hypotheses. Chapter 2 is also a summary of current laboratory research. Chapter 3 reviews field research and offers conclusions that synthesize field and laboratory research. These findings suggest a much different assessment of the influence of pretrial publicity than is offered in current reviews. The second question is: If publicity might plausibly influence the opinion of jurors, how might it do so? This question requires a shift from psychological theories of information processing to media theories about how information might be noticed in the first place. Chapter 4 delves into theories of media effect and offers a cultivation explanation as the means by which media might most plausibly influence trials. Original data will be offered to explore the cultivation predictions about pretrial publicity. Psychological theories are not discarded, but are reviewed in chapter 5. In general, theories such as the Elaboration Likelihood Model provide explanations for why pretrial publicity effects might be so modest. A third question is: What remedies might eliminate any pretrial publicity effect? Having taken the laboratory and field research into account, our suggestions are offered at the end of chapter 3. A series of relatively low-cost remedies might counteract any biasing influence of pretrial publicity. Throughout, we explore evidence for the cumulative remedy hypothesis, which supposes that remedies working in combination with one another might be more powerful than remedies studied in isolation, and additionally that pretrial publicity can have an effect only when all remedies fail simultaneously. Our final question is: How does pretrial publicity relate to the overall fairness in the legal system? Straying (but not far) from our native fields of study, we review legal theories and conclude that realism offers useful insights into and evocative descriptions of the legal system. Given the centrality of economic prowess to litigant success, we conclude that a focus on a single potential source of bias—pretrial publicity in this case—may run the risk of misdirecting attention onto a highly visible but relatively insignificant factor in a system that purports to dispense justice. Research findings on the ways that defendants might actually benefit from pretrial publicity point to a larger issue of economic fairness. In the end, we hope that our efforts can suggest cheaper remedies and ways to reprioritize resource expenditures in the legal system to make it more fair to everyone, and not simply to those very few defendants who have the misfortune of becoming famous for all the wrong reasons.

CHAPTER TWO

What We Think We Know

The exclusive use of *p* values has become a disease. It is fostered by journals and by granting agencies. It is not at all unusual to see one, two, or three stars in every article of most journals in the social and psychological sciences. This is a form of statistical Star Wars. It has the effect of misdirecting attention from understanding the structure of the phenomenon to a decision format that is often not the goal. (I. Olkin, *The Future of Meta-Analysis*, 1990, p. 5)

Highly publicized trials are unsightly things that nobody seems to like very much. Judges make demeaning comments about "letting the jackals in" (a phrase attributed to Lance Ito following his decision to televise the Simpson trial), defense attorneys howl ceaselessly about how their clients are being convicted in the press, and even the poor Marcia Clarks of the world seem completely exhausted by the end of it all. This ugliness leads to the widespread suspicion that something must be wrong with a process this unbecoming, and this visceral negative reaction to the circus on the part of academics and legal scholars led, as much as anything, to the *Sheppard* decision. But First Amendment issues are tricky precisely because the speech most in need of protection is often the speech that most people least want to hear, and the unpleasantness of the discourse usually has to be sharply distinguished from its value or harm. There is much more uproar about the process than there is hard evidence that pretrial publicity actually puts defendants in an unfair position. This chapter sorts through that evidence in an attempt to summarize what we know about pretrial publicity at present and to answer the first major question of this book: Is there a pretrial publicity effect at all? There are more detailed questions to pursue, of course, and it is easy to imagine that the important question isn't whether there is a pretrial publicity effect, but when and how it might emerge. These sexier questions are deferred until chapter 3, and in the interest of putting carts and horses in the correct order this chapter ponders whether there is a pretrial publicity effect at all. As it turns out, the answer to the question is elusive enough to justify a thorough search.

Finding an answer will require sifting through a lot of literature and coming clean about some of the issues simplified in the introductory chapter. There are actually more divisions in the literature than just the laboratory or field nature of the research. Some studies have included trials, whereas some have not. Some studies have polled respondents who have witnessed naturally occurring levels of coverage but have not shown them trials, whereas some studies have conducted mock trials but relied on experimentally manipulated publicity. The first order of business is to identify those studies of concern, a second agenda item is to come up with a way of categorizing the studies, and a final preliminary goal is to establish criteria for evaluating them.

The first step is the easiest, and identifying research to include is a fairly straightforward process. This section concerns itself only with published research on the empirical effects of pretrial publicity. The studies reviewed next were selected on the basis of four criteria. To be included, a study had to include a sample group, include pretrial publicity as a variable, conduct a significance test, and be published in a printed journal. Overall, 36 studies were identified that met those criteria. It should be mentioned that the last criterion excluded four theses and dissertations and some unpublished results reviewed elsewhere (see Steblay et al., 1999). The decision to exclude unpublished material was made for two reasons. First, unpublished work is much more difficult to access and by its very nature un-indexed, and thus it is probably not possible to review every unpublished study. At least, it is possible to know the universe of published studies and how thorough your review of them might be; even knowing the size of the unpublished universe is a daunting task. The alternative seemed to be including all published research and all the unpublished research we could find, which in the end seemed as random as a knuckleball. We decided that consistency was an important goal and one difficult to attain if we sought to include unpublished results. Second, although it is far from a perfect process, peer review for publication does generally serve as a quality screen. Although not all published research is good and not all unpublished research is bad, it is a generally accepted professional standard that research needs to pass through peer review before its conclusions are widely accepted. Rather than review all published work and some unknown proportion of the unpublished research, we thought it better to draw an easily implemented bright line.

The second task is to find a way to categorize the studies, in a proverbial attempt to compare apples to apples and oranges to oranges. These 36 studies are divided into five groups. The first group includes studies, conducted either with laboratory manipulations or on naturally occurring phenomena, that did not include trial evidence in their design. These studies are informative, but quite obviously only speak to what might happen to mock jurors who are exposed to pretrial publicity in the absence of a trial. The second group of studies are those laboratory studies that have found a pretrial publicity effect, a third group are those laboratory studies that only provide partial support for a pretrial publicity effect, and the fourth group is those laboratory studies that have not found any pretrial publicity effect. The fifth and final group of studies, the smallest by far, are those field studies that have compared highly publicized with less publicized trials, which are reviewed in chapter 3.

Our third and final preliminary task is to establish some criteria for evaluating the studies. Academic studies, of course, are not good or bad in a vacuum devoid of context, but provide information that is more or less useful depending on the questions that have been asked. The central question of this book is not whether a pretrial publicity effect can be established in laboratory research, but whether such an effect can be extrapolated to actual trials. This is a fairly simple point, but the discussions about the value of laboratory research have been heated enough to warrant a little more discussion. The issue gets to the heart of what laboratory research means in the social sciences. In the physical sciences, of course, the difference between laboratory or "pure" research and field or "applied" research is an old and well-established one (although not without controversy in the postmodern age). The reasons are easy enough to figure out. If, for instance, a scientist wanted to study copper, the scholar could isolate its properties in the laboratory and figure out its density, tensile strength, conductive properties, how shiny it might be as an earring, or any intrinsic property it had that the scientist might be interested in. A field researcher might be interested in the features of copper as it naturally occurred—where it would get deposited, what other rock it was usually found with, how much of it could be found at a given spot. The two strands of research could proceed pleasantly side by side and complement each other: the natural research exposing how copper might be found and extracted (among other things), and the laboratory research studying its properties and what might be done with it once it had been extracted. Both strands of research might be brought together by an industrialist interested in creating tubing and eventually incorporated by a plumber. The whole thing works for the physical sciences because there is a difference between copper in its natural state and what it might be molded into with human intervention. Of course, "pure" research might be valuable in its own right, and it might be a worthy thing just to know about copper in the abstract.

What separates the study of copper from the study of human social behavior is matters of choice and of consciousness. Copper can't choose to appear to be zinc for the sake of pleasing the scientist, or feel embarrassed or excited by the various manipulations worked on it in the laboratory. Although it is true that the process of observation itself can change the physical properties of some matter (the much-discussed and often misinterpreted Heisenberg principle), those changes are not presumed to be the result of choices or emotional reactions on the part of subatomic particles. Human social behavior, however, takes place in a context that gives it much of its meaning. Divorcing human behavior from its context may be necessary to conduct laboratory research, but it introduces a problem of validity—that is, how confident are we that we're still studying what we set out to study? In different contexts, people make different choices, influenced by a variety of factors related, in part, to their sense of what is appropriate or desirable for them to do under these circumstances.

When copper is removed from its natural environment and brought to the laboratory, it doesn't try to figure out what kind of coppery behavior is appropriate to this new place. It would be unusual for human beings to be similarly indifferent to the social demands of a new context. Among the considerations people have as they acclimate themselves to a new social situation is how they will react to stimuli in the environment. Men and women brought together to form a mock jury in a laboratory know to one extent or another to regard each other differently than if they were brought together in a frat party or a wedding. Factors such as sexual attraction, relative alcohol tolerance, or dancing ability may be ignored as bases for deciding with whom one will talk in the laboratory, but may be considered urgent in another social context. People's beliefs about how others will evaluate them and their behavior are also contextual. As much as their own choices are influenced by different factors in different contexts, people know that others have expectations of them in one context that would be inappropriate in another context, and they adjust their behavior accordingly; behaving like a responsible juror will not get you invited to future frat parties.

The potential for publicity to influence people's beliefs about a defendant depends in no small part on the social context in which people confront the publicity. Publicity is only *pretrial* publicity when there is an expectation that a trial will ensue at some point. The context in which most people, even those who will become jurors, confront what lawyers consider pretrial publicity is more likely to be one in which the publicity is pre-dinner publicity, or pre-bedtime publicity, or pre-breakfast publicity.

Because pretrial publicity does not exist outside a context, trying to study its "pure" features is a futile effort. Who cares if social scientists can create a condition where pretrial publicity does produce an effect in the laboratory if those conditions never occur during actual trials? Is it worth knowing that social scientists can create biased trials even if trials aren't biased in actual practice? What's the point in knowing that, absent deliberation, pretrial publicity will produce bias, if all actual trials have deliberation? Such research might have value in reminding us all of the importance of deliberation, but it can hardly be taken as evidence that pretrial publicity is biasing actual trials. The present review takes the perspective that laboratory research is important and that it contains important information that can inform the scholarly discussion, but that questions of generalizability (the sole focus of this chapter) must be clearly separated from questions of value. As others (e.g., Jones, 1991) have noted, research can contain a wealth of interesting information and still not speak to questions of courtroom application. That is to say, the studies discussed here are generally excellent and their authors have been extremely conscientious in their research decisions and are usually fully open about the limits of their own research. Nothing presented here is intended to suggest that any research has been poorly done or is invalid. There are many good reasons that laboratory researchers will create careful controls to explore specific questions. However, not all quality laboratory research will necessarily speak to the question of whether pretrial publicity biases actual trials. The exclusive focus of this chapter is not whether research has been done well or poorly, but whether the research can be extrapolated to actual trial contexts.

The yardstick for measuring whether laboratory research can be extrapolated to actual courtrooms should be whether or not a study's manipulations create conditions that differ from actual courtrooms in ways that are likely to alter the outcomes. Toward that end, the studies reviewed next are evaluated against five criteria (different criteria are offered elsewhere; see Studebaker et al., 2002; Vidmar, 2002). In general, these criteria are based on the assumption that for research findings to extrapolate, the sample must have the same characteristics as the population to which the findings are to be applied. This is basic sampling theory (see, e.g., Spiegel, 1990, chap. 8).

The first criterion is that the jurors or mock jurors in the sample should be demographically similar to jurors who hear actual trials. Review methodologists have isolated sample similarity as a crucial factor in analysis (Hedges, 1990). Of the 43 independent tests Steblay et al. (1999) reported, 23 used only student samples and 6 included student samples. It is obvious that jury populations differ from undergraduate student populations in a number of important regards, beginning with simple demographic features. Because demographic factors generally reflect different life experiences, they can alter the ways that jurors process trial information (e.g., Fairchild & Cowan, 1997; Newman, Duff, Schnopp-Wyatt, Brock, & Hoffman, 1997; Skolnick & Shaw, 1997). It is therefore inappropriate to study a sample group that is known, a priori, to differ from the population the study is ultimately concerned with. Many scholars concur with the need to utilize realistic samples (e.g., Freedman et al., 1998; Kerwin & Shaffer, 1994; London & Nunez, 2000; Padawer-Singer et al., 1974, 1977), and thus studies based solely on undergraduate samples are suspect.

There are contrasting opinions. Bornstein (1999) reviewed 26 studies that had both student and nonstudent samples and discovered that only 5 reported significant differences between the groups and only 2 studies reported significant interactions with other variables. Bornstein concluded that "These findings bode well for the feasibility of generalizing from simulation studies to the behavior of real jurors" (p. 88). Three points may be made here. First, as Bornstein noted elsewhere (Bornstein & Rajki, 1994), a student sample might not be a concern in itself, but if the sample covaries with other factors that are important, generalizability will be frustrated. The most obvious factors that student status might covary with are demographic ones. Such concerns might be eliminated if the effect size of demographic variables is "only modest," as Bornstein suggested (p. 77). Others have come to similar conclusions and noted that demographic variables do not predict case outcomes as well as attitudinal variables (Bornstein & Rajki, 1994; Fulero & Penrod, 1990; Palmer, Baer, Jasperson, & DeLaat, 2001; Peacock, Cowan, Bommersbach, Smith, & Stahly, 1997) or are generally weak predictors overall (Olczak, Kaplan, & Penrod, 1991). The effect sizes these conclusions are drawn on range from between 3% (the Olczak et al. conclusion based on Penrod's 1979 dissertation) or 8% (Bornstein's reported citation of Hepburn's 1980 research). The midpoint of these effect sizes is nearly identical to the effect size reported for pretrial publicity by Stebaly et al. (1999), who report an overall r of .16, or 3% of variance. In other words, although the effect sizes for demographic variables are not especially large, they are almost the same as the effect sizes for pretrial publicity. It would be odd indeed to discount the influence of demographic variables for the purposes of concluding in favor of a pretrial publicity effect when the effect sizes of those different variables are practically identical. A first reason to reject Bornstein's conclusion is that demographic factors are not inconsequential, at least not in relation to pretrial publicity.

Second, of greatest importance is not necessarily whether student samples differ from nonstudent samples, but whether the variable interacts with other crucial factors (Studebaker et al., 2002). Such interactions have rarely been studied; Bornstein's (1999) review concerned itself with student samples and trial media as possible threats to ecological validity, and noted that the interaction between those two variables had never been studied. It is possible that student status might interact with other important variables in ways that have also not yet been studied. For example, it is easy to imagine that a group of students in their late teens and early twenties might react differently to judicial authority and instructions than would older persons, a possibility Bornstein reviewed and found mixed evidence for. It is also not difficult to imagine that deliberations might interact with student status; simply imagine the differences that might be expected between any hour-long discussion by a group of college students and a discussion by a group made up of people found on jury rolls on the same topic. Coalitions might be critical; Daudistel et al. (1999) studied actual court decisions in Texas and found that juror racial characteristics did matter, but only when a critical mass of ethnic people was on the jury panel. Thus, not only might juror demographic characteristics be important, but so might be the overall composition of the jury panel. An individual student juror might not alter the outcome of a jury panel but a group of college students might produce a different verdict than a group of nonstudents. At any rate, these various possibilities are poorly understood and rarely studied, a fact that should warrant caution when generalizing from student samples.

A third point concerns the meaning of a 21-to-5 split in study counting. As commentators about reviews pointed out (Cook & Leviton, 1980), neither meta-analyses nor the method of comparing raw counts of studies that do and do not find significant differences can change the meaning of an averaged effect—one that is the summary conclusion of a number of studies. For example, if five studies find an effect and five do not, the "average" result is zero, but it is of course most likely that in reality an effect exists, and good social science will try to tease out why the studies came to differing results rather than simply concluding that no effect exists by relying on the averaged effect. If some studies find an effect and others do not, three possibilities exist: The significant differences can be a methodological artifact (perhaps of poor control), the nonsignificant differences can be a methodological artifact (perhaps of low power or poor manipulation), or the effect might emerge in some situations but not others. Those factors that make the effect emerge might not be readily apparent to either researchers or reviewers. In the present case, we are left to explain why significant differences between student and nonstudent samples did emerge in five studies. There is some evidence to suggest that demographic variables emerge as important only in certain situations, such as when race is salient and when it is not (Sommers & Ellsworth, 2001). It may therefore be that, to the extent that student status covaries with other demographic variables, and those differences emerge only in certain conditions that are largely un-contemplated in pretrial publicity research, the 21-to-5 article count reveals that student status can emerge in ways that researchers are not yet able to predict. Such a circumstance again warns against wholesale adoption of student-sample research.

Finally, it is worth noting that Bornstein (1999) ultimately concluded that trial factors are the most crucial ones, a finding consistent with the conclusion that trial evidence is the most important factor in determining trial outcomes. If we believe that trial evidence is more important than experience before the trial, it is not difficult to come to the conclusion that in actual practice pretrial publicity is not an insurmountable threat and might be subject to remedy. We can only conclude that student status is unimportant in determining the way jurors will process information they come to via pretrial publicity if we believe that, of all the pretrial experiences jurors have had, the exposure to a few articles of news coverage is more important and unchanged by years of differing experience based on race, class, gender, and other demographic factors. Such is unlikely to be the case. For these reasons, we believe student samples do not necessarily speak to actual practice, Bornstein's defense of them notwithstanding.

The second criterion is that conviction rates in academic studies should match those of actual trials. Criminal conviction rates are quite high in actual trials, around 80% (Federal Judicial Center, 2001). In some experiments, the trials to be decided by mock jurors are chosen because they have been shown to produce a 50% conviction rate among previous mock juries. This design presumably offers the best opportunity to clarify the effect size of any pretrial publicity effect. A study that pretests for a 50% conviction rate, therefore, chooses to study one sample (a group of criminal cases for which conviction rates are 50%) that differs systematically from the population that the researcher would like to know about (criminal cases for which conviction rates are 80%). In no other area of social science would such a move be accepted uncritically. There are many points to be made about ceiling effects and other statistical phenomena that might confound the interpretation of any findings, but the point here is more basic. Extrapolation requires that the cases under study not differ in known ways from the cases the findings are to be extended to. Imagine a study done on ways to improve the free-throw shooting of basketball players. A study conducted on players who can make 50% of their free throws might conclude that training them to focus on the back of the rim improves their free-throw percentage. It is not necessarily true that the same training would help a group who could make 80% of their free throws. The 80% group might already focus on the back of the rim, or have a number of habits (keeping the ball on their finger tips, positioning their feet correctly, etc.) that make focusing on the back of the rim a net liability (so to speak). Of course, the researcher would never know what separates the 50% shooters from the 80% shooters without further study. All that is known in advance is that they are probably different in some important way. For this reason, assuming that what is true of one group will extrapolate to the other is a dubious intellectual move. This point is not controversial and is about as basic as sampling theory gets.

Although error sometimes does not distort results in a predictable direction, in this instance the sampling procedure can only inflate the chances of finding a pretrial publicity effect. The possibility that *any* source of bias, based on publicity or anything else, might influence the jury's decision is highest when the trial evidence is inconclusive (Kaplan & Miller, 1978; Kerwin & Shaffer, 1994). It is difficult to imagine any situation where studying close cases would reduce the chances of finding a pretrial publicity effect. In sum, studies should examine a sample of cases that has the same characteristics as the population in question, for both theoretical and practical reasons. It is inappropriate to conclude that a source of bias that alters outcomes in a pool of cases that produces 50% conviction rates will also alter outcomes in a pool of cases that produces 80% conviction rates.

Third, the amounts of pretrial publicity should match actual levels of exposure. Obviously, research based on studies with vast exposure cannot be easily applied to cases with minimal exposure. What constitutes a lot of exposure? Some researchers believe that exposure to a single article is an awfully weak manipulation (Kovera, 2002), and others find that in general pretrial publicity has relied on fairly weak manipulations (Studebaker et al., 2002). These conclusions have not been based on comparisons to actual coverage levels. Eighty-one percent of actual federal murder trials are not covered at all, roughly 11% are covered in only a single article, roughly 7% are covered with two to four articles, and only 1% are covered with more than five articles (Bruschke & Loges, 1999). Thus, any case receiving more than five articles worth of coverage represents a relatively extreme coverage condition. This number is undoubtedly a low-ball figure; the existence of an article does not mean that all potential jurors have read it. Vidmar (2002) reported a telling example. A sample of 109 respondents were all given one to three newspapers to read and instructed to read them as they normally would. The papers included a front-page story on the drug trade with the headline "Unmasked: Our New Drug Bosses" and a large color photograph with the name of the defendant and the caption "Top Heroin Distributor." Included also were two accompanying stories; some respondents were also given subsequent newspapers with follow-up stories on the drug trade. The paper identified the defendant with the drug distributor's nickname "Uncle Six" 17 different times. Respondents were contacted again 2 weeks later. None of 109 respondents in the experimental condition could spontaneously link the defendant to "Uncle Six" even with prompting that included other possible drug-dealer names. When directly questioned, only 1 of 109 respondents could link the defendant to "Uncle Six." Although with prompting respondents could link the name to drug trade, they also linked a fictitious control name of a similar cultural heritage to the drug trade to the same degree. Vidmar concluded that this research and other research on the media "raises important questions about the effects of even highly prejudicial news stories that are subject to selective exposure, that occur in isolation, that occur without additional indication of interest among members of the community, and that are removed in time from jury selection" (p. 90). The figure of five articles constituting a "high publicity" case, therefore, is a very conservative guess, and it can safely be said that in actual practice jurors read five or more articles about a crime in less than 1% of actual criminal trials.

We note in passing that some critics of our work assume that virtually all trials receive coverage and that coverage on the scale of the Simpson or McVeigh trials is typical of "high-publicity" cases or that it is only slightly elevated from coverage typically received. Instead, those trials are truly exceptional and of historic proportion (Kulish, 1998; Walton, 1998) and serve to set the benchmark for the most obscene abuses of overcoverage rather than defining what is typical.

Fourth, any manipulation should include some form of jury deliberation, for at least two reasons. First, generally speaking, there is reason to believe that deliberation can alter the outcome of trials. It is true that some commentators believe that jury deliberation does not eliminate potential pretrial publicity biases or may exaggerate them (Fein, McCloskey, & Tomlinson, 1997; Kramer et al., 1990; Padawer-Singer & Barton, 1975; Studebaker & Penrod, 1997). These claims notwithstanding, there is a host of research that supports the notion that decisions reached individually are different than decisions reached in groups (Hans & Doob, 1976; Kaplan & Miller, 1978; Kline & Jess, 1966; Thompson, Fong, & Rosenhan, 1981) and that deliberation does change the nature of jury decisions (Davis, 1986; Kramer et al., 1990; Otto et al., 1994). Some research suggests an especially powerful influence of deliberation—in particular, that deliberations plus instructions can eliminate bias even when either remedy applied in isolation fails (Kerwin & Shaffer, 1994; London & Nunez, 2000). Without taking a position on the effectiveness of jury deliberations in eliminating a pretrial publicity effect, it is clear that group decisions differ from individual decisions. The field of small-group communication has presented a host of theoretical reasons why this is the case (for a textbook summary of the theories see Infante, Rancer, & Womack, 1997, chap. 9). Once again, there is danger in trying to extrapolate from a population that is making decisions individually to a population that *always* makes decisions in groups. To put the point another way, no actual defendant has ever been convicted on the basis of a predeliberation verdict, and there is danger in trying to base conclusions about postdeliberation decisions on studies that have examined only predeliberation verdicts.

A second reason deliberations are crucial is that some research indicates that the failure of deliberations to succeed in some situations may be due to a methodological flaw in disconfirming studies. Noting that studies that found a postdeliberation pretrial publicity effect also typically required that mock jurors render predeliberation judgments, Freedman et al. (1998) conducted two studies. The first study did not request a predeliberation verdict and was unable to uncover a pretrial publicity effect. The second study manipulated predeliberation verdicts as an independent variable and found that pretrial publicity effects emerged only when mock jurors provided predeliberation judgments. Most profoundly, this suggests that all evidence in favor of a pretrial publicity effect may be a methodological artifact, but at a minimum the results suggest that deliberation can serve as an important mediating variable that would be hazardous for pretrial publicity researchers to ignore.

Fifth, the delay between exposure to publicity and presentation of trial evidence should simulate actual conditions. As Davis (1986) stated: "Measurement of processes by which jurors either succumb to or reveal bias, and the manipulation of time intervals in pretrial publicity research, are crucial but largely missing elements" (p. 593). Others concurred with the point (Greene & Wade, 1988; Mullin, Imrich, & Linz, 1996; Pember, 1984; Sherard, 1987; Vidmar, 2002; Wilcox, 1970), and Hvistendahl (1979), an early researcher in the area, was careful to note this limited his own findings. Since Hvistendahl it has been more common for commentators to repeat the point than it has been for researchers to consider it carefully. A delay between exposure to a media message and a trial is the sort of "natural" remedy that might reduce any biasing effect of pretrial publicity. There is some evidence that many jurors simply can't remember the coverage by the time a case comes to trial (Bauer, 1976), and strong evidence that viewers in general do not retain much information they get from the media (Robinson & Levy, 1986; Steblay et al., 1999; Vidmar, 2002; see Pember, 1984, 1990). Relying again on the drug-dealer study and general media research, Vidmar (2002) concluded: "These findings also raise questions about the ecological validity of simulation studies that provide one-shot exposure to brief synopses of prejudicial materials and then require the subjects to render verdicts on a defendant shortly afterward, sometimes within minutes" (p. 90). It is a questionable practice to extrapolate to a population where there is always a notable gap between exposure and trial evidence from a sample where there is no gap between publicity exposure and the presentation of trial evidence.

These, then, are the criteria. A laboratory study is taken here to be similar to an actual trial to the extent that it (a) relies on actual jurors and not student samples, (b) uses cases with conviction rates that are similar to actual trials, (c) examines common rather than extreme amounts of coverage, (d) allows mock jurors to deliberate, and (e) allows for a natural delay between exposure to publicity and presentation of the trial. This list is not exhaustive. Studies may include manipulations that are different from actual courtrooms in any number of ways. When appropriate, comments are made about additional weaknesses (or strengths) of the studies reviewed next. However, this list does encompass some obvious and potentially important points, and it should serve as a useful yardstick when assessing the realism of a study. All three preliminary tasks have now been accomplished. The set of studies to be reviewed has been selected, the studies have then been grouped into five different types, and a set of criteria to evaluate them has been established. The next step in assessing what we know is to review the extant research.

LABORATORY STUDIES THAT DID NOT INCLUDE TRIAL EVIDENCE

Of the five different groups of studies, those that did not include trial evidence are the least relevant to actual practice. A defendant convicted without a trial would have much more to worry about than too much pretrial publicity. The extreme importance of evidence is a point that is developed in some depth later, and trial evidence may serve as the most important natural "remedy" to pretrial publicity. Nonetheless, there are patterns in this section of the literature that are informative, and no review should proceed in ignorance of this work if for no other reason that to guard against babies being thrown out with bathwater. Twelve studies examined pretrial publicity in the absence of trial information (Constantini & King, 1980–1981; Greene & Loftus, 1984; Hvistendahl, 1979; Moran & Cutler, 1991; Ogloff & Vidmar, 1994; Riley, 1973; Rollings &

Blascovich, 1977; Shaffer, 1986; Simon & Eimermann, 1971; Sohn, 1976; Tans & Chaffee, 1966; Vidmar & Judson, 1981). The findings all point to the similar conclusion that respondents exposed to pretrial publicity will generally be biased against defendants prior to the introduction of trial evidence, and that the more information that respondents retain, the more likely they are to prejudge guilt. This view is consistent with the idea that jurors act as "optimal decision makers"—that is, they will use all the information at their disposal to try to reach a just verdict (Bornstein & Rajki, 1994). This proposition is referred to as the "knowledge–guilt" hypothesis.

Three studies are particularly informative. Vidmar and Judson (1981) conducted phone interviews about a high-profile business fraud case in Canada and found that respondents who had any knowledge of the case at all were more likely to conclude the defendant was "probably guilty" (76%) than were respondents with no knowledge of the case (67%). Constantini and King (1980–1981) studied three publicized cases in California, and measured knowledge about the case on a 7-item quiz. Based on the number of correct answers to scale, respondents were divided into groups designated as poorly, moderately, or well informed. Although poorly informed respondents concluded that the defendants were guilty between 2% and 30% of the time (depending on the case under study), well-informed respondents concluded guilt 54% to 61% of the time. Very similarly, Moran and Cutler (1991) studied a drug case in Illinois and a homicide case in Florida and asked respondents five to eight specific questions about the case. They found a clear, linear relationship between the number of questions that could be answered correctly and the conclusion that there was "a lot of evidence" against the defendant. For example, in the Illinois case only 11% of respondents who could answer no question about the case correctly concluded that there was a lot of evidence against the defendant, whereas 60% of the respondents who could answer seven or more questions correctly came to that conclusion. Using slightly different methods, three other studies came to similar conclusions (Ogloff & Vidmar, 1994; Riley, 1973; Shaffer, 1986; Simon & Eimermann, 1971; Sohn, 1976; Tans & Chaffee, 1966).

Two studies lend only equivocal support to the conclusion that pretrial publicity biases potential jurors in the absence of trial evidence. Hvistendahl (1979) studied story placement and defendant characteristics across six conditions, and found a significant biasing effect in only one condition. Rollings and Blascovich (1977) studied the Patty Hearst trial and found that there was not a prodefendant shift in public opinion following Heart's arrest and publicization of her "brainwashing" defense, and concluded that the influence of pretrial publicity may have been overstated. Although that conclusion is very much in line with the position taken in this book, there are obvious limitations to the reasoning of Rollings and Blascovich. The effect that they expected to find was a prodefendant shift following the publicity surrounding Hearst's defense.

Discovering that there was no prodefendant shift is quite different from finding that antidefendant publicity could infringe on defendant's rights, and it would be an obvious error to conclude that if the media can't help defendants it must not be able to hurt them either. In addition, the study did not ask respondents for their personal belief about whether Hearst was guilty, but instead asked their opinion about whether she would be found guilty by the court. Once again, it is obviously suspect to equate opinions about guilt with opinions of what others think about guilt, if for no other reason than the well-established finding that people tend to overestimate the extent to which the media influence others (called the "third-person" effect in media research; Davidson, 1982).

A final point about Rollings and Blascovich is that their data, more than their conclusions, support the knowledge–guilt hypothesis. Note that 94% of respondents concluded that Hearst would be found guilty before her arrest (when all publicity was antidefendant) and 91% concluded she would be found guilty afterward (when her defense was presumably disseminated by the press). It may have been the case that Hearst had already been judged guilty by the time of her arrest and the assertion of her defense didn't change matters, or it may have simply been that her defense was implausible. It is striking that in the Hearst case, where most respondents had probably been exposed to pretrial information, over 90% believed that Hearst would be found guilty. It is easy to observe these data and believe that those exposed to pretrial publicity but not trial evidence tend to presume defendant guilt.

This interpretation of the findings of Rollings and Blascovich aside, one study has suggested that the knowledge–guilt hypothesis may work in reverse and that prodefendant information may bias cases in favor of the defense. Greene and Loftus (1984) advanced the idea that general stories of injustice against criminal defendants could bias public opinions in favor of defendants (Tans & Chaffee, 1966, found similar evidence in this regard). Although the idea is an interesting one, scant evidence is offered in its defense. The authors conducted two studies. The first was not designed to test for external influences, but was a simulated trial study that took place over several months. The authors noted that during a month when a story about injustice appeared in the media the conviction rates in their simulated trial dropped. Quantitative analysis, however, revealed that the drop was not statistically significant. The second study was concerned with a *Reader's Digest* story about an injustice. *Reader's Digest* subscribers (who might have been exposed to the prodefendant story) were compared against nonsubscribers and no differences were found. However, when subscribers who could recall the story ($n = 13$) were compared with subscribers who could not ($n = 23$), differences were observed. Overall, Greene and Loftus's conclusion is based on a sample of only 36 respondents, and for two of three comparisons they conducted significant differences were not obtained.

The possibility that general stories of injustice might bias trials in favor of criminal defendants is an interesting one that does raise some fascinating questions. Should a criminal defense attorney facing pretrial publicity counter by releasing stories about wrongfully convicted defendants in general? Are such stories useful remedies? Ought pretrial publicity be countered by competing media images (an idea that sounds absurd on its face, but may be the most effective if trial-time remedies are as useless as current reviews suggest)? These questions will be explored in more depth later in the book, but three points suffice for now. First, whatever its possibilities, a prodefendant effect for general stories of injustice received very minimal support by Greene and Loftus. It is at present little more than a useful idea to explore. Second, such prodefendant coverage is rare. Much more common are reports that violate American Bar Association (ABA) standards of coverage. Third, such a finding does not contrast with the general knowledge–guilt hypothesis. It may be the case that both propositions may have merit. It may be true that the more specific knowledge potential jurors have about a case, the more they will presume guilt, and it may also be the case that potential jurors who see stories about wrongful convictions will tend to presume innocence. It is unknown whether these two different phenomena might cancel each other out.

In sum, research conducted in the absence of trial evidence is generally supportive of the knowledge–guilt hypothesis. Potential jurors who are exposed to pretrial information will generally be more likely to prejudge against the defense. Furthermore, in a linear fashion, the more information that jurors can retain the more likely they are to carry antidefendant attitudes. The studies in this group, by their very designs, offer no information about whether pretrial publicity can influence jury verdicts (or even individual juror opinions) after trial evidence and deliberation, but they do offer some compelling information about the ways that pretrial publicity can influence potential jurors before a trial starts, and the news is not good for criminal defendants.

STUDIES THAT INCLUDED TRIAL EVIDENCE AND FOUND A PRETRIAL PUBLICITY EFFECT

Eight studies have included trial evidence and found a pretrial publicity effect. However, virtually all of these studies have been conducted under circumstances that differ from actual trials in very important ways. The eight studies are considered in the chronological order of their publication. An interesting theme that begins to emerge in these studies is the importance of trial evidence. Without really attempting to study the relative importance of trial evidence in relation to pretrial publicity, a careful reading of the findings of this set of studies shows that even if pretrial publicity does emerge as a biasing factor (it does in this set of studies but not in others), the influence is much smaller than the influence of trial evidence. This is, of course, encouraging for the course of justice. At any rate, these eight studies represent the best case that can be made for a pretrial publicity effect, and this review tries to assess whether that case is convincing.

Sue, Smith, and Gilbert (1974)

These authors created a case that involved a robbery or murder, gave respondents a four-page booklet describing the trial, and exposed them to pretrial publicity that reported that the defendant had a gun and then either did or did not connect the gun to the crime. Respondents exposed to the version of publicity that connected the gun to the crime convicted more frequently (43%) than respondents exposed to the publicity that reported the gun but did not link it to the crime (23%), and the authors concluded that there was therefore a pretrial publicity effect. There are at least four reasons these findings are difficult to extrapolate. First, there was no condition that included a "no publicity" control group, and thus it is not known how respondents who were not exposed to either form of publicity would react. Second, the overall conviction rate averaged to 33% even though all respondents were exposed to some form of antidefendant pretrial publicity. Given that actual criminal conviction rates are around 80%, it is difficult to conclude that conditions that produce 33% conviction rates are especially damaging to defendant interests. In any event, the conviction rates obtained in the study differed substantially from actual conviction rates. Third, there was no deliberation. Fourth, there was no delay between exposure to the potentially damaging publicity and the presentation of the trial evidence. In sum, this preliminary but suggestive study provided useful information but did not convincingly speak to how pretrial publicity might operate during actual trials.

Padawer-Singer and Barton (1975)

The article contained two studies. The first involved a mock murder trial that ultimately produced a conviction rate of 45% to 55%. All of the 120 jurors (drawn from actual jury rolls) read pretrial publicity. The "prejudicial" condition included information about a retracted confession and criminal background, both bits of information that would be inadmissible. The "neutral" condition included information that was admissible at trial. The participants were grouped into juries; only 3 of 12 juries reached verdicts after 6 hours of deliberation. The votes of individual jurors demonstrated higher conviction rates for the prejudicial publicity condition (78% vs. 55%), but the authors ran no significance tests due to a lack of independence in the observations (for statistical tests to be valid, each data point, in this case each juror verdict, must be independent of each other data point; Spiegel, 1990). The second study was a replication of the first and was conducted with 266 mock jurors drawn from actual courts in New York. Once again, hung juries were a common outcome and only 14 of 23 juries came to a verdict. The authors combined majority guilty and unanimous verdicts and found a higher conviction rate for the prejudicial publicity condition (70% vs. 31%).

In general, the study was well done and used an excellent sample, allowed the participants to deliberate, and the amount of pretrial publicity did not seem unusual. The authors were admirably reluctant to conduct statistical tests that might have been misleading and were unwilling to attach too much significance to the verdicts of individual jurors rather than juries. The nature of the publicity, however, may have been especially onerous. A retracted confession may be especially damaging and is certainly probative. There was no delay between exposure to the pretrial publicity and the trial, and the conviction rates were quite different from those obtained in actual trials. Even the conviction rates found in the high publicity condition were lower than those found in actual trials.

One critical element is the large number of hung juries. The authors resort to counting majority votes to estimate the results of hung juries, but the use of this method might make the finding inapplicable to actual trials. In actual cases (depending, of course, on local court rules), a single juror can hold out and force a retrial, which is by itself a victory for a defendant, especially in a system that produces 80% convictions. In addition, the second trial introduces a "natural" continuance, mitigating against any pretrial publicity factors at a second trial. At any rate, it is one thing to show that after 6 hours of deliberation a majority of jurors would vote guilty, and quite another to show that a majority of juries would vote guilty (a point others have made). It is something else still to show that after 6 hours of deliberation most juries are hung, which this study does, and something that's probably good for defendants.

The nature of the publicity in this mock case may provide clues about when and how pretrial publicity might be the most biasing. Basically, the study involved a case that had very weak evidence at trial but very important information in the pretrial publicity. This is the description of the prosecution case provided by the authors:

> A prominent woman in Washington, D.C., was found shot to death in a park. A man was found in the area and arrested. He was identified by someone who had seen him from over 100 feet away as the man who bent over the victim a short time after the witness had heard the victim's cries. The gun was never found. The prosecution claimed that all official exits were closed only minutes after the murder had been committed. The defense established the existence of other unofficial, unmarked exits. The defendant did not take the stand. (p. 129)

By any account, this is a weak case for the prosecution. There is no physical evidence and the eyewitness testimony could not even establish that the defendant was the shooter, but only that the defendant was near the body. The pretrial publicity, meanwhile, revealed that the defendant had originally confessed to the crime (and later retracted that confession) and that the defendant had a criminal history. What this study may demonstrate most clearly is that in the instance where the trial evidence is weak but extremely probative information is contained in pretrial publicity, jurors may lean on whatever probative information they have at their disposal. How often this situation occurs in actual trials is unknown.

Two remaining factors mitigate against the conclusion that this article provides evidence of a pretrial publicity effect. First, the study used a voir dire procedure, conducted in the study but reported in a separate article (Padawer-Singer et al., 1974), which was effective in eliminating any pretrial publicity bias. This data set thus shows that pretrial publicity biases trials only in the absence of voir dire. Of course, actual trials have some jury selection procedure. Second, there was no true control group; all participants read "one 'neutral' clipping dealing with facts which were admissible in court" (p. 129). Information that is admissible in court may still work contrary to defense interests when reported in the press, especially if the knowledge–guilt hypothesis is correct. Thus there was no true control group unexposed to publicity. There is also no guarantee that all admissible facts will be introduced at trial.

In sum, this study fully satisfies three of the five criteria. It did not, however, have a delay between exposure to the publicity and exposure to the trial, nor did it select a case with conviction rates mirroring those of actual trials. The fact that conviction rates were only 40% in the group exposed to "neutral" publicity suggests that jurors may not be unduly influenced by pretrial information and lends further credence to the conclusion that pretrial publicity evidence is most damaging when it is probative. The study lacked a true control group and the authors' own results, published separately, indicate that when voir dire procedures are implemented any effect of pretrial publicity is successfully mitigated. This study certainly provides some information suggesting a pretrial publicity effect, but the evidence is far from conclusive, and ultimately the data are more supportive of the contention that pretrial publicity can be remedied.

Sue, Smith, and Pedroza (1975)

In a very similar study to the prior effort of the first two authors, 158 undergraduates were given a four-page booklet describing a robbery and murder. The "pretrial publicity" condition included an article that mentioned that the defendant had been found with a gun that ballistics tests proved had been the murder weapon. It further mentioned that the gun had been suppressed as evidence at the trial. The "no publicity" condition made no mention of a gun. The results showed that those exposed to the prejudicial pretrial publicity were more likely to convict (53% vs. 23%), that the personality trait of authoritarianism was not linked to guilt outcomes, that pretrial publicity influenced ratings of evidence strength, and that those mock jurors who admitted bias were more likely to vote guilty. The study falls short of four of the five criteria instantly; the study used a student sample, the conviction rates were far askew of those in actual trials and much lower, there was no deliberation, and there was no delay between exposure to the pretrial publicity and exposure to the trial. There was also no control group that had no exposure to press accounts of the crime.

On the final criteria, the amount of exposure, the manipulation in this study seems acceptable. The nature of the publicity, however, was incriminating in the extreme (Freedman et al., 1998). Much as with the Padawer-Singer and Barton article, this paper might demonstrate that the probative value of the publicity is a crucial variable. Information that the defendant was in possession of the gun that was definitively proven to be the murder weapon speaks to guilt even more than a retracted confession. Once again, it seems plausible that pretrial publicity might influence jurors when it includes information that speaks to guilt more clearly than the evidence at trial. This finding is again supportive of the knowledge–guilt hypothesis, and demonstrates that specific knowledge about the case can lead to presumptions of guilt.

Also interesting is the finding that pretrial publicity influences perceptions of evidence strength. Such a finding suggests that perhaps perceptions of evidence strength mediate any relationship between pretrial publicity and the trial outcome. Other research has shown that mock jurors have difficulty separating evidence out and isolating their evaluations of it. For example, instructions to disregard evidence may fail and actually make jurors pay more attention to the evidence (Rieke & Stutman, 1990, p. 61). Research on trials with joined offenses has found that as the defendant is charged with more counts conviction rates go up (Tanford & Penrod, 1982), even compared to the situation where the offenses were tried sequentially. Even more suggestively, the Tanford and Penrod study found that the strongest predictor of verdict was perception of evidence strength, leading the authors to conclude that study participants in all conditions based their decisions on their perception of the strength of the evidence, but that in the joined offense condition the cumulative effect of the evidence strengthened perceptions that there was a lot of evidence against the defendant. These findings are consistent with research that has found that evidence strength is a crucial, and perhaps dominant, factor in determining verdicts (Visher, 1987).

All these findings, taken together, point to the conclusion that perceptions of evidence strength are crucial, that they may mediate any pretrial publicity effect, and that evidence perceptions are cumulative. Thus, when pretrial publicity contains evidence that very clearly speaks to guilt, such as the mention that the defendant was found with a gun that ballistics determined to be the murder weapon, such information may shade the way that jurors process the rest of the evidence. This view is more nuanced than that of other reviews, and suggests a different picture from that suggested elsewhere. Jurors, it appears, are not influenced by emotionally charged images, and do in fact try their best to base their decisions on the evidence presented at trial. The fact that only 53% of mock jurors who heard that the defendant was found with the murder weapon ultimately voted to convict may actually prove, more than anything else, that jurors will try mightily to remain unbiased, even when they have probative but inadmissible evidence at their disposal. If jurors are faithful to their task of deciding the case on the basis of the evidence and nothing more, pretrial publicity is most onerous when it includes information that will influence perceptions of evidence strength.

It is interesting to notice that thus far in all three studies that have found a pretrial publicity effect the pretrial publicity included probative information not available to jurors elsewhere—information that linked the defendant to the crime very directly (via either retracted confession or possession of a murder weapon) but that was not presented at trial. By any account, this represents a very extreme publicity condition, and if most trials that involve publicity do not involve the reporting of inadmissible but probative evidence the results of these studies may not be generally applicable. At a theoretical level, these findings suggest that the characteristic of pretrial publicity most important to whether or not it influences a jury is its probative value.

Kramer and Kerr (1989)

These authors were primarily concerned with how trial complexity interacted with pretrial publicity. After choosing a case that was pretested to have conviction rates that fell between 40% and 50%, 529 undergraduates were shown either a long (100-minute) or short (10-minute) version of a trial. Half of the participants were exposed to videotaped pretrial publicity varied to contain high or low factual or emotional content. In the weakest pretrial publicity condition (low emotional/low factual bias) it was simply reported that a crime had occurred and that the defendant had been arrested, whereas in the strongest publicity condition (high emotional/high factual bias) news reports contained information about a prior criminal record and suppressed but incriminating evidence found at the defendant's girlfriend's house. The report went on to strongly imply that the defendant had hit and killed a 7-year-old girl with his car and then left the scene, and the publicity included pictures of the girl's weeping mother. The results showed that either emotional or factual publicity increased conviction rates (53% vs. 43% guilty for factual publicity and 57% vs. 43% guilty for emotional publicity) and that the shorter trial increased conviction rates (53% vs. 44% guilty). The two factors did not interact, however, and thus the length of the trial did not exacerbate the publicity effect. Pretrial publicity increased sentence lengths.

As with the prior studies, this investigation immediately fails four of the five criteria. The sample was composed of undergraduates, the conviction rates were intentionally suppressed by the authors, there was no deliberation, and there was no delay between exposure to the publicity and exposure to the trial. On the final criterion, degree of exposure, the amount of publicity seems typical of most cases but once again the manipulations seem especially damaging. In addition to including information of probative value (evidence found at the girlfriend's house), the emotional publicity painted the defendant in an especially depraved light. Imagine how different the O. J. Simpson trial would have been, for example, had Simpson run over and killed a 7-year-old girl during his famous Bronco chase. In sum, this study proves that undergraduates exposed to extreme publicity immediately before a trial will, in the absence of deliberation, render guilty verdicts about 10% more often than unexposed jurors, but will even then vote guilty just barely over half the time. On its face, this effect of pretrial publicity does not seem especially damaging, especially compared to 80% conviction rates in actual trials. The gap between these conditions and those of an actual trial is large, however, and there is reason to believe that these findings might be much different from those obtained in more realistic circumstances.

Once again, there are details in the study that point to the importance of trial evidence. The authors believe their trial length manipulation might have inadvertently introduced an evidence effect. They wrote: "We suspect that this [trial length] effect has less to do with trial length, per se, than with uncontrolled differences in the quality or perceived quality of the evidence against the defendant between the long and short trial" (p. 97). Such a conclusion, of course, lends further support to the viewpoint that evidence may be the key determinant in legal trials. In addition, the study was the fourth of four studies reviewed thus far that included probative but inadmissible information in the pretrial publicity manipulation.

Kramer, Kerr, and Carroll (1990)

In one of the best studies ever done on pretrial publicity, the authors recruited 791 mock jurors, 617 recruited from jury rolls and 174 students, and used the same publicity manipulations as Kramer and Kerr (1989), reported earlier. Pretesting of the case revealed that conviction rates were between 40% and 50%. Study participants were exposed to pretrial information and a mock videotaped trial and then made an initial predeliberation choice and were put into juries and allowed to deliberate for 1 hour. One group of participants was exposed to the pretrial publicity an average of 12 days before the trial. In all cases, the mock jurors rendered individual postdeliberation verdicts. There was no pretrial publicity effect at all for the predeliberation verdicts (49.6% guilty), and half the juries were hung. The authors then converted the verdicts to a continuous scale (with 1 = conviction, 2 = hung, and 3 = acquittal), ran a different statistical test, and found that juries exposed to pretrial publicity were more conviction prone (mean of 1.89) than nonexposed juries (mean of 2.31). The delay condition eliminated the biasing effect of factual but not emotional publicity. An examination of the postdeliberation verdicts of individual jurors generally confirmed these trends. The final counts for jury verdicts for the emotional publicity condition were 18 guilty (31%), 29 hung (50%), 11 not guilty (19%), and in the low publicity condition the results were 4 guilty (11%), 17 hung (47%), 15 not guilty (42%). The authors conclude that pretrial publicity has an effect on verdicts and that a "continuance" is only effective against factually biasing information.

The results do represent the best case made for pretrial publicity having a biasing effect. The sample is certainly impressive, a deliberation was present, and some of the jurors did experience a delay between their exposure to the publicity and the trial evidence, a feature of the study the authors referred to as "continuance." However, it should be noted that what the authors deem a continuance is actually only a description of how most actual jurors experience pretrial publicity, coming to it casually a few weeks or so before the trial. An actual continuance granted by a judge following a motion at trial would be much longer. It should also be noted that, in fact, the participants in the Kramer et al. study did not come by the pretrial publicity casually. At some level of consciousness they must have known that the publicity they saw was different from their everyday perusal of the morning paper. In addition, the deliberation lasted only an hour, which would be an extremely short time for a jury to return any verdict. Thus, it is more accurate to say that this study examined abbreviated deliberations rather than full deliberations. Finally, the study falls short on the remaining two criteria. Conviction rates were pretested and differed vastly from actual conviction rates, and the manipulation of publicity suffered the same limitations as the Kramer and Kerr (1989) study. The factual publicity condition included probative but suppressed evidence and the emotional bias was not only extreme but probably probative: Knowing that the defendant had killed a small child and run from the scene certainly speaks to character.

The function of deliberation described in the study is interesting. The authors made much of the fact that publicity effects emerged only after deliberation, and concluded that deliberation can't reduce pretrial publicity effects and may make matters worse. Other research, of course, came to the opposite conclusion. The authors' case against deliberation may be overstated. Recall that prior to deliberation, all publicity conditions produced conviction rates of around 50%. After deliberation, when hung juries are considered, conviction rates drop to 31% for emotionally biasing conditions and 11% for no-emotional-bias conditions. Deliberation, in all cases, moved in the direction of leniency, a common finding (see Davis, 1986; London & Nunez, 2000). It is thus more accurate to say that deliberation did not cause as large a prodefendant shift in the emotional publicity as in the no-emotional-publicity conditions, but it is hard to conclude that deliberations produce an effect contrary to defendant interests. Even if it can be assumed that half of the 29 hung juries eventually would have resulted in conviction, the resulting number of convictions (33) would raise conviction rates to 56%, only modestly higher than the predeliberation conviction rate of roughly 50%. This reasoning is borne out with a comparison of individual juror verdicts. For the high emotional bias condition, the predeliberation conviction rate was 51.8%, and after deliberation it only shifted to 55%.

The proportion of hung juries that Kramer et al. observed is much higher than real trials produce, and may be due to any number of factors in the research design, including the short deliberations and the diminished urgency of reaching a verdict when everyone knows there is nothing "really" at stake. Apparently frustrated by this unreal result, Kramer et al. turned their attention to the attitudes of individual jurors. In research terms, this is a problem of a gap between a unit of observation (i.e., the thing a researcher observes) and a unit of analysis (the thing about which a researcher wants to draw conclusions). A chief strength of the Kramer et al. study is its initial focus on jury verdicts—collective decisions that follow deliberation—as their unit of analysis. The switch to individual jurors as their unit of observation and then their attempt to extrapolate from the biases of jurors to the original unit of analysis is the problem. The phenomenon they really want to understand is the effect of pretrial publicity on verdicts, but they end up with conclusions about jurors, negating the value of their initial focus. It is not sufficient to argue that because jury verdicts are always the result of votes by individual jurors one can draw valid conclusions about verdicts by studying jurors, any more than to say that because a baseball team's performance is always the result of each player's contribution, one can predict the outcome of a game by studying each player's individual statistics. (Any Hall-of-Famer who played his entire career with the Chicago Cubs or Boston Red Sox—such as Ernie Banks or Carl Yastrzemski—can vouch for that.)

The entire treatment of hung juries posed a difficult issue for the researchers. As noted earlier, others have come to the conclusion that once group deliberations have occurred, individual decisions are not independent and statistical tests are inappropriate (Padawer-Singer & Barton, 1975). The decision required a difficult judgment call, especially because the degree to which the lack of independence skewed the results was unknown. Methodologically, to the extent there was a substantial degree of distortion, it might be inappropriate to generalize from these results. Substantively, it may be difficult to conclude that a hung jury represents a midpoint between conviction and acquittal. In a system with high conviction rates, a hung jury means a new trial for the defendant, a new lever to use in a plea bargain, and an additional delay between initial publicity about the case. A truly innocent defendant can hope that exonerating evidence will arise in the interim between the two trials. A prosecutor might decide not to prosecute a case a second time, or witnesses might not give the trial a second go-round. In short, a hung jury probably represents more of a victory for a defendant than a draw. Statistically, if the three points on the scale (conviction, hung, acquittal) do not fall at even intervals but take on more of an ordinal shape, different statistics are in order and the interval calculations will not do. For these two reasons, it may not be appropriate to give the scale-based results of the study much weight.

Finally, it should be noted that the entire case for pretrial publicity rests on a crucial distinction between emotional and factual publicity. The authors concluded that emotional-bias information has an effect but factual-bias information does not. Subsequent analyses discarded that distinction. Citing the work of Kramer et al. and others, Wilson and Bornstein (1998) began their own research by noting that "a few studies have made a distinction between emotional and factual PTP ... the results of these studies have yet to provide strong evidence for the value of this distinction" (p. 586). Their research concluded that "there was insufficient evidence to conclude that emotional PTP was significantly more prejudicial than factual PTP. This provides evidence that if the amount and duration of PTP as well as its degree of bias ... are held constant, then the effect of PTP is not significantly different for emotional and factual PTP" (p. 594). In a study of the factors that affect people's ability to remember news reports, Valkenburg, Semetko, and de Vreese (1999) found that emotional news (cast in a "human interest frame") was the least likely to be remembered. In the end, the ability of the emotional pretrial publicity to survive deliberation found by Kramer et al. may be the product of the extreme nature of the publicity (running over an innocent child in an unrelated crime) rather than an overall pretrial publicity effect. In fact, the existence of the emotional publicity effect may be due to the joined-charge effect reported by Tanford and Penrod (1982). Jurors hearing a trial about a second offense (murder in this case) when they have already heard reports of guilt in a separate offense (hit-and-run vehicular manslaughter) may be more likely to convict not because they heard emotionally charged publicity, but because they are hearing what appears to be a second trial about a second charge.

Thus, taking the findings at face value, the most straightforward interpretation of this study is that when jurors are exposed to probative factual and extremely emotional pretrial publicity, hear a weak case that is likely to produce 50% conviction rates, and allowed jurors to deliberate for an hour, the most likely result will be a hung jury. After deliberation there will still be no factual publicity effect, but the prodefendant shifts will not be as large for the extreme emotional bias condition. Conviction rates, pretested to be 50%, will drop sharply in all other conditions, and will rise no higher than 55% in the extreme emotional bias situation. If the emotional/factual distinction does not hold or the emotional publicity manipulation is confounded with a joined-offense condition the results may be even more suspect. If hung juries represent victories for the defendant rather than a draw, the results are even more suspect. Such is not compelling evidence for a pretrial publicity effect.

Dexter, Cutler, and Moran (1992)

Interested in whether voir dire could offset pretrial publicity effects, these authors exposed half of their sample of 68 undergraduates to seven newspaper stories about a murder suspect. The stories included information about a prior record, negative statements about the defendant's character, a retracted confession, allegations of drug use by the defendant, and tales of the defendant's physical abusiveness; none of this information was presented at the trial. Mock jurors were asked whether they had an opinion about guilt or innocence and to rate defendant culpability at the conclusion of reading the pretrial publicity so that jurors would "rehearse" the information they encountered in the publicity. There was a one-week delay between exposure to the publicity and the trial. Mock jurors were then subjected to either a minimal or extended voir dire process by actual attorneys taking the role of prosecution or defense, watched a 6-hour mock trial on video, and rendered independent verdicts without deliberating (jurors did deliberate and render postdeliberation verdicts, but the authors chose not to present those results because only 8 juries were formed). The mock trial was chosen because pretests demonstrated conviction rates of 40%. Although extended voir dire did reduce convictions, there was a pretrial publicity effect (47% convicted in the pretrial publicity condition vs. 33% with no publicity). The two factors did not interact, so extended voir dire, although it depressed convictions, had no special ability to remove pretrial publicity effects.

Whether the data show voir dire to be an effective remedy depends, as always, on the point of reference. The authors' conclusion is certainly valid: In either voir dire condition, conviction rates are higher in the pretrial publicity condition than in the no-pretrial-publicity condition. However, it is also true that acquittal rates are higher in the extended voir dire condition (65%) than in the minimal voir dire condition without pretrial publicity (53%). Thus, a criminal defendant receiving pretrial publicity but with voir dire is in a better position than a criminal defendant without pretrial publicity but also without voir dire, suggesting that the quality of voir dire, manipulated as either extended or minimal in this study, is more important than the degree of pretrial publicity.

The study fails all five criteria. The sample was composed of undergraduates, the conviction rates differed greatly from those of actual trials, there was no deliberation, and the delay between exposure to publicity and exposure to the trial was modest (although present). In addition, the sheer number of articles of pretrial coverage exceeded both those of any other study reviewed here and typical levels of coverage in actual trials. The decision to ask mock jurors their opinions in advance and rehearse the publicity they encountered both runs afoul of the way media consumers process media information and introduces the possibility of bias warned against by the research of Freedman et al. (1998). In addition, the information was especially damaging and included information that the defendant had confessed to the crime, had a prior criminal record, used drugs, and was physically abusive. Despite all the negative pretrial information, only 47% of mock jurors voted for conviction. Once again, the results, although suggestive, hardly make a compelling case for generalization to actual trials, and depending on the point of reference suggest that voir dire might be more important than pretrial publicity.

As with other studies, this research found a very strong correlation between the verdict and perceived evidence strength. The authors wrote: "The correlations between verdict ... prosecution case strength, and defense case strength ... were substantial in magnitude ($rs > .50$) and statistically significant ($p < .01$)" (p. 827). The variables were so tightly associated with one another that the authors actually combined them into a single index of defendant culpability and used the index as the dependent variable. Although the choice to combine the variables into a single index is certainly within the purview of acceptable research procedure, another interpretation of the correlations is that perception of evidence strength is a crucial mediating variable between pretrial publicity and the trial verdict. Once again, evidence strength emerged as a key factor, and perhaps the dominant one, in juror decision making.

Wilson and Bornstein (1998)

The authors were primarily interested in whether the medium of pretrial publicity made a difference and also studied emotional versus factual pretrial publicity. The mock case involved a daughter who had murdered her mother, and the verdict choices presented to the jury were murder or manslaughter. Eighty-eight undergraduates were divided into groups; those exposed to pretrial publicity saw either a newscast containing eight inadmissible items or read a newspaper account containing those same eight items. The authors were careful in selecting their eight pieces of inadmissible evidence; participants in a pilot study rated 50 fabricated pieces of evidence and only items rated as most likely to produce guilt were included in the main study. Manipulation checks verified that the emotional pieces of information did produce greater emotional arousal. After exposure to pretrial publicity, participants rendered individual verdicts without deliberation. Conviction rates for murder in control groups ranged between 31% and 47%. There was a significant effect for pretrial publicity (73% convicted in publicity conditions vs. 39% in no-publicity conditions), but not for the medium of transmission or for the type of information (factual or emotional).

The article falls short of all five criteria. The sample was composed of undergraduates, conviction rates in control conditions suggested different conviction rates from actual trials, there was no deliberation, and there was no delay between exposure to publicity and exposure to the trial. The amount and type of exposure was extreme; each publicity condition contained eight inadmissible facts, a figure that actual reporters would be hard pressed to include even if they were trying to violate court rules. A comparison to the work of Imrich et al. (1995) is striking. Imrich et al. studied actual crime coverage in 14 newspapers over an 8-week period and coded the articles for the presence of any information that fell into the one of the nine ABA categories of prohibited publicity. They found that 27% of the defendants received coverage that violated at least one ABA guideline. The authors don't report the total number of articles or how often a defendant was subject to more than one prejudicial piece of information, but a little extrapolation can put the matter into perspective. The authors do report that the category occurring with the greatest frequency was present in 8.5% of criminal cases. Assuming a random distribution across the categories and assuming that every type of ABA-violation information occurred with a frequency of 8.5% (an artificially inflated number), the chance that any one defendant would encounter coverage that included pieces of damaging information from eight different categories is 0.003 in a million. Even without these statistical machinations, even a cursory reading of Imrich et al. makes it clear that it is not at all common for criminal defendants to face even two different types of damaging publicity. Eight different pieces of damaging information would be a truly astounding situation for any criminal defendant. Further, the authors pretested their items and specifically selected them only if, to a statistically significant degree, they were more likely to produce judgments of guilt in comparison to other inadmissible items.

Finally, because it was a foregone conclusion that the defendant had killed her mother and the only question was whether the act was murder or manslaughter, virtually all the information had probative value for the question before the jurors, whether or not it was factual. For example, one included item, "the defendant ran back to the bedroom and started to crush her dead mother's skull with a baseball bat," although emotionally arousing, certainly speaks to the issue of whether the defendant was committing an act worthy of murder rather than manslaughter. The factual information was certainly probative, and there is good reason to believe that the emotional information, while more emotionally arousing than its "factual" counterpart, did include content that could have been substantive for mock jurors.

In sum, the article does demonstrate that undergraduates will vote for murder quite often when they are exposed to large amounts of prejudicial information and are asked to render a judgment of murder or manslaughter immediately after exposure to the publicity and without deliberation. The results do not give one confidence that in most actual cases publicity can harm a defendant's interests. The study again suggests that evidence might be an important mediating variable. If it is true that what jurors focus on the most is the evidence presented, it stands to reason that probative pretrial information will be the most prejudicial. Given the extreme probative nature of the pretrial manipulation in this study, the results may be read as supporting the ideas that (a) jurors focus on evidence when making their decisions, and (b) probative information is especially harmful to defendant interests.

Bornstein, Whisenhunt, Nemeth, and Dunaway (2002)

Taking as a starting point the conclusion that pretrial publicity influenced criminal trials, the authors were interested in whether such an effect would be present for civil trials as well. The case selected involved an ovarian cancer claim; the authors pretested 30 pieces of hypothetical evidence and selected for inclusion only the most incriminating or exonerating items, and further pretested "to insure that both the defendant and plaintiff PTP article produced significant bias" (p. 6). A sample of undergraduates read either a proplaintiff, prodefendant, or control story, read a one-page summary of a trial, and completed a series of dependent measures that included verdicts. The prodefense publicity condition produced a liability judgment (similar to a criminal conviction) rate of 25%, the control 47%, and the proplaintiff publicity condition 75%. A second study focused solely on defendants and manipulated the placement of jury instructions in three conditions: a control, jury instructions after the trial, and jury instructions before and after the trial. A sample of 202 undergraduates followed the same procedures utilized in the first study and found a main effect for pretrial publicity (across jury instruction conditions liability convictions jumped between roughly 13 and 20 points) and a main effect for jury instructions (the before-and-after instruction condition had the lowest conviction rates). In pretrial publicity conditions, final conviction rates were 81.1% for the jury instruction control condition (65.5% without publicity), 80.0% for the situation where jury instructions were given only after the trial (58.3% without publicity), and 75.8% for instructions given before and after the trial (52.6% without publicity). Jury instructions did not eliminate the biasing effect of pretrial publicity but simply lowered liability convictions overall. Thus, the results are quite similar to those obtained for deliberation by Kramer et al. (1990); instructions can cause a prodefendant shift, and that shift is not as pronounced when pretrial publicity is present. As in the first study, the pattern generally held for other dependent measures. The authors concluded that instructions fail and pretrial publicity has an effect.

The authors noted that the study lacked ecological validity but were untroubled by the fact, citing Bornstein's (1999) review of laboratory research.

Given this stance, it is not surprising that the study fell short on the criteria identified here. Both sets of samples were undergraduate student populations. The control conviction rate in the first study was 47% and 58.3% in the control publicity/jury instructions after trial condition in the second study (the equivalent condition to the first study). Both rates are low relative to overall criminal conviction rates, and especially low given that the study used the civil "preponderance of evidence" standard rather than the criminal "beyond a reasonable doubt" standard. Exposure levels were not unnaturally high but they were unusually damaging; it is of course not normal journalistic practice to pretest 30 possible biasing items and include only the 5 most damaging, nor do newspapers pretest their stories to insure that they produce bias over control versions. There was no deliberation or delay in the study. This study examined only civil and not criminal trials, which may put its focus beyond the scope of this book, and at any rate it did lack ecological validity, as the authors were careful to note. Little about this study was similar to actual trial conditions.

Summary

The articles reviewed so far present the best case that can be made for an overall pretrial publicity effect. Every study we review after this section produced findings less supportive of a pretrial publicity effect than the eight reviewed in this section. However, even the articles already reviewed do not provide strong evidence in favor of a pretrial publicity effect that will replicate in actual trials. Most deviate from actual courtroom settings in important ways, and usually in ways that would exaggerate a publicity effect. Laboratory research certainly has its place; the question posed here is not whether the research has been done "correctly," in some abstract sense, but whether the information generated by these studies can be generalized to actual trial settings. None of these studies bears enough of a resemblance to actual courtroom settings to suggest that they will.

Two themes do emerge from a review of the studies, however. First, each study in this group used extremely probative information in its publicity manipulation. Sue et al. (1974) linked the physical evidence (a gun and the gun's use in the crime) to the defendant, the same manipulation as Sue et al. (1975). Padawer-Singer and Barton (1975) and Dexter et al. (1992) each included a retracted confession and a criminal history. Kramer and Kerr (1989) and Kramer et al. (1990) included physical evidence (a gun linked to the crime), a criminal history, and the "emotional" suggestion that the defendant hit and killed a 7-year-old girl with his car. Wilson and Bornstein (1998) went to extraordinary lengths to include information that was screened for factual and emotional value, as did Bornstein et al. (2002). Freedman et al. (1998) evaluated the situation this way:

It may be that the crucial factor is whether the pretrial publicity contains conclusive (or nearly conclusive) evidence of guilt. In Kramer et al., both kinds of publicity included information that virtually proved the defendant was guilty (the weapon found in the girlfriend's apartment and the defendant's presence at the scene of the crime when he denied being there), as did the publicity used in other studies that found effects on post-trial opinions (e.g., Sue et al., 1974, 1975). (p. 267)

Whatever else might be said about these studies, it is clear that they have examined pretrial publicity effects only in the situation where the pretrial information has weighty probative value.

Second, the studies do suggest that evidence may be the key factor determining trial outcomes. Sue et al. (1975) found that pretrial publicity influenced juror perceptions of evidence strength. Kramer and Kerr (1989), while attempting to study differences in trial length, believed that the differences they eventually found could have been due to unintended differences in evidence quality. Dexter et al. (1992) found the links between evidence strength and verdict so strong that they collapsed the measures into a single dependent variable. Wilson and Bornstein (1998) and Bornstein et al. (2002) each manipulated the evidentiary value of the items included in the publicity. As reviewed in more depth latter, the viewpoint that evidence is a powerful determinant of trial outcomes is widely accepted in other social science research (Ostrom, Werner, & Saks, 1978; Reskin & Visher, 1986; Saks & Hastie, 1978; Tanford & Penrod, 1982; Visher, 1987), and although hardly surprising, it is at least encouraging. Pretrial publicity might be studied in isolation in laboratories, but in actual courtrooms it always interacts with a number of other factors. One factor that might (thankfully) exert a much more powerful influence than pretrial publicity is the strength of the evidence in the case.

Finally, if the suppositions of Freedman et al. (1998) are correct, all these findings might be a methodological artifact produced by asking jurors for a predeliberation verdict.

LABORATORY STUDIES THAT PARTIALLY SUPPORT THE EXISTENCE OF A PRETRIAL PUBLICITY EFFECT

Each of the studies reviewed so far produced a statistically significant relationship between the study's publicity manipulations and its measures of trial outcome. The studies reviewed in this section have produced equivocal results; that is, they contain some findings suggesting that a pretrial publicity effect may exist and some evidence to suggest the contrary conclusion. In at least some instances, they affirm the effectiveness of one remedy or another. They are reviewed in chronological order below.

Kline and Jess (1966)

Forty-eight male sophomores were divided into eight juries who watched a live mock trial concerning a traffic injury; half were exposed to pretrial publicity. The publicity took the form of newspaper articles that reported that the defendant had a bad driving record, had been arrested for drunk driving and reckless driving, and had left the scene of the accident. Kline and Jess found that all four juries discussed the pretrial publicity information, but three juries rejected it, as the judge instructed. The remaining jury found against the defendant. Thus, the study found that pretrial publicity did bias one trial, but that three juries followed judicial instructions and discarded the inadmissible evidence. (Other jury instruction research is reviewed later.) A control group unexposed to pretrial publicity also found against the defendant in one of four trials. Conclusions are difficult to draw from this study; the sample included only eight juries composed entirely of undergraduate males. The study did allow deliberation but not delay; the other two criteria (i.e., conviction rate control and publicity level) are not applicable to this research design. The study does not fare particularly well against the five criteria. Perhaps the most instructive finding points to the conclusion that juries will try to follow judicial instructions and do their best to base their decision on relevant evidence but may not always be successful in doing so.

Hoiberg and Stires (1973)

In the only published study involving high school students, 337 participants read a newspaper article containing either "heinous" facts (the sexual nature of a crime and vivid descriptions of its brutality) or "incriminating" facts (the defendant was arrested as a suspect, and the existence of a retracted confession), all of which were later revealed at a trial presented on an audio tape. The study concerned a rape-murder and guilt was measured on a 10-point scale rather than as a dichotomous verdict. The publicity affected women only, and for women the type of pretrial publicity (heinous or incriminating) did not matter. The case was pretested to insure 50% conviction rates, and final guilt ratings averaged between roughly 5 and 7 on the 10-point scale. The results were equivocal, because the pretrial publicity effect only emerged for female and not male respondents. A gender effect in a similar pattern has not emerged in any subsequent study.

The results of this study are very difficult to generalize. The dependent variable was measured as a continuous scale rather than as a verdict, and the sample was composed entirely of high school students who would not be eligible for actual jury service. The initial conviction rates were low, there was no delay, and no deliberation occurred. If taken at face value, the interpretation of this study would be that pretrial publicity affects women but not men, a conclusion difficult to give much credence.

Padawer-Singer, Singer, and Singer (1974)

The authors were concerned with whether voir dire eliminated pretrial publicity effects. Using a sample drawn from actual jury rolls in New York, the researchers exposed 266 respondents to publicity concerning the defendant's
prior record and a retracted confession. Attorneys from the District Attorney's
office and the Legal Aid Society conducted voir dire. Overall, there was an effect for pretrial publicity (across conditions, conviction rates jumped from
about 50% to about 60%), although voir dire in the publicity condition reduced conviction rates from 78% to 60%. The authors concluded that voir dire
was very effective. The publicity used in the study was not overly extensive, it
utilized an impressive sample, and it incorporated deliberation. It failed two
of the criteria in that the overall conviction rates were much lower than those
obtained in actual trials (to the extent that current conviction rates obtained in
1974) and that there was no delay between exposure to publicity and exposure
to evidence. The findings are equivocal because, although a modest pretrial
publicity effect was present, the practice of voir dire eliminated the bias to a
substantial degree.

The principle issue raised by the study is whether voir dire is an effective
remedy; a number of other scholars have concluded that it is not (Dexter et
al., 1992; Fein, 1997; Kerr, 1994; Kerr et al., 1991; Moran & Cutler, 1991;
Studebaker & Penrod, 1997; VanDyke, 1977). Perhaps the differences are less
real than apparent. Although other studies tend to find that lawyers aren't
very good at determining whether potential jurors will vote for or against
the side the lawyer represents, Padawer-Singer et al. (1974) specifically examined the question of whether voir dire could reduce pretrial publicity effects.
The authors found that it could. Furthermore, it did not come at the expense
of the prosecution; there was not a prodefendant influence for unexposed jurors. Voir dire seemed to eliminate publicity bias but did not create a general
prodefendant shift.

The findings that most contrast with those of Padawer-Singer et al. (1974)
are those of Dexter et al. (1992). The results of Padawer-Singer et al. are more
realistic on at least two fronts: The study used jurors drawn from actual jury
rolls and not a student sample, and the jurors were allowed to deliberate. As
discussed in greater length later, deliberation may be a crucial factor. As noted
earlier, it is also true that in the Dexter et al. study a defendant with extended
voir dire and pretrial publicity was still in a better position than a defendant
with no publicity but no voir dire. A more thorough discussion awaits, but
whatever else might be said about this confusing situation it is true that the
more realistic of the two studies points to the conclusion that voir dire is effective. Ultimately, the most important question for voir dire is how it fits into the
overall package of remedies that a court can apply when trying to reduce publicity bias. Even if voir dire is only partially effective or effective in some situa-

tions but not others, it might still form an important component of a remedy process that is most effective when various remedies combine. In sum, this study lends limited support to the conclusion that pretrial publicity can be biasing, but stronger evidence to support the belief that courtroom procedures can attenuate that effect.

Greene and Wade (1988)

Concerned about a "general" pretrial publicity effect, the authors wanted to know if media reports about a similar case could alter the outcome of a particular case at hand. In the first of two studies, 120 undergraduates read either a story about an unrelated heinous crime (the antidefendant condition), a story about an innocent person being convicted in an unrelated case (the prodefendant condition), or a control story. The trial was presented via a booklet. Guilt was judged on a 4-point scale, and the results showed that, compared to the control group, the prodefendant publicity helped the defendant but the antidefendant story did not hurt the defendant's chances. A second study using the same general methodology on a different group of 140 undergraduates manipulated whether the publicized case was similar or dissimilar to the case before the jury, and found once again that there was a strong effect for the prodefendant manipulation, but only a marginal effect for whether the reported case was similar to the case before the simulated jurors.

Although this study did demonstrate a pretrial publicity effect, it was in a direction that benefited defendants. Generalizations are difficult, as the study fails four criteria: The sample was composed entirely of undergraduates, there was no deliberation or delay between the publicity and the trial, and conviction rates are difficult to even estimate since the dependent variable was measured on a scale rather than as a dichotomous verdict. Other research has failed to uncover a prodefendant effect for prodefendant coverage (Riedel, 1993; Rollings & Blascovich, 1977). In sum, the study is not especially compelling, but it does suggest that publicity about failings of the criminal system in general rather than the defendant in particular might work in favor of defendant interests. This finding has applications to potential remedies, understandings of how publicity might be processed, and the structural paradox hypothesis. These implications will be explored in more depth in chapter 3.

Otto, Penrod, and Dexter (1994)

A group of 262 undergraduates read a collection of newspaper articles. Some articles contained no negative pretrial publicity, and others included one of five sorts of damaging pretrial information: negative comments about the defendant's character, weak inadmissible statements by a neighbor about the defendant, strong inadmissible statements by a neighbor (i.e., that the defendant was a drug user), information about the defendant's prior record, or information about the defendant's low status job. After exposure to the publicity, participants watched a videotape of an actual trial involving a disturbance of the peace charge. The data were analyzed with a path analysis, and only three types of information influenced predeliberation verdicts. Statements about character and strong inadmissible statements hurt the defendant whereas weak inadmissible statements helped the defendant. There were no direct pretrial publicity effects on postdeliberation verdicts, although there were some unremarkable indirect effects. The authors describe the results as showing "consistently modest results for pretrial publicity" (p. 466).

Perhaps the most interesting thing about this study is the behavior of the nonpretrial publicity variables. In addition to the publicity measures there were five additional variables that mediated the relationships between the pretrial verdicts and the final trial. Path analysis produces beta scores to describe the strength of relationships. The beta scores do not have a straightforward inferential relationship to a population like the familiar Pearson's r, but they do indicate the magnitude of the relationship between the independent variables and the dependent variable relative to the other independent variables. The direct relationship between the pretrial verdict and the final verdict was .17. Three of the five mediating variables made larger contributions: defendant persuasiveness (−.27), strength of prosecution case (.56), and sympathy for defendant (−.22). Two mediating variables, the defendant not being likeable (.14) and the defendant being a typical criminal (.13), made contributions of roughly equal size.

What is most apparent from these findings is that, although the individual merits of each remedy may be debated, what happens at the trial is much more important to the outcome than what happens before the trial. Whatever bias jurors come into a trial with (their pre-deliberation judgments in this case) is massively swamped by the trial itself. A defendant's persuasiveness, for example, is roughly twice as important as any pretrial judgment, and the strength of the prosecution's case is three times as important. This has important implications for the knowledge–guilt hypothesis. Thus far, the knowledge–guilt hypothesis states that potential jurors with access to pretrial information about the case will tend to presume guilt, but takes no stance on how those pretrial suppositions influence the final verdict. These results demonstrate that pretrial judgments will be much less important than opinions formed during the trial. Of course, it is fair to say that, all things being equal, a defendant with negative pretrial publicity might be in a worse situation than a defendant without such publicity. Things are rarely always equal in actual trials, however, and a criminal defense strategist would do much better allocating scarce resources to winning the case at trial rather than waging a pretrial publicity fight. The implications of all these strange doings will be worked out in the final chapter, but for now it is worth noting that pretrial judgments are less important to trial outcomes than the case presented at trial.

It is also worth noting that some obvious connections between the types of pretrial information and the final verdict were not statistically significant. Negative statements about a defendant's character, mention of a prior record, and mention of a low status job were not related to whether or not a defendant was likeable (no pretrial information, in fact, was linked to likability). Neither was any type of pretrial publicity related to defendant persuasiveness, and thus a criminal defendant's ability to speak in his or her own defense was not harmed by pretrial publicity. Pretrial judgments of guilt were, strangely, associated with more sympathy for the defendant (beta = .16) and more skepticism of the prosecution's case (beta = −.16).

The moral of all these fascinating and unpredictable findings is one that warns against simpleminded interpretations of statistical significance. Although it is true that pretrial publicity demonstrated a statistically significant relationship with the final verdict through a number of indirect paths, it is also true that the relationship was no stronger than some unpredicted and counterintuitive findings, including the backward relationship between pretrial judgments and perceptions of prosecution case strength and sympathy for the defendant and a negative relationship between weak inadmissible statements and pretrial judgments of guilt (beta = −.20). Taken on their face, these findings suggest that a defendant receiving pretrial publicity including weak statements actually has a better chance than a defendant with no publicity. They also show that a defendant judged guilty before the trial starts actually has a better chance than a defendant presumed innocent because the prejudgments of guilt combine to increase sympathy for the defendant (beta = .16) and weaken perceptions of the prosecution case (beta = −.16) more than they directly lead to guilt in the final verdict (beta = .17). These figures may warn against taking the findings on their face. The bottom line is that while this study does have some findings suggesting that pretrial publicity is bad for a defendant, it has an equal number of findings that are counterintuitive, and there is no good reason to accept some of the findings while ignoring the others. To focus narrowly on the statistical significance of the pretrial publicity measures while ignoring the other larger and counterintuitive findings is to miss the forest for the trees.

Finally, two other findings of this study affirm the proevidence themes found in other studies. First, the dominant factor, by far, was evidence strength. The strength of the prosecution case had the largest influence on the final verdict (beta = .54), twice as large as any other factor, and more than three times larger than most. The authors did conduct a test to determine whether trial evidence changed the influence of pretrial publicity and concluded that "trial evidence weakened the effects of character pretrial publicity—however, changes in other pretrial publicity coefficients did not approach significance, which suggests that their effects may be more resistant to evidentiary influences" (p. 463). This may be true, but it is not the point being made here. It may be the case that if a strong inadmissible statement produced a beta of .05 on the final verdict the trial evidence might not change it, but it would remain true that perceptions of prosecution case strength would produce a much larger beta of .54. In other words, trial evidence can't change the effect of pretrial publicity, but it is a lot more important. Another way to think about the author's tests is that while they show trial evidence doesn't eliminate publicity factors, many of those factors were not significant in the first place. Finding that trial evidence didn't lower the beta for weak inadmissible statements below .01 is unremarkable. The single most important factor determining the final verdict was the strength of the prosecution's case, and none of the other tests makes that fact any less important.

Second, information that was most probative had the largest effect. Strong inadmissible statements were positively associated with pretrial judgments of guilt (beta = .17), whereas weak inadmissible statements, it has already been said, lowered pretrial judgments of guilt. Negative statements about character do appear to negatively influence pretrial judgments of guilt (beta = .34), but character statements were the one sort of evidence the authors concluded was offset by trial evidence. Furthermore, the case had to do with disorderly conduct, and thus information about a defendant's character and whether it was the sort of person likely to be "disorderly" may have had probative value. At any rate, the more probative information (the strong inadmissible statements) was roughly three and a half times more damaging to the defendant than the less probative information (weak inadmissible statements).

The authors conclude that careful control is necessary to detect pretrial publicity effects and that evidence reduces but does not eliminate pretrial publicity bias. Such a conclusion is modest and consistent with the ultimate finding that once evidence was introduced there was no direct path linking pretrial publicity to a final verdict. A careful look at the path coefficients for even the predeliberation model shows that the strength of the prosecution's case was the strongest contributor to the verdict and individually was a much better predictor of trial outcome than all direct and indirect effects of publicity combined. Finally, the study failed three criteria: It used a student sample, it did not include deliberation, and it did not include a delay. The conviction rates are difficult even to measure because a continuous rather than a dichotomous measure was used. This study did reveal a number of interesting nuances and the authors are admirably reluctant to draw sweeping conclusions from their data. Trial evidence was once again the dominant factor and probative evidence was again the most damaging; weak information actually helped defendants. Ultimately, it is difficult to read this study and come away with the conclusion that pretrial publicity is an insidious, irrepressible influence on jurors. Freedman et al. (1998) put the point this way:

Otto et al. (1994) used five different kinds of pretrial publicity and found that none of them had a significant direct effect on final verdicts. A path analysis showed that although there were no direct effects, one of the five types (negative information about the defendant's character) did have an indirect effect on verdicts. The authors concluded that they had demonstrated a negative effect of pretrial publicity, but the results could plausibly be interpreted to have demonstrated the opposite. (p. 258)

Fein, Morgan, Norton, and Sommers (1997)

Primarily concerned with whether the defense could cast doubt on pretrial publicity, the study exposed 86 undergraduates to five or six newspaper articles, some of which contained general coverage of the crime in question, but one of which was an editorial specifically calling for conviction. The case involved assault and was pretested to obtain a 50% conviction rate. All materials, including the trial, were written and mailed to participants who rendered individual verdicts. In various trial conditions, the defense tried to cast "suspicion" on the motives of the prosecution and argued that the pretrial publicity was either racially biased or suspect in general; in some versions race was not mentioned by either side or in the pretrial publicity. Pretrial publicity increased conviction rates from 44% in the control condition to 78%, but the racial suspicion condition had conviction rates of 45%, almost identical to the control condition. Conviction rates were highest (over 90%) when race was not mentioned but the defense tried to create suspicion.

The results are equivocal because, although the study did find a pretrial publicity effect, it found that one specific defense strategy—questioning the prosecution and media motives on racial grounds—effectively eliminated the pretrial publicity effect. Other strategies either failed or made things worse for the defense. Generalizability is questionable; the sample was composed of undergraduates, the conviction rates were sharply lower than those obtained in actual cases, and there was no deliberation. Although the authors believed they had included a "small amount" of pretrial publicity, five or six articles is actually a fairly large number in comparison to actual levels of coverage. There was a limited delay, although it was only roughly 3 days. Thus, the study failed on three of the criteria and probably fell short on the other two. The evidence in favor of a pretrial publicity effect is weak and the evidence in favor of an effective defense strategy is limited; creating suspicion worked, but only in specific circumstances. In all, this study provides minimal support for the existence of a pretrial publicity effect in actual courtrooms but some evidence that some defense strategies might effectively counteract the pretrial publicity.

Fein, McCloskey, and Tomlinson (1997)

In a replication and extension of their earlier work, 91 undergraduates read a case about a man who murdered his estranged wife. Those in the pretrial publicity condition read three or four articles indicating that the defendant had beaten his wife, that his fingerprints were on the murder weapon, that an eyewitness had identified him, and that he was an alcoholic. One article was an editorial openly calling for his conviction. In the "suspicion" condition (a condition where the defense attempted to create suspicion about the motives of the press and prosecutor), participants read an additional newspaper article denouncing the sensationalism of the coverage. As an additional suspicion manipulation the defense attorney made comments during the trial that questioned the motives of the media hype and suggested that the District Attorney planted the stories to obtain a conviction. The control condition produced conviction rates of 45%, the pretrial publicity condition had conviction rates of 80%, but the pretrial publicity plus suspicion condition had conviction rates of only 35%. A second study demonstrated that suspicion could also help discount inadmissible evidence at trial (in addition to pretrial publicity), and the authors concluded that suspicion could help counteract a large amount of antidefense information.

The case the authors make for the utility of suspicion as a defense tactic is much more compelling than the case they make for pretrial publicity. The sample was drawn exclusively from undergraduates, the participants did not deliberate, and there was no delay between exposure to the publicity and the trial. The pretrial information was fairly high (more than three articles), highly charged (an editorial calling for conviction), and very probative (fingerprints on the murder weapon). Although the conviction rate for the pretrial publicity condition was 80%, the control condition only produced 45% conviction rates. Thus, the study seems to fall short on all five criteria. Again, Fein, McClosky, and Tomlinson (1997) made a good case for one effective way to counteract pretrial publicity, but their case in favor of an overall pretrial publicity effect is more tenuous.

Studebaker, Robbennolt, Penrod, Pathak-Sharma, Groscup, and Davenport (2002)

The primary concern of this article was making a case for the use of the Internet as a way to improve ecological validity; as part of that overall argument the authors presented some data they gathered in connection with the McVeigh trial. Mock jurors were recruited via e-mail and were e-mailed trial summaries at six different points in the trial (although dependent measures were reported for only two measurement points). Respondents reported their exposure to pretrial publicity about McVeigh (which, a separate content analysis by the same authors revealed, was heavily slanted against the defendant; Studebaker et al., 2000) and a series of dependent measures. Before the trial started, exposure to pretrial publicity did not correlate with proprosecution attitudes, but did correlate with knowledge about the bombing, belief that

McVeigh was involved, and belief that evidence favored the prosecution. After the first trial summary, which included the judge's remarks and opening statements, exposure to pretrial publicity was not correlated with guilt judgments but was correlated with knowledge about the bombing, which was, in turn, correlated with guilt judgments.

Although the authors concluded that "PTP was clearly related to bias against the defendant in this case" (p. 36), the conclusion is difficult to square with their ultimate findings. At the two measurement points for which they presented data neither of their direct measures of bias—proprosecution attitudes before the trial or guilt judgments after the first trial summary—was significantly correlated with bias. Even the indirect relationship the authors note is incredibly small; the effect sizes are such that exposure explains 6.7% of knowledge about the bombing, which in turn explained 7.3% of the guilt. Thus, exposure explained 6.7% of a factor that explained 7.3% of guilt, or less than 0.5% of guilt judgments.

It is possible to compare the sample obtained in this study against population characteristics, because the authors very admirably included population demographics from the Statistical Abstract for the same year as the study. The comparison reveals that the sample was more likely to be White (95.8% in the sample vs. 82.1% in the population), male (60.4% vs. 48.9%), and educated (66.7% with a college degree vs. 16.4% in the population) than was the population. Conviction rates are not reported and were presumably measured continuously rather than dichotomously. No deliberation took place. The authors did an excellent job of utilizing realistic publicity; all exposure and delay rates were perfectly natural or slightly longer than in actual trials, given the delay between the time actual jurors heard the case and when summaries were e-mailed to study participants.

One additional feature of the study that makes it differ from actual trials in a way that might strengthen publicity effects is that, due to sample attrition, the authors report only the data after the first trial summary. At that time the defense had not yet presented its case. The results were therefore obtained after the participants had been exposed to the heavily antidefense news coverage and after opening statements but before hearing evidence from either side in the case.

Finally, the correlations between knowledge about the case and guilt ratings, which were among the strongest reported, offer intriguing evidence about the knowledge–guilt hypothesis. Measures taken before the trial started showed that knowledge about the bombing had relatively strong correlations with belief in McVeigh's participation in the bombing (.23) and perceived pressure to convict (.35). The strongest correlation found (.76; roughly double the size of the next-largest correlation) was between belief that the evidence favored the prosecution and belief in McVeigh's involvement in the bombing. These findings rather strongly support the contention that the primary factor juries pay attention to when making decisions is the evidence before them, and that to the extent pretrial publicity has an effect it is through a coloring of the evidence. There is also some support for the notion that knowledge about the case results in judgments of guilt, although it is important to note that knowledge was not significantly correlated with proprosecution attitudes or belief that the evidence favored the prosecution. Much as with the work of Otto et al. (1994), this research demonstrates that those with knowledge about a case will tend to presume guilt before the onset of a trial, but there is little evidence to suggest that such a belief will survive the trial.

Summary

This group of studies has suggested some interesting possibilities that may shed light on why laboratory studies don't replicate in field research and might even begin to prove that there is no pretrial publicity effect at all. The studies show that some, but not all, juries will follow instructions. Some, but not all, defense strategies can counteract some, but perhaps not all, types of pretrial publicity. Voir dire might just eliminate any pretrial publicity effect that does exist. Some defendants will benefit from general stories about wrongful convictions. Finally, some defendants will actually benefit from some types of negative publicity, especially "weak inadmissible statements." What does all this mean? Mostly, we believe that it adds support to the cumulative remedy hypothesis. The overall effect of jury instructions, voir dire, and defense strategy, although only partially effective in isolation, produces an overlapping system of double-checks that make it difficult for any pretrial publicity effect to emerge. These legal remedies combine with other nonlegal remedies, such as a normal delay between exposure to publicity and exposure to the trial, or the prodefendant effects of certain types of publicity. In the end, it may still be possible for pretrial information to influence the outcome of a trial in very specific circumstances, but it is difficult to believe that this will happen very often.

The second major conclusion that can be drawn at the end of a review of these studies is that, once again, trial evidence seems awfully—in fact, wonderfully—important. Even if pretrial publicity has an effect on verdicts, it is not the only factor that does, and evidence ends up being a much larger contributor to the final verdict. Of course, a fair trial may require that all biasing elements be removed, and the normative issue of how much bias is enough to create concern is different from the empirical question of how large the effect is. In terms of pure description, however, it appears that we are safe in saying that other factors, especially the evidence presented at trial, are much more important to the outcome of the trial than pretrial publicity.

LABORATORY STUDIES THAT DID NOT FIND
A PRETRIAL PUBLICITY EFFECT

Contrary to other reports (e.g., Studebaker & Penrod, 1997), there are at least seven published studies that provide data indicating the absence of any pretrial publicity effect. We use the same five criteria we used to evaluate studies that support claims of an effect of pretrial publicity to evaluate studies that fail to support such claims. However, it's worth recalling the purpose of these criteria: to clarify the difference between experimental conditions and the more complex circumstances of the courtroom. The advantage of experiments is the isolation of phenomena so that their unique properties have the best opportunity to manifest themselves. If any of the studies reviewed next fail these criteria, it can be said that pretrial publicity failed to demonstrate an effect even though the design of the study made a positive finding especially likely. This review also continues to explore the themes identified in the reviews of other studies, especially the importance of evidence, the possibility that probative information is the most biasing, and the cumulative remedy hypothesis. They are again presented in chronological order.

Simon (1966)

In a study that was very sophisticated for its time, the author had 107 registered voters read two articles about a crime that contained reports about the arrest of a defendant, evidence found in the defendant's home, and reports that the defendant had a prior criminal record. Half of the participants listened to an audiotaped trial. Although pretrial publicity did produce significantly higher pretrial judgments of guilt, the conviction rates between the pretrial publicity and no-publicity conditions became virtually identical after the trial (25% vs. 22%). The author concluded that pretrial dangers were exaggerated. Freedman and Burke (1996) obtained very similar results three decades later (reviewed later in this chapter), and the finding lends further support to the idea that evidence is the dominant factor determining the outcome of a trial. The study contained an excellent sample and allowed deliberation, although it contained no delay between exposure to publicity and the trial, the publicity tended to be especially prejudicial, and the conviction rates were low. All three of these factors, of course, should have exaggerated the chances of finding a publicity effect.

One confound in the study design is that trial evidence and deliberation both intervened before the verdict outcome. This is not necessarily a bad thing; all actual trials, of course, allow both trial evidence and deliberation. The only consequence of the research decision is that it is unclear whether it is the introduction of trial evidence, the jury deliberation, or the two factors in combination that eliminated the pretrial publicity effect. In sum, this rather realistic study found that the trial process eliminated any effect of pretrial publicity.

Davis (1986)

Manipulating a case involving breaking and entering and rape, 224 undergraduates read a single article that was either sensational or neutral, and the participants were further divided into 1-week-delay and no-delay conditions. The sensational story reported the crime rate, the victim's name, the suspect's prior record, the suspect's opportunity to dispose of evidence, and a pejorative comment about the defendant by a former employer. The neutral version mentioned the crime rate and victim name but also included the number of suspects, the lack of clues, and statements by the police claiming confidence in their ability to solve the crime. The trial was presented via videotape, and jurors rendered individual verdicts asking how they would rule as a one-person jury. Jurors were also placed into juries, and both the jury-level and individual-level data were analyzed. Posttrial conviction rates were all around 30%. In general, participants found the sensational report to be biased and discounted it. There were no significant predeliberation or postdeliberation effects for pretrial publicity. Those exposed to the sensational reports were actually slightly more likely to favor defendants. Deliberation caused a general prodefendant shift. At the jury level, negative pretrial publicity produced more hung juries than neutral publicity, but in either condition the delay increased the number of acquittals. At the individual level, negative publicity in the delay condition had a tendency to cause jurors to be less suspicious of what they considered to be noncredible news accounts, leading the author to tenuously suggest a "sleeper" effect, saying, "Some of the present data support this interpretation" (p. 603). Davis concluded that "the jury verdicts and (individual) juror measures revealed considerable resistance to the influence of prejudicial news" (p. 601), and analyses of the deliberations revealed that jurors did discuss extralegal matters but were not confused or unduly influenced by them.

The sample group in this study was not characteristic of actual jury compositions and the final conviction rates obtained were rather low, but the jury was allowed to deliberate and a delay was included as part of the study (although compared to actual trials the delay was fairly short). Because there was no group that was not exposed to publicity at all, the study lacked a true control group. In short, this study could not find a difference in conviction rates between participants exposed to sensational publicity and those exposed to neutral publicity, although some of the data did support the conclusion that a delay in exposure might actually worsen things for the defendant. Davis aligned his work with that of Simon, and this study may be read as a second set of data that, similar to Simon, found that evidence and deliberation went a long way toward eliminating a publicity effect. Importantly, this study did demonstrate the importance of including a delay and deliberation in the design. Davis concluded, "Research methods in publicity studies ought to manipulate the time interval between the news and trial presentation, and should permit longer periods of deliberation" (p. 605).

Riedel (1993)

In a laboratory study of a rape trial, 342 undergraduates read four unrelated stories and then either a story about a man mistakenly convicted of rape or a man who was mistakenly acquitted of a rape charge and then raped and killed a woman 2 weeks later. Participants then watched a videotape of a trial. In terms of verdicts, the only significant difference was that men who watched the mistaken acquittal story were more likely to find the defendant not guilty. In other words, the negative pretrial publicity improved defendant chances for male jurors. There was a significant difference in the sentence lengths, with participants in the mistaken acquittal condition recommending longer sentences. The study was limited on each of the five criteria. Furthermore, the study only examined a "general" pretrial publicity effect because none of the coverage was tied specifically to the defendant. Taken on its face, this study found that at the trial stage negative pretrial publicity helped defendants (in limited circumstances) if it did anything.

Mullin, Imrich, and Linz (1996)

Much like Riedel, these authors found a boomerang effect for antidefendant pretrial publicity in a rape trial. Each participant observed two sets of 10 articles, 1 week apart from each other and 1 week before the trial. In each set of 10 articles, two were antidefendant. A negative pretrial publicity condition included articles with information about the defendant's prior criminal record and indictments of the defendant's character. A neutral condition mentioned that the defendant had been arrested and that an investigation was in progress. Finally, a general pretrial publicity condition included an antiacquaintance rape article written to mirror the style typical of women's magazines. Sixty-six undergraduates were exposed to the publicity manipulations and then observed a video of a rape trial that had been pretested for a 50% conviction rate. Study participants rendered individual opinions without deliberation. The only significant effect was for the general antiacquaintance rape pretrial publicity condition; men observing the general pretrial publicity were more likely to acquit (75% vs. 21% conviction rates). A second study on 62 undergraduates found no significant verdict effects at all. In the end, only one of two studies found any pretrial publicity effect, that effect was a prodefendant effect, and that effect only occurred for men. Aside from the disturbing social implications of the findings, on its face the study does suggest pretrial publicity effects may not exist.

Although this study does fall short of being realistic on a number of fronts—it used an undergraduate sample, a case with 50% conviction rates, and the participants did not deliberate as actual jurors always do—the method of exposure did seem more realistic than the manipulations of most studies. Most readers scan their entire paper looking for something interesting and do not read crime stories in isolation; the study manipulation that included two crime articles in a packet of 10 more nearly approximates that reading pattern than most. In addition, the 1-week delay between exposure to the media and the trial is also more realistic, although short of the delays typical of many actual trials. These two manipulations—designed to make the study more realistic and not used in combination in any other study—resulted in a study that did not find a pretrial publicity effect. These two remedies are "natural" in the sense that they are not imposed by the court, and the findings of this study thus lend support to the cumulative remedy hypothesis.

Freedman and Burke (1996)

The Paul Bernardo rape-murder case was one of the most sensational in Canadian history and the coverage included a host of misinformation against the defendant. This study asked 155 adult Canadians how much they knew about the case and found that the amount of knowledge significantly correlated with assessments of guilt. The participants then read a 400-word summary of the trial and were again asked to render a verdict on the murder charge. After reading about the trial evidence all pretrial publicity effects disappeared, although there remained a nonsignificant tendency for the most publicity-saturated groups to render guilt judgments more often. When the rape charge was added to the murder charge, even this difference disappeared.

Although the account of the trial was obviously fabricated and simplistic, the exposure to publicity was fully realistic, the sample was drawn from the general population, and there was a natural delay between the exposure to the publicity and the "trial." This study allowed for no deliberation, and the conviction rate was lower than that found in most U.S. criminal cases. Overall, this study found no pretrial publicity effect when evidence was introduced, a finding very similar to that of Simon (1966) and Davis (1986).

Freedman, Martin, and Mota (1998)

Two studies were conducted to test the hypothesis that trial evidence and deliberation might be able to eliminate the influence of pretrial publicity. The first study exposed undergraduates to an edited, 1-hour version of an actual trial. Publicity was manipulated by having participants read four or five articles that included information actually released about the case but that stopped short of conclusively proving defendant guilt. Pilot testing confirmed that the "negative" articles were more biasing than the "neutral" ones; there was a 1-week gap between the reading of the articles and the exposure to the trial. Neither guilt ratings nor verdicts "even approached significance" (p. 261), and the pattern of means showed that participants in the negative publicity condition actually had more positive feelings about the defendant. Judicial instructions lowered ratings of guilt, although it was difficult for the authors to assess whether instructions effectively eliminated bias since there was no bias to correct. The authors concluded that mock jurors seemed to "bend over backward" to give the defendant the benefit of the doubt when biasing information was present.

In a second study, the authors largely replicated the first but also added a condition where some study participants expressed an opinion about guilt before the introduction of trial evidence. The "negative" publicity was altered so that major pieces of evidence that would appear in the trial were also included in the publicity. A pretrial effect for negative publicity did emerge. After trial evidence was introduced a pattern emerged where those who saw negative publicity and were asked to express a pretrial opinion were much more likely to convict (63%) than those exposed to negative publicity but not asked for a pretrial opinion (20%) or those exposed to neutral publicity (31% overall). The authors concluded that "asking jurors for their opinions before they have heard the trial will magnify pretrial publicity effects" (p. 268) and added, "Our opinion is that the laboratory studies overestimate rather than underestimate the effects" (p. 268).

The study did depart from natural conditions, although in ways that were likely to enhance pretrial publicity effects. The respondents were all undergraduates, conviction percentages in control conditions ranged between only 18% and 35% (the trial stimulus included videotaped footage of an actual case where the defendant was acquitted), and there was no deliberation. The authors listed the student sample and lack of deliberation as limitations to their work. Levels of exposure may not have been "natural"—a great deal of media coverage was reduced to four or five articles—but more so than other researchers the authors took special efforts to make their publicity materials mirror those that might appear outside the laboratory. The design did include a 1-week delay, which, although rather short when compared to what one might expect at an actual trial, was more realistic than no delay at all. In short, this study is a quite exemplary example of researchers working hard to mirror actual courtroom conditions and discovering either that no differences between publicity conditions emerged or that differences that did appear could be explained by study methodology.

Perhaps the most compelling feature of this research is the suggestion, and subsequent empirical support, of the claim that asking for predeliberation verdicts is a key factor that can explain on methodological grounds the results of much of the laboratory research. If the point they make is correct, much of the evidence in favor of a pretrial publicity effect can be explained as an artifact of research design.

Kovera (2002)

In this very sophisticated study of a possible agenda-setting media effect on pretrial publicity, the author followed the lead of others and pretested a general prodefense or proprosecution television report of rape to determine that each version had a distinctly prodefense or proprosecution slant. In a first study, undergraduate participants watched a version of the story or a control and were given a brief description of a rape case; no trial information was given and instead jurors were asked to list the types of evidence they would need to see to render a guilty verdict. The results confirmed that pretrial stories did influence the amount and type of evidence mock jurors would need to convict in predicted directions—those viewing a prodefense news story wanted more evidence about consent, more evidence from witnesses, and more evidence overall.

A second study had undergraduates watch 10 TV news stories, one of which was either prodefense, proprosecution, or a control. Participants then watched a videotape of a date-rape trial and completed several measures, including rape attitudes and verdict judgments without deliberation. Control groups returned a conviction rate of 57%. Again, an agenda-setting influence was present but only for those with neutral rape attitudes and only for the proprosecution condition. Mock jurors with prodefense attitudes who were exposed to rape media of either slant viewed the victim as more credible, whereas mock jurors with provictim attitudes viewed the defendant with less credibility than control participants. Therefore, and quite strikingly, exposure to publicity had the effect of actually reversing bias for both litigant ratings and verdicts, and both effects emerged without differentiation in regard to whether the media exposure was proprosecution or prodefense. Similarly, prodefendant mock jurors exposed to rape media produced more convictions (50%) than prodefendant mock jurors not exposed to media (27%), whereas provictim mock jurors convicted less often when exposed to rape media (68%) than provictim mock jurors who were not exposed to rape media (89%). No differences were obtained for those with neutral attitudes.

An extremely poignant facet of this study is that it actually measured mock juror bias before the introduction of media information. This design decision made it possible to compare not just an overall biasing effect for media but one that measured changes from preexisting biases. The pattern of results is so startling that it bears repeating: Pretrial publicity actually offset preexisting biases in a highly desirable way: It eliminated bias against the defendant for those predisposed to support the victim, it eliminated bias in favor of the defendant for those predisposed to support the defendant, and it did not alter opinions for those without strong prodefendant or provictim attitudes. Taken at its face, the results of this study suggest that pretrial publicity, far from being a daunting force to be removed, is an effective remedy against preexisting bias. (As promising as this is, one must wonder whether in reality people are likely to spontaneously expose themselves to media content that challenges their biases.)

Also telling are the results of the agenda-setting examinations. Publicity was found to influence the types and amounts of evidence jurors would need to see to produce convictions, and it did so primarily for jurors without strong rape attitudes. This suggests initially that, once again, to the extent that pretrial publicity can influence the outcome of a trial it does so by altering perceptions about the evidence. Further, it suggests that it may be general coverage of crime issues that frames the way jurors process evidence. As the author noted:

> The present research suggests that participants' beliefs about what constitutes a plausible rape scenario can also be influenced by media exposure. As people are more likely to remember information that is consistent with their preexisting schema, participants' expectations for what evidentiary patterns are plausible indications that a crime occurred have important implications for juror decisions. (p. 68)

In regard to levels of realism, the sample was composed of undergraduates, conviction percentages were low, there was no deliberation, and there was no delay between media exposure and the trial. The exposure levels were not striking; a single article does not seem more or less powerful than media in typical trials. However, mixing the stories into a group of nine other media stories does simulate to some extent the manner in which actual media consumers are exposed to crime news. Although the author concludes that the rape media exposure was especially brief (a 2-minute news story), the exposure scenario seems relatively realistic.

In short, this is a simulation study that shows that pretrial publicity can actually counteract preexisting biases, can do so regardless of the slant of the coverage, and to the extent that it might introduce bias will do so by altering standards for and perceptions about evidence. It further suggests that general pretrial publicity might indeed be a crucial influence. The study is especially noteworthy because it measured biases before the introduction of publicity and is especially significant because its findings so directly refute the conclusion that publicity introduces bias, although it might alter juror decision-making schemata.

Summary

Three major themes emerge from this group of studies, and all of them relate back to the central question of this chapter, which is whether there is a pretrial publicity effect at all. First, the very existence of these studies is surprising. One could read Studebaker and Penrod (1997) and conclude that no study had ever been done that failed to find a publicity effect. It must be acknowledged that there is a group of studies that has failed to find a pretrial publicity effect, and that those studies are no worse than the group of studies that has uncovered a publicity effect and might in some ways may be more realistic. Second, remedies do seem to be effective, at least part of the time. The work of Simon (1966), Davis (1986), and Freedman and Burke (1996) showed that trial evidence can eliminate a publicity effect. Davis concluded that deliberation was generally effective. The work of Mullin et al. (1996) suggests that natural delays and distractions might eliminate any biasing effect for those exposed to pretrial publicity. These studies are not necessarily conclusive on the point, but the results are very suggestive and again lend support to the cumulative remedy hypothesis. Enough remedies have shown up as being effective in enough different studies and enough different situations to make it seem likely that, in combination, one remedy or the other can usually manage to offset a publicity effect. Third, some types of publicity actually seem to help some defendants in some situations. The boomerang effect of sensational publicity found by Davis certainly speaks in favor of this conclusion. Much like the work of Otto et al. (1994), who found that weak inadmissible statements actually increased the chances of acquittal, the work of Riedel (1993) and Mullin et al. suggests that coverage espousing the evils of rape actually makes male jurors more prone to acquittal. This is not, of course, a good thing—God only knows why exposure to the evils of rape makes men more likely to acquit, and most of the possible explanations are horrifying—but in relation to the question of whether there is a publicity effect these findings can't be ignored. Kovera's (2002) results are especially noteworthy, and suggest that regardless of its slant, media exposure can offset preexisting biases. We are not ready to suggest that the ideal juror is one who had been exposed to especially slanted coverage, but evidence is gathering to support the conclusion that sometimes even bad publicity helps defendants.

Is there a pretrial publicity effect? Our final answer to this question will not appear until after the field research has been reviewed, but at this point it is no stronger than: Maybe, but not always. At least sometimes trial evidence will correct for or simply outweigh negative publicity. At least sometimes jurors will forget the publicity they have seen, sometimes deliberation will weed out kernels of misinformation, and sometimes the publicity will actually help defendants. If there is a pretrial publicity effect it is an elusive bugger and one that only shows up now and then. It is not the omnipresent, unkillable ogre suggested by other reviews. Figuring how pretrial publicity works and when it biases trials will take refined thinking and require more subtle conclusions than a simple declaration that it is always a threat and survives all remedies.

PUTTING IT ALL TOGETHER: ISSUES RAISED AND ANSWERED IN THESE STUDIES

Several questions are raised by this review, and the answers to these questions will take us back to the central questions of the book. If things work out, all these questions and answers might result in a better set of remedies. The first question raised simply has to do with the quality of this review. How can this review of the same topic and the same literature produce such different conclusions from the other two most recent reviews? Surely, if the other reviews are right and this one is wrong, little has been gained by the enterprise. The second issue raised returns to the methodological issues. As noted in the first chapter, scholars sharply differ on the consequences of the differences between laboratory research and field practice. Some suggest that the differences invalidate the laboratory research completely and some maintain the differences are of no consequence at all. At the conclusion of the review, what can be said of these methodological disputes? With these two issues addressed, we can return to the central questions of the book: Is there a pretrial publicity effect in actual trials? When does it show up? If it does exist, what do we know about it?

This Review Compared to Others

Although other reviewers have concluded that the preponderance of studies demonstrates a pretrial publicity effect (e.g,. Gibson & Padilla, 1998; Kerr, 1994; Steblay et al., 1999; Studebaker & Penrod, 1997), this review of all published empirical research points to a starkly different pattern where there are roughly as many studies that failed to find a pretrial publicity effect as there were studies that did, and a roughly equal number of studies that produced equivocal results. Who's right? A careful comparison of this review to the others is warranted. In the particular case of the Studebaker and Penrod article, one of the most comprehensive and well reasoned to date, studies that do not find a pretrial publicity effect seem simply not to appear in the review. Of the seven studies cited earlier that do not demonstrate a pretrial publicity effect, four are not cited at all (Davis, 1986; Freedman & Burke, 1996; Mullin et al., 1996; Riedel, 1993) and two studies were published after the review was completed (Freedman et al., 1998; Kovera, 2002). The Simon article (1966) is cited, but no mention is made of the fact that Simon discovered that all differences between publicity and no publicity groups disappeared after trial evidence and deliberation. Similarly, no mention is made of the author's ultimate conclusion that fears of pretrial publicity are overstated. In fact, Simon is not cited at all in either the section dealing with trial evidence or the section dealing with deliberation. In both sections the same article, Otto et al. (1994) is relied on heavily to demonstrate the failure of trial evidence and deliberation. For reasons delineated earlier, the Otto et al. study may not provide sufficient evidence to warrant this conclusion. The most that can be said for the Otto et al. study is that it demonstrated that only one of five types of pretrial publicity has any effect at all on the final verdict, and that effect was indirect and dwarfed by assessments of trial evidence. The study was not done poorly, it was done exceptionally well, but its results do not demonstrate a large, pernicious effect for pretrial publicity. Citing the study as evidence for the failure of deliberation is especially odd, because the description of the procedures included in the article does not indicate that participants deliberated with each other at all. At any rate, relying so extensively on a study that describes its own results as "modest" while simultaneously failing to consider at least four published studies with contrary evidence should cast suspicion on the conclusions of the article. Notice that these issues are completely separate from the questions of realism and methodology (a topic returned to in the next section), and instead have to do with how to interpret the current findings if they are taken at face value. In sum, it appears as if Studebaker and Penrod overstated the case for a pretrial publicity effect by ignoring contrary studies and interpreting some studies in a way that goes beyond even the conclusions of the authors of those studies.

The second recent review, the article by Steblay et al. (1999), is especially difficult to square with the present review. How could their meta-analysis come to such a different conclusion than this review? Is it not the case that the more rigorous procedures of meta-analysis those authors relied on is more valid than the admittedly subjective assessments offered here? The first step in comparing a meta-analysis with other reviews is to understand what a meta-analysis can and cannot do. As a basic starting point, even an unabashed advocate of meta-analysis noted that it is not a panacea for research synthesis and that quantitative sophistication should always be an aid to clear thought and not a substitute for it (Wolf, 1986). A fairly reasonable view is that both traditional reviews (such as that offered here) and meta-analysis have their strengths and limitations, and that neither method is inherently superior (Cook & Leviton, 1980). What really counts is how well each review is done, and in particular how the various features of each study are dealt with (Wolf, 1986). Both meta-analysis and traditional reviews involve a large number of subjective judgments; these judgments have a significant impact on the results of the meta-analysis (Hedges, 1990). The danger is in accepting the conclusions of a meta-analysis solely on the basis of its appearance as a more "objective" method of review:

> In order to take the precision of an effect size seriously, one must assume that there is equal bias across studies.... While qualitative reviews may be equally prone to bias, the descriptive accuracy of a point estimate in meta-analysis can have mischievous consequences because of its apparent "objectivity," "precision," and "scientism." To naïve readers, these lend a social credibility that may be built on procedural invalidity. (Cook & Leviton, 1980, p. 455)

In short, there's no reason to prefer a meta-analysis to a traditional review just because it's a meta-analysis. The point is an easy one, but the social credibility that Cook and Leviton warned against is all too easy to grant.

There are two other features of meta-analysis that might make the work of Steblay et al. (1999) less than definitive. First, meta-analysis is most suspect when the number of studies is small and the results are heterogeneous. There is, of course, no test for how many studies is too few, but two essays (Cook & Leviton, 1980; Wolf, 1986) have pointed to the reviews of Zuckerman (1979) and Arkin, Cooper, and Kolditz (1980), who reviewed 13 and 23 studies, respectively, as paradigm cases of reviews that meta-analysis could not deal with well because of the low number of studies. Twenty-three is the exact number of studies utilized by Steblay et al. The heterogeneity of the studies was addressed earlier, and thus there is every reason to believe that the present situation—a small number of studies with heterogeneous results—is exactly the sort of condition that does not lend itself well to meta-analysis. Second, meta-analysis cannot detect bias that is in one direction (Cook & Leviton, 1980). Thus, if some feature of the research designs produce an artificial finding across a number of studies, the meta-analysis will not be able to ferret out the offending characteristic. If, as argued earlier, the literature to date has consistently biased results in the direction of a positive finding, a meta-analysis can only reproduce those biases. The work of Stebaly et al. is thus exemplary in its attention to methods and scrupulous in its coding of different study features, but the method may have been applied to a situation where it was not capable of untangling overlapping and conflicting issues. The situation might be likened to taking a Honda Civic off-roading in the jungle; the car might be brilliantly engineered, but simply isn't designed to handle the terrain.

Turning to the more specific question of why our review and that of Steblay et al. (1999) might differ, two explanations may serve to illuminate, one dealing with studies included in the review and the second focusing on the features of those studies considered significant. The first explanation is simply that the same studies were not under consideration in the two different reviews. Steblay et al., who include five unpublished articles in their meta-analysis, did not review 10 of the published studies cited here (one additional study, Kovera, 2002, was reviewed in its unpublished form), and reviewed 6 studies that we have chosen not to review because they did not include trial evidence. Thus, our review and that of Steblay et al. reviewed 13 studies in common, we have reviewed 10 studies they have excluded, and they have reviewed 11 studies we did not include. Our reviews thus have 13 studies in common and 21 studies that are not common to both reviews. The difference is further magnified by the number of "independent tests" included in the differences; Steblay et al. report 44 independent tests in the 23 studies, or roughly two tests per study. Without counting specifically, the differences in the number of independent tests might be twice as large as the differences in the number of studies. Not surprisingly, methodologists have warned that differences in the sampling of studies can have a large impact on the results obtained (Hedges, 1990), and given the sizeable differences in which studies were reviewed a difference in studies selected could easily account for the differing conclusions.

Is there a pattern to the differences that could explain the discrepancies in conclusions? There is. A publication bias, or the tendency of journals to only publish studies that produce significant findings, has plagued meta-analysis from the outset (Kotiaho & Tompkins, 2002; Wachter & Straf, 1990; Wolf, 1986). Recent research demonstrated that publication bias can completely invalidate any meta-analysis. Kotiaho and Tompkins (2002) wrote:

> If we accept that there is extensive publication bias, it seems evident that there is no possibility for a meta-analysis to fail. This is because, if only about 9% of the published work reports non-significant results (Csada et al., 1996), it follows that when an overall effect size from this data set is calculated, a meta-analysis cannot fail to find a significant effect. (p. 552)

There is some evidence of publication bias in the pretrial publicity literature. Steblay et al. (1999) found five unpublished studies in their review and report that the average effect size for the unpublished studies (.09) is half that of the published studies (.18). Of course, including those studies is an attempt to deal with the biasing effect, but if it is imagined that there are other unpublished studies that were not recovered for the meta-analysis and that those studies have the same effect size as the other unpublished studies, the warning of Kotiaho and Tompkins is ominous indeed. Further, there is reason to believe that the effect size for unpublished studies may be smaller still. Of the five unpublished studies, the largest effect size (–.22) is negative, roughly double six of the seven other effect sizes, and from a sample roughly half as large as the other six independent tests combined ($n = 358$ vs. 615). If that effect is taken as evidence disconfirming an antidefendant bias, which it surely must, a weighted average effect size, accounting for sign, is only .03, now one-sixth of that in published research.

What matters, ultimately, is not whether publication bias exists, but whether such bias creeps into the meta-analysis. In other words, the concern with published and unpublished research is important because there should not be a bias such that studies that find significant differences are overrepresented in the sample of studies. In the present case, of the eight studies reported here that did find an effect six were included, and the only two that were not were those unavailable as of the Steblay et al. (1999) publication date. Of the eight studies that demonstrated only a partial effect, only three were included, although three were unavailable as of the publication date. Of the seven studies reviewed here that did not find significant results, three were not included at all in Steblay et al., and one was included in its unpublished form. Only one study was unavailable as of the Steblay et al. publication date. On the final scorecard, Steblay et al. included six studies that found an effect, three that found an equivocal effect, and four that found no effect. Excluded were two that found an effect, five that were equivocal, and three that found no effect. These comparisons are further exaggerated depending on how one assesses the six studies that lacked trial evidence included by Steblay et al. and discarded by us; all six studies produced significant results and, as the results Steblay et al. present demonstrate, show effect sizes roughly two to three times larger than other studies in the sample. The studies included for review in Steblay et al. do appear to have been slanted in favor of finding an effect.

The second major explanation for a difference between our study and that of Steblay et al. (1999) has to do with which features of a given study are most salient. As meta-analytic methodologists have noted, the most crucial factor in any review, and especially in meta-analysis, is deciding which features of the study to code (Cook & Leviton, 1980; Wolf, 1986). Minor variations have major impacts (Hedges, 1990). The most important comparisons involve theoretical variables that can explain differences in outcomes across studies (Cook & Leviton, 1980, see p. 464). In more vernacular terms, a single study that includes a crucial variable is more revealing than a thousand studies without the variable. Meta-analysis, of course, hopes to deal with this issue by coding for the presence or absence of a particular study characteristic. There are two particular choices where the coding of Steblay et al. may have failed to capture key variables focused on in this review, in the first instance because the coding may simply reflect a methodological artifact and in the second case because the coding was impossible. The first case is our decision to exclude studies that did not include trial evidence, for the theoretical reason that no defendant has ever been convicted in the absence of trial evidence (at least, not in any court with minimal concerns for justice). Steblay et al. included these studies in their review, and coded studies for the timing of the verdict judgment, as either before trial, after trial and before deliberation, or after trial and deliberation. The theoretical decision has methodological implications, if Freedman et al. (1998) are correct that asking for pretrial (or predeliberation) opinions can completely explain any residual pretrial publicity effect. At any rate, the theoretical choice could be telling; Steblay et al. report an effect size for these studies (.28) roughly three times as large as predeliberation verdicts (.10) and twice the size of postdeliberation verdicts (.15). Simply excluding those studies could, of course, radically change the results. To the extent that it is valid to conclude on theoretical grounds that pretrial publicity effects in the absence of trials is of little interest, 17 independent trials reported by Steblay et al. are irrelevant. To the extent that the research choice to include the predeliberation data collection produces a research artifact that greatly explains the remaining effect, a pretrial publicity effect might disappear entirely.

A second consideration is the cumulative remedy hypothesis suggested here, which is not captured in the coding scheme of Steblay et al. (1999). Of course, the cumulative remedy hypothesis is at its heart an interaction effect that supposes that remedies in interaction with one another might succeed when each alone fails. There is the general viewpoint that meta-analysis should consider interactions for theoretical reasons (Wachter & Straf, 1990), but Hedges (1990) very forcefully made the point that meta-analysis is incapable of testing for an interaction effect not contained in an original study. As Cook and Leviton (1980) put it,

> Our guess is that, with their stress on broad generalization, meta-analysts are even more prone than qualitative reviewers to overlook or to down play the importance of contingency-specifying interactions that in most situations have an inferential precedence over statements about main effects. (p. 464)

If, as our cumulative remedy hypothesis predicts, deliberation and delay and instructions and voir dire all combine to eliminate pretrial publicity effects, individual studies that examine only remedies in isolation will never provide a fair test that speaks to remedies working in combination. A meta-analytic synthesis of the individual studies is structurally incapable of providing an interaction test not included in the original studies. If there's anything to the work of Freedman et al. (1998) or that of London and Nunez (2000), scholars would do well to pay attention to the possibly profound interactions suggested elsewhere rather than the intoxicating summation of meta-analysis.

In sum, there are three reasons to believe that the conclusions of Steblay et al. (1999), if contradictory to those reported here, are not to be preferred. First, the method of meta-analysis might not be well suited to the current situation, characterized by a small number of studies and heterogeneous results. Second, the articles reviewed by the two contrasting efforts are substantially different and different in a way that might exaggerate the presence of a pretrial publicity effect in the work of Steblay et al. Third, two substantive differences, the theoretical choice by Steblay et al. to include studies without trial evidence and our choice to exclude them, and our belief in the cumulative remedy hypothesis combined with the inability of meta-analysis to test for such an effect absent specific research on the issue, could point to substantive reasons that the reviews differ. To the extent that trial evidence and a cumulative remedy effect are important considerations, the results of Steblay et al. do not contrast with the findings offered here so much as they are irrelevant to them.

None of this is to suggest that the review includes major errors. Indeed, Steblay et al. (1999) were quite careful in their coding of the studies, and the issues raised here concerning study sampling and coding are hardly peculiar to the meta-analysis performed by Steblay et al. Nonetheless, we conclude that the meta-analysis does well that which meta-analyses do well, which is summarize the average effects of current research. What we hope our review has done is to push the envelope a little further, and suggest some factors that might render the summed effects of present research questionable. It is finally worth noting that Steblay et al. conclude that the effect of pretrial publicity is modest and difficult to detect:

> The PTP effect, particularly in simulation studies, is relatively small; thus, without adequate sample size a statistically significant result would not be obtained. The data indicate a small average effect size, $r = .16$, with the range across studies including zero and negative as well as positive effect sizes. (p. 229)

In other words, the conclusions of Steblay et al. are more consistent with the type of effect we suggest, one that is not entirely consistent across studies, potentially contingent on a number of circumstances, and not all that powerful. We differ, of course, on whether remedies might be effective. The results of the Steblay et al. meta-analysis do not support the views of Studebaker and Penrod, who report a consistent effect that is both powerful and completely resistant to remedy. Given the historical tendency of traditional reviews to produce more conservative results than meta-analyses (Cook & Leviton, 1980), it is notable that the results reported by Steblay et al. are much more modest than those opined to exist by Studebaker and Penrod.

Questions of Methodology

As noted in the introduction, opinions vary widely about the meaning of the differences between laboratory and field research. At this point, the case for the generalizability of laboratory findings turns on three issues. First, the results of the laboratory research may be overstated, as the prior section has addressed. If the laboratory results are overstated, the case for generalizability is difficult to maintain; no pretrial publicity effect will show up during actual trials because such effects only appear in some carefully controlled (and perhaps artificial) laboratory situations. Second, if the methodological issues are inconsequential, as some claim, pretrial publicity effects should be apparent in field studies. Putting the cart just slightly ahead of the horse, field research (reviewed and presented later) has demonstrated that highly publicized trials show no differences in conviction rates when compared to trials with no publicity whatsoever. The work is best considered preliminary and suggestive at this point, but these early findings do not suggest that the results of laboratory research can be replicated in the field. If field tests fail to replicate laboratory research, there is a second strike against the generalizability of a pretrial publicity effect.

The third and final point critical to the issue of generalizability concerns the particular claims made by those asserting that the differences are inconsequential and point to research to support the conclusion. Thus far we have skirted the issue, offering our own criteria and justifications for it, but it is worth addressing the justifications others offer for laboratory research directly. It should be noted that of all the various assessments of the methodological adequacy of extant research, the only one that is in direct contrast to the conclusions offered here is the view that the artificialities of laboratory research are of no consequence at all. For this reason, the justifications of others warrant further discussion.

The Studebaker and Penrod (1997) article does the best job of supporting the claim that "a number of studies have determined that the artificialities of the typical trial simulation study generally do not bias verdicts" (p. 435). The authors provided six citations as evidence for the claim, but even accepting the references at face value does not establish either the validity of laboratory research overall nor the irrelevance of the five criteria used here. The cited works do provide some evidence that speaks to a variety of issues concerning generalizability. One study is cited to demonstrate that shorter trial lengths "are not inherently distorting" (Kramer & Kerr, 1989, p. 99). Another demonstrates that videotaped trials are generally viewed as equivalent to actual trials (Miller, 1975). Others prove that mock jurors take their jobs seriously (Kerr, Nerenz, & Herrick, 1979) and that leniency effects are not limited to college students (MacCoun & Kerr, 1988). However, there are also studies—in fact, aspects of studies reviewed by Studebaker and Penrod—that conclude that laboratory artificialities are cause for concern, some of which are not cited by or were unavailable to Studebaker and Penrod. These included the finding that deliberation is a crucial factor (Kerr et al., 1979; London & Nunez, 2000; MacCoun & Kerr, 1988), that minimal evidence use is troublesome (Kramer & Kerr, 1989), and that human memory is faulty and thus delays are crucial (MacCoun & Kerr, 1988, p. 23; Vidmar, 2002).

At any rate, even the authors of studies cited by Studebaker and Penrod (1997) did not interpret their own results as blanket validation of simulation research. Kramer and Kerr (1989) wrote:

> We do agree with the moral of much of the criticism of jury simulation research—that such research should not be automatically or carelessly generalized to actual juror/jury behavior.... These findings certainly do not establish the irrelevance of stimulus material length or complexity for the magnitude of any (much less all) treatments of possible interest. (p. 99)

Kerr et al. (1979, p. 351) took a similar view: "We hasten to add that these results do not suggest that one may indiscriminately generalize results obtained with mock, laboratory juries to actual juries." They added the caution that

> By characterizing the mock jury research as high on experimental realism, we do not wish to imply that the verisimilitude of jury simulation studies is unimportant. To the contrary, until we better understand which of the de-

partures from typical courtroom procedure are important, it is desirable
that such simulations be as "true to life" as possible. (p. 353)

The very authors cited by Studebaker and Penrod as validating simulation research would seem to champion the sort of careful assessment of laboratory
research attempted here.

All told and with rare exception, those studies that did find an effect for pretrial publicity contained many manipulations that make them difficult to generalize from, and the case against a pretrial publicity effect seems stronger
than the case for it. Contrary views seem to have given too little weight to
studies that have found no pretrial publicity effect and too much weight to laboratory research.

So What Do We Know?

Most of the current research on pretrial publicity has proceeded in a largely
atheoretical fashion. Focused narrowly on the question of whether or not pretrial publicity influences jurors, most research has been very application focused and has not addressed broader questions about why publicity might bias
jurors or connected to the larger literature on whether media accounts can
change personal opinions and, if they can, how they might do so. The remainder of the book takes up the challenge of linking pretrial publicity research to a
broader theoretical literature or field tests, and suggests a number of ideas
that are speculative. This chapter, instead, has focused on what the laboratory
literature to date has proven and what conclusions are warranted by our current knowledge base.

First, we know that there is not a general pretrial publicity effect. We know
that the laboratory results are mixed. Many studies have found no effect at all
and many studies have produced mixed results. If a pretrial publicity effect does
exist, it is weak and difficult to detect (Otto et al., 1994; Steblay et al., 1999). In
laboratory terms, this means that careful controls must be used to detect the effect. In the field, this means that a number of factors usually correct for or
swamp pretrial publicity, and it usually doesn't alter the outcome of trials.

Second, we have good reason to believe the cumulative remedy hypothesis.
Remedies that only work some of the time in isolation have a good chance of
working together. Because almost all trials have a number of remedies—deliberation, evidence, voir dire, instructions, delays, different exposure patterns for
jurors—there is a chance for the remedies to double-check each other. Pretrial
publicity only influences the outcomes of trials when all remedies fail at once.

Third, even though there is not a strong, general pretrial publicity effect,
there is reason to believe that there are some cases where pretrial publicity
might pose a real threat to a fair trial. When a case becomes the focus of intense scrutiny and moves from being one that simply attracts some media at-

tention to one that has become a "media trial" it becomes likely that the extreme publicity situations studied in the laboratory obtain—here we recall that paradigmatic Sheppard trial. When the publicity includes information that has probative value and speaks to guilt, there is special cause for concern. The knowledge–guilt hypothesis suggests that the more jurors know about a case, the more likely they are to assume guilt. When the trial evidence is weak, publicity is most likely to make a difference to jurors who are trying their best to evaluate the evidence.

There is cause for optimism and cause for vigilance. Pretrial publicity is not the pernicious ogre previously reported. On the other hand, it may have been blocked from the legal system because of the efficacy of extant remedies, which suggests that the issue is not one to dismiss as irrelevant but instead that careful attention ought be given to appropriate remedies. The search for smarter, more effective remedies can only improve the course of justice.

CHAPTER THREE

Field Research

While many of these professors are brilliant scholars who make immeasurable contributions to the law, some publish virtually incomprehensible articles that have little relation to reality. (Stephen Bright, 1997, p. 833)

LITERATURE REVIEW

There are two features of the extant field research that will make even a casual reader suspicious: There aren't very many of such studies, and they've all been written by us. In relation to the latter shortcoming, we can only say that at least it wasn't our idea. The concept of correlating publicity with the outcomes of actual trials was an idea first expressed by Kerr (1994; see the quotation in chap. 1). Kerr's call gained some prominence with the publication of Studebaker and Penrod's (1997) work. If pretrial publicity does indeed influence trials and it does indeed survive all remedies, one would expect that highly publicized trials have higher conviction rates than trials without any coverage at all. In relation to the first concern, we're not sure why there isn't more research of this type, but at least one serious possibility is that it is very hard to do. Accessing court records is not easy, and coding media stories is time-consuming and expensive. Regardless of the amount of research in this area and who has done it, the results are interesting and speak for themselves.

The only published research to date that has attempted to correlate actual coverage with the outcomes of a large number of trials is Bruschke and Loges (1999). The study examined all federal murder trials over a 3-year period and examined newspaper coverage of those cases. Cases were divided into categories of no publicity, low publicity (1 to 5 articles), moderate publicity (6 to 10 articles), and high publicity (11 or more articles). High- and no-publicity conditions produced roughly equal conviction rates (79.9% and 79.0%, respectively), defendants fared better under moderate- (68.0% conviction rates) rather than low-publicity conditions (92.0%), but for defendants who were sentenced, any degree of publicity was associated with a longer sentence when compared to defendants receiving no pretrial coverage. Defendants fared the best in the moderate-publicity condition and fared the worst in the low-publicity condition. The core finding of the study was that no-publicity and high-publicity conditions produced identical conviction rates, and that any pretrial publicity effect, to the extent that it did exist, did not exhibit a simple, linear pattern.

In relation to the five criteria, it is both true and unsurprising that field research scores as more realistic than laboratory research. The sample was composed of actual juries, the conviction rates were realistic—in fact, they were real—the amount and nature of publicity were natural rather than created (eliminating any concern that an observed effect was the product of artificial stimulus materials), and deliberation and delay were both present and natural. What was gained in realism was of necessity lost in control. Nothing is reported about the content of the coverage; which, if any, remedies were applied; or whether any juror saw any of the publicity surrounding the cases. If some unknown factor—the heinousness of the crime, for example—drove both the publicity and the conviction rates, then this study did not provide a fair test of publicity in isolation. What was undoubtedly studied, however, was publicity as it actually occurs, and it is quite striking that in the only study to examine a large number of actual cases no difference was found in conviction rates between high- and no-publicity cases.

NEW RESEARCH

We subsequently collected data that continue to explore the basic pretrial publicity questions and also branch out to explore two additional questions. The first new area concerns the type of crime under study. Current research has studied a variety of criminal cases, spanning murder, rape, robbery, sexual abuse, business fraud, and drunk driving (Steblay et al., 1999, provide a complete listing of offenses used in pretrial publicity research). Although various crimes have been studied, comparisons across crime types have been limited (e.g., Tanford & Penrod, 1982; Tans & Chaffee, 1966). Tans and Chaffee (1966) found no differences based on the type of crime; replicating such a finding (now three decades old) would lead to the important practical conclusion that whatever rules are formed about pretrial publicity could be applied uniformly across crime types. We pose the question: RQ 1: Does the effect of pretrial publicity on trial outcomes depend on the type of crime with which the defendant is charged?

The second question guiding this research has to do with extending research into legal forums other than trials as part of an effort to study legal cases in context. A criminal trial is actually a very rare event in the legal system and the far more frequent result is a plea bargain. Across all federal criminal cases in 1995 (n = 29,036), 77.3% of the time defendants entered pleas of guilty (Federal Judicial

Center, 1997). There is reason to believe that pretrial publicity may influence plea bargains as much as it influences trial outcomes. Although jurors can be screened for their exposure to pretrial publicity, the ultimate dispositors in a plea bargain—the prosecutor and defense attorneys—are under no such censure and are, in fact, more likely to be acutely aware of any press coverage surrounding the case. A prosecutor may be less inclined to offer a good deal to a defendant in a highly publicized case for fear of appearing soft on crime (Pritchard, 1990). Further, a defendant in a highly publicized case might feel more pressured to accept a plea bargain, fearing that a jury would be more likely to come back with an even more unfavorable sentence. The second question is: RQ 2: Does pretrial publicity influence plea-bargained sentences?

Overview

The present data set is used to analyze actual court trials and compare cases with large amounts of pretrial publicity against those that were not covered widely. Three major cities, Atlanta, Detroit, and Los Angeles, were selected for the study. These cities were selected for their rough geographical diversity and because the major newspapers in every city were included in the Lexis / Nexis newspaper database. Every federal murder or bank robbery case that appeared before the federal district courts in those cities between 1993 and 1995 was included in the study. The defendant names were searched in the Lexis / Nexis electronic newspaper database. Any article that appeared before the start of the trial or plea bargain and included either the defendant's name or a reference to the crime was tallied.

As noted earlier, this approach was outlined by Kerr (1994). It should be noted that Kerr was skeptical about the ability to find an adequate sample of "matched cases" to serve as the "no-publicity" control group. The concern is certainly valid, but we believe our choice of method is still valuable for three reasons. First, the cases we compare have been deemed identical by the legal system. Federal rules do not distinguish, for example, between different types of first-degree murder. Thus, although we do not know whether our sample of "high-publicity" and "low-publicity" cases are identical in all respects save for publicity, we do know that the legal system has deemed that the cases deserve identical charges. Substituting the judgment of a researcher for that of a professional prosecutor is foolhardy at best. Second, if the high- and low-publicity cases do differ in some important respect that draws publicity to one group but not the other, such a bias introduces Type I error. That is, such a condition makes it more likely that differences will be observed in conviction rates. However, because we suspect that no differences may be obtained, such a disconfirming finding would be especially telling and supportive of the viewpoint that pretrial publicity is relatively inconsequential. Thus, a positive finding of differences between low- and high-publicity groups will not be able to distinguish whether the differences observed are due to publicity or some unknown factor about the cases that generated publicity, but a negative finding of no difference is supportive of the conclusion that whatever remedies are in effect do seem to produce identical conviction rates even in different publicity circumstances. Finally, as a practical matter, even if researchers can separate cases that are identical in every respect and then decide not to apply publicity to one case, defense attorneys have no similar option. For example, even if some unknown factor causes some first-degree murder cases to get more publicity than others, defense attorneys must cope with the coverage only in those cases that generate publicity. The relevant question, from an applied point of view, is whether those cases that generate publicity can be dealt with in a similar fashion as cases that do not contain some feature that generates publicity, even if an unknown third variable accounts for both the publicity and the differences in conviction rates.

Court Records

The Federal Judicial Center (FJC) compiles information on many aspects of each federal case, including the trial disposition and the sentence length, if any, of the criminal defendants. This information is made publicly available through the Inter-University Consortium for Political and Social Research (ICPSR) at Ann Arbor, MI; all first-degree murder and bank robbery cases for the cities in question were identified in that data set (Federal Judicial Center, 1997). However, although the FJC includes the docket numbers for each case, it does not include defendant names. In order to obtain the names of defendants, the docket numbers were cross-referenced against the Public Access to Court Electronic Records (PACER) databases maintained by the federal courts. The PACER system is a network of electronic databases maintained by the federal court system; each district maintains its own database. In 24 cases the defendant number listed in the FJC database did not return a defendant name in the PACER system; those cases were excluded from the analysis. If multiple defendants were tried together, each defendant was treated as a separate unit of analysis. In all, between 1993 and 1995 there were 51 first-degree murder defendants and 798 bank-robbery defendants identified for this study.

Measuring Pretrial Publicity

The name of each murder defendant was entered into the Lexis/Nexis database, a full-text compilation of thousands of newspapers around the world that is updated daily. The database is searchable with individual words and will locate the occurrence of any search term in any article in the database; the result is that typing in a given name should produce a listing of all articles in which that name appeared. Although limiting a search to the Lexis/Nexis database does present limitations—television coverage is not measured—Lexis/ Nexis does represent a state-of-the-art system and is the most complete collection of newspaper coverage available.

A number of research decisions had to be made to insure the uniformity of database searches and article counting. In relation to what counted as pretrial publicity, we decided to err on the side of inclusion, based on the broad definitions of pretrial publicity utilized in prior research and the research designs (cited earlier) that were based on the premise that tangential material can influence a defendant's chances. Thus, any article that contained the defendant's name in relation to the crime in question was included. Further, any coverage of the crime that identified the victim's name but not the defendant's name was included. In sum, an attempt was made to identify all stories related to the defendant or the alleged crime. Any article preceding the verdict date or plea date was counted.

Some papers produced multiple versions of the same edition; coverage of the same defendant on the same day of the same paper with the same headline was counted as only one article, even if it appeared differently in the database as a "metro" and a "downtown" edition. In relation to search term selection, one difficulty was that the defendant's name could have appeared differently in press coverage than it did in court records. Nicknames, pseudonyms, and shorter versions of first names (i.e., "Jon" from "Jonathan") were searched only if they appeared as an "also known as" entry in the court records. Because the Lexis/Nexis search terminology is fairly complex, an experienced Lexis/Nexis user was employed to search the defendant names. A second experienced Lexis/Nexis user re-searched 48 names. Perfect agreement on the number of articles was obtained in 47 of 48 cases. In the one instance of disagreement the official court records had misspelled the defendant's name, and the double-check uncovered articles that the first researcher did not find. Overall, independent searches of the Lexis/Nexis database appeared to produce highly reliable article counts.

One final issue involving the measurement of pretrial publicity involves the Detroit sample. In July 1995, an especially nasty newspaper strike disrupted the normal conduct of the printed media in Detroit ("Detroit Newspaper Strike Ends," 1997). Thus, for 5 months of the 24-month period of this study the Detroit papers may have had their coverage sharply altered by the strike; although the papers did not miss a day of publication (Slaughter, 1997), their circulation did drop from 899,000 to 620,000 ("Detroit Newspaper Strike Ends," 1997). Nonetheless, the strike did not influence the present study. A review of the data indicated that all but one Detroit case was disposed of prior to July 1995, and that case was disposed of in August, only 2 weeks after the onset of the strike. As a final check against a corrupting influence, where appropriate the data analyzed later in this report were considered with the Detroit data excluded altogether.

General Description of Press Coverage

Press coverage was not uniform in this sample of cases. Article frequency counts are reported in Table 3.1; in 81.4% of the cases no coverage was present at all. In the remaining 158 cases, more cases were covered by only a single article than any other article count. Only five cases were covered with more than seven articles. These data make it apparent that press coverage is not the norm, and that most cases that are covered are covered only in a single article.

When word counts rather than article counts are considered, the mean number of words per case is 151.9 with a very large standard deviation of 1,079.0 words. There are regional differences in the amount of coverage given to these cases; a one-way analysis of variance (ANOVA) treating the total number of words on each defendant as the dependent variable produced significant results ($F = 3.373$, $df = 2/846$, $p < .05$). The highest amount of coverage existed in Atlanta ($M = 371$, $n = 117$, $SD = 2506.0$), followed by Los Angeles ($M = 131$, $n = 651$, $SD = 621.1$) and Detroit ($M = .27$, $n = 81$, $SD = 2.4$). Of the 849 cases retained for analysis, 128 went to trial, 675 involved a guilty plea by the defendant, and 37 were disposed of in some other fashion.

Publicity Effects on Case Outcomes

There are two legal outcomes of particular concern to this study; the first is a determination of guilt or innocence, and the second is the sentence length for

TABLE 3.1

Frequency Counts for Article Coverage

Number of Articles	Frequency	Percent	Cumulative Percent
.00	691	81.4	81.4
1.00	92	10.8	92.2
2.00	29	3.4	95.6
3.00	18	2.1	97.8
4.00	10	1.2	98.9
5.00	2	0.2	99.2
6.00	2	0.2	99.4
7.00	1	0.1	99.5
9.00	1	0.1	99.6
10.00	1	0.1	99.8
23.00	1	0.1	99.9
71.00	1	0.1	100.0
Total	849	100.0	100.0

those found guilty. Addressing the first concern, levels of publicity do not appear to be related to determinations of guilt or innocence. Due to the distribution of press coverage, some accounting had to be made for the fact that the vast number of cases include no coverage at all. All attempts to categorize the level of publicity in different ways produced identical, nonsignificant results. In addition, determinations of what "guilt" means can vary according to different trial outcomes (see later discussion). All attempts to categorize the case outcomes in different ways produced identical, nonsignificant results. Thus, no matter how publicity was categorized, and no matter how guilt was categorized, no significant relationships emerged.

Questions of guilt or innocence are fairly abstract; a more objective measure is whether the defendant was sentenced to serve time. The FJC codes case outcomes in 15 different ways, including: dismissed, acquitted by court, acquitted by jury, plea of guilty, convicted by court, convicted by jury, nolle prosequi, pretrial diversion, mistrial, dismissed without prejudice, not guilty by reason of insanity, and guilty but insane. Case outcomes were recategorized as resulting in the defendant either receiving a sentence (convicted or pleaded guilty) or not receiving a sentence (all other outcomes).

Publicity was measured in three different ways. First, cases were divided into two levels, those that received any amount of publicity and those that received none. All subsequent references to this division are identified as the "2-level publicity" variable. A 2×2 chi-square produced nonsignificant results ($\chi^2 = 0$, $df = 1$, $p = .991$). Second, the cases were divided into three levels, one including no publicity, one including cases receiving 300 or fewer words worth of coverage ($n = 73$), and one including cases receiving 301 or more words worth of coverage ($n = 85$). All subsequent references to this division will be identified as the "3-level publicity variable." The results were again not statistically significant ($\chi^2 = 1.603$, $df = 2$, $p = .449$). Finally, an independent-groups t-test was conducted comparing the total words of coverage between defendants who were ultimately incarcerated and those who ultimately were not. Not only were the results not significant ($t = .528$, $df = 838$, $p = .598$), but non-incarcerated defendants were covered more extensively ($M = 233.7$ words, $SD = 942.0$) than were defendants who were ultimately incarcerated ($M = 148.6$, $SD = 1092.8$).

When the dependent variable was changed to sentence length, however, there did appear to be a relationship between newspaper coverage and the length of the defendant's sentence. Because federal law mandates longer sentences for murder than bank robbery, sentence lengths were converted to z-scores within offense categories for further analysis. All subsequent references to sentence lengths refer to their z-score values. A significant correlation emerged between the amount of newspaper coverage measured in total words and the length of the sentence (Pearson's $r = .172$, $p < .01$). The unequal distribution in newspaper coverage resulted in a huge group of cases without any coverage at all; when the "no-coverage" group was excluded, along with the four most highly publicized cases (which appeared to be outliers), the size of the correlation nearly doubled (Pearson's $r = .304$, $p < .01$, $n = 155$). Very similar results were obtained when the cases without any coverage were randomly excluded to equalize the number of coverage and no coverage cases (Pearson's $r = .271$, $p < .01$, $n = 321$). An additional source of noise in the data was the regional effect of press coverage. When only the data from Los Angeles (the city with the largest number of cases) were considered and the sizes of coverage and no-coverage groups were equalized, the correlation again jumped (Pearson's $r = .369$, $p < .01$, $n = 247$), and when no-coverage cases were excluded altogether the correlation again made a large increase (Pearson's $r = .514$, $p < .01$, $n = 130$).

The Type of Crime

Although murder cases received more coverage (M total words = 781; $SD = 3,856.1$) than did bank robberies (M total words = 111; $SD = 527.8$), the effect did not appear to be statistically significant. Chi-square tests comparing the 2-level publicity variable and crime type were not significant ($\chi^2 = 1.696$, $df = 1$, $p = .193$), and neither were tests comparing the 3-level publicity variable and crime type ($\chi^2 = 1.696$, $df = 2$, $p = .428$). A t-test comparison of the total words of coverage produced significantly unequal variances (Levene's $F = 62.615$, $p < .001$) and when corrections were applied to adjust for unequal variances between the groups the t-test was not significant ($t = 1.240$, $df = 50.12$, $p = .221$).

The type of crime did appear to interact with the amount of coverage to produce different sentence lengths. A stepwise multiple-regression test was conducted treating the length of the prison term as the dependent variable. Three independent variables were entered. The first was a dummy-coded variable designating the type of crime (murder or bank robbery). The second variable was the total number of words of pretrial newspaper coverage. The third variable was an interaction between the first two variables, constructed by multiplying the variables together (Jaccard, Turrisi, & Wan, 1990). The final equation explained roughly 6% of the variance ($R = .242$, $R^2 = .059$, adjusted $R^2 = .057$) and included the interaction term ($t = 5.130$, $p < .01$, beta = .526) and the total words of coverage term ($t = 3.177$, $p < .001$, beta = $-.326$).

The direction of the effect was difficult to interpret. The positive value of the beta score for the interaction term indicated that publicity had a stronger effect for bank robbery than it did for murder; in order to make the results more interpretable Table 3.2 presents average sentence lengths for three different levels of press coverage. It appears that for murder defendants, moderate levels of publicity (22–300 words) result in the longest prison sentences, whereas high levels of publicity (301 words or more) result in the longest prison sentences for bank robbery defendants. (It should be noted that an

TABLE 3.2

Mean z-Scores for Prison-Term Length by Publicity Level

Crime	Publicity Category		
	No Coverage	0–300 Words	301+ Words
Murder	−.18	.73	.04
Bank robbery	−.01	−.08	.24

ANOVA crossing those two variables produced nonsignificant but suggestive results; $F = 2.380$, $df = 5/843$, $p = .093$.) In other words, publicity seems to have a curvilinear association with murder sentences but a linear association with bank robbery sentences.

Most startling was the direction of the remaining publicity measure. Once the interaction effect was accounted for, the remaining influence of publicity seemed to be one that reduced sentence length, and thus favored defendants.

Plea Bargaining

Defendants who entered guilty pleas received lower prison sentences (z-score $M = -.08$; $SD = .66$) than defendants who did not plead guilty (z-score $M = 1.06$; $SD = 1.76$; $t = 12.745$, $df = 810$, $p < .001$), an unsurprising finding because defendants pleading guilty usually enter into plea-bargain agreements that reduce the sentence in return for the admission of guilt. The length of a pleaded sentence did not appear to depend on the amount of publicity; an ANOVA including the 2-level publicity variable and a conviction-type variable with two levels (convicted at trial vs. guilty plea) and the length of sentence as the dependent variable produced nonsignificant differences for the interaction between the independent variables ($F = 2.658$, $df = 1/788$, $p = .104$). When the 3-level publicity variable was substituted, the results were again nonsignificant ($F = 1.356$, $df = 2/786$, $p = .258$).

However, cases with guilty pleas and cases that went to trial did differ in the amount of coverage they received. Trial cases averaged 471.1 total words ($n = 128$; $SD = 2628.5$), guilty plea cases averaged 86.1 words ($n = 675$; $SD = 276.6$), and all other cases averaged 283.7 words ($n = 37$; $SD = 175.9$). A one-way ANOVA indicated significant differences between these groups ($F = 7.164$, $df = 2/837$, $p < .01$) and Scheffé post-hoc tests revealed significant differences between trial and guilty plea groups ($p < .001$) but for no other comparison.

Discussion of the New Research

We were primarily interested in whether publicity affected trial outcomes in actual legal cases. The present results indicate that pretrial newspaper coverage does not influence determinations of guilt or innocence but is associated with sentence length. This is the same finding reported by Bruschke and Loges's (1999) field research and Riedel's (1993) laboratory research. One possibility, therefore, is that pretrial coverage may vary with sentence length but does not influence verdicts.

This finding points to some of the issues we dwell on at more length later, although some preliminary comments are in order. Early conceptions of what it meant to have a fair trial derived from a very different context than is faced in contemporary America. Two centuries ago, plea bargaining was much less commonplace and pretrial coverage existed on a different scale. Would the founders who crafted constitutional protections have concluded that defendants were receiving a fair trial if they believed that verdicts were not influenced by extensive coverage but that sentences were? More to the point, is our modern polity content with that state of affairs? The answers to these questions are difficult at best, but the present research findings suggest that they may be pertinent.

Methodologically, these findings suggest important shifts in a number of research orientations. Prior research seems to have selected the dependent variable in a haphazard fashion. Some studies utilize dichotomous guilt/innocence judgments, some use sentence lengths, and some use Likert-type probability of guilt continuous scales. The present findings suggest that the choice of dependent variable is crucial, and might account for the seeming disparity of findings to date. Further, present findings suggest that remedies should focus on the posttrial rather than pretrial phase. Research should, for example, expand its focus and consider sentencing remedies in addition to pretrial procedures such as jury selection. Finally, researchers might look for a third variable that can explain both the publicity and the sentence lengths. The heinousness of crime, for example, might explain both the amount of coverage and the length of sentence, with more heinous crimes generating both more publicity and longer sentences.

The first research question asked: "Does the effect of pretrial publicity on trial outcomes depend on the type of crime with which the defendant is charged?" The answer here is more complex than imagined by the question. Once again, the verdict is not affected by the type of crime. However, in murder cases pretrial coverage seems to have a curvilinear relationship with sentence length, whereas for robbery cases there is a simple linear pattern. The curvilinear pattern of pretrial coverage on sentence length in murder cases is similar to the finding reported by Bruschke and Loges (1999).

It is interesting to speculate why this pattern might exist. One difference between murder and robbery is that murder is a more severe offense. Pretrial publicity might exert a curvilinear influence on sentence lengths for severe crimes but a linear influence for less severe crimes. A second possibility is that because murder cases generated more publicity than robbery cases, the observed influence is simply a result of different levels of press coverage. If this is the case, pretrial publicity may exhibit a curvilinear influence on sentence lengths overall, but because crimes with lower levels of coverage never generate enough publicity to move into the higher publicity categories where additional coverage lowers sentence lengths, the effect appears linear.

The second research question asked: "Does pretrial publicity influence plea-bargained cases?" Although trial cases received more coverage than guilty-plea cases, and guilty-plea cases received lower sentences than non-pleaded cases, there was no interaction between the coverage level and whether or not the case was plea-bargained. Thus, any influence of publicity is not more pronounced in guilty-plea versus nonpleaded cases. This suggests that the plea bargain is a potentially effective defense strategy in a publicized case. A plea bargain should stave off publicity, and defendants in publicized cases (who face an 80% to 90% chance of being found guilty) should receive a lower sentence via a plea bargain than if they went to trial. Of course, a truly innocent defendant who can win at trial (overcoming the 80% conviction rates) would still do better by taking his or her case to court.

These findings have implications for theories about pretrial coverage. Simple cause/effect explanations for the relationship between pretrial coverage and a fair trial do not appear adequate to describe the relationship between the variables. Theories should distinguish between trial verdicts of guilt or innocence and sentence lengths and account for the type of crime in question. Further, there is the interesting possibility that once the interaction between crime type and publicity level is accounted for, the remaining direct effect of publicity may actually benefit defendants. This is consistent with other evidence that certain types of negative publicity might actually improve a defendant's chances (e.g., Mullin et al., 1996; Riedel, 1993; see earlier review).

At present, the following propositions may serve as useful summaries of current knowledge and possible hypotheses for future research:

1. Pretrial publicity in criminal trials may influence sentence lengths but not verdicts.
2. Pretrial publicity will probably have a curvilinear influence on sentence lengths in murder trials but a direct linear influence in robbery trials.
3. Pretrial publicity is more likely to affect the outcome of jury trials as compared to plea-bargained cases.

Much more research needs to be done. The present study, one of very few naturalistic studies to date, did not account for television or radio coverage. Although there is research that indicates that newspaper coverage is the primary medium through which media consumers base their opinions about legal trials (Freedman & Burke, 1996; Nietzel & Dillehay, 1983), the vast influence of television is undeniable and future research should consider the influence of all media. In addition, the present study and that of Bruschke and Loges (1999) examined only federal-level offenses. There may be many important differences in the way cases are handled at the federal and state levels, and expanding research focus to include state-level cases would be useful. A separate issue involves cell size equalization. A finding in the present study that comports with that of Bruschke and Loges is that the number of "no-coverage" cases will vastly exceed the number of cases that have any coverage at all; future research should develop models that account for the vastly different size of publicity conditions in naturally occurring cases.

Two other issues for future research deserve deeper consideration. The first involves the amount of coverage that is damaging. Although this study and that of Bruschke and Loges did find differences between low-publicity, no-publicity, and high-publicity cases, the special case of the "low-publicity" condition complicates explanations. Although it is fairly straightforward to assume that pretrial publicity exerted no influence on the trial in the no-publicity condition, and it is at least a reasonable inference that highly publicized trials produce coverage that at least some potential jurors are exposed to, it is less clear that when a defendant has been covered in, say, one to five stories, any jurors are even aware that the coverage exists. To give a rough estimate, if an average metropolitan newspaper included only 50 stories per edition, in a 2-year period between a crime and a trial, roughly 163,000 articles would appear in the newspaper. It seems rather unlikely that any given juror would read and would remember the 3 out of 163,000 articles that were potentially biasing. In fact, it seems most likely that no juror serving on a case covered by one to five articles would have read any of the coverage, and yet two studies have now found differences between low- and no-publicity conditions. This suggests two questions for future research. First, how much coverage has to exist before most jurors are likely to be exposed to at least some of it? Second, if jurors in the low-publicity conditions haven't read any of the coverage, why do low- and no-publicity groups differ?

The second, more profound issue has to do with causation. How could pretrial publicity influence a case if few of the jurors have been exposed to publicity or if they don't remember it? As argued elsewhere (Vidmar, 2002), both exposure and retention rates are likely to be very low. Laboratory studies are able to very carefully control a number of variables and ensure juror exposure. This approach has obvious benefits, especially when researchers are providing explanations for the observed findings. Scholars using laboratory methods are less given to grasping explanations about the potential confounding effect of an unmeasured variable because variables are relatively easy to add to the design. The downside of the laboratory approach is that much of the control comes at the expense of realism, and thus scholars are in danger of making very good predictions about situations that are unlikely to exist in normal courtroom situations. The naturalistic approach is in no danger of producing a finding that is the result of artificial laboratory conditions, but the number of variables that can be included in the design are subject to a much larger number of practical limits. Rather than simply manipulate various factors in the design, each variable that is added requires direct observation of each case and independent coding. Although this is unfortunate, large jumps in knowledge may only come about with direct observation of a large number of actual trials and the coding of a large number of variables. Such research will be much more time-consuming, expensive, and laborious, but the corresponding improvement in data quality should be equally impressive.

Obviously, more field research is needed. No field research has yet studied television coverage, which might influence trials differently than newspaper coverage. If, as Steblay et al. (1999) and Otto et al. (1994) contend, it is necessary to carefully control all the variables that might alter trial outcomes to find a pretrial publicity effect, there can be little doubt that our work made no effort to apply the manipulations necessary to uncover a subtle effect. Nonetheless, this study does provide a useful picture of the amount of coverage typical in most criminal trials, and it is striking that in the only two studies to date of a large number of actual cases, high- and no-publicity conditions produced virtually identical conviction rates.

THE STATE OF KNOWLEDGE AFTER CONSIDERING FIELD RESEARCH

The entry-level condition for any discussion of remedies for pretrial publicity is some demonstration that pretrial publicity is in need of correction, and the first major question of this book is whether there is a pretrial publicity effect at all. The work of this chapter thus far has been to demonstrate that a general fear of pretrial publicity is largely unfounded. The claim that laboratory research unequivocally shows an effect is unwarranted. Concerns about methodology cannot be dismissed by simply citing prior research. Most importantly, the findings of laboratory research do not replicate in the field. What is to be made of this? Should pretrial publicity be treated as the insidious force that prior reviewers have characterized it to be? Should it be dismissed as an artifact of laboratory research? Is there anything to worry about?

In a word, yes, there are circumstances when pretrial publicity might be cause for concern. However, it is not an insidious and nearly unstoppable force (as the conclusions of prior reviews might seem to identify), but one that appears only rarely. There are two reasons for this. First, as described by the cumulative remedy hypothesis, a host of court-imposed and natural remedies exist in actual courtrooms that can, in fact, simply correct pretrial publicity. A natural delay might cause jurors to forget publicity that they have seen. A solid defense strategy can make jurors discount publicity. Sometimes, a juror will bring up an inadmissible point during deliberation and other jurors will successfully get the point discounted. Sometimes, a good lawyer will be able to select a jury that has not been exposed to the publicity. These checks overlap one another, and even if they do not always work well in isolation, pretrial publicity can only influence the trial outcome when they all fail simultaneously.

The second reason that pretrial publicity may not show up in actual trials has to do with cumulative probability rather than cumulative remedy; simply put, it is a small enough contributor to the outcome of a trial that it is usually swamped by other, more important factors. Consider what is meant by a "statistically significant" relationship and what it means for laboratory research to uncover one. Steblay et al. (1999) describe a result that they call modest with an overall r of .16. They further note that it is detectable only in a study with a large sample size and therefore a lot of statistical power. These are certainly accurate claims. However, it is also a true and oft-repeated point that, given a large enough sample size and enough power, even trivial differences will emerge as statistically significant. Statistical significance, after all, only means that any observed differences didn't emerge by random chance, and a criterion score between groups (conviction rates in this case) is not exactly identical. The magnitude, or size, of the effect is quite another question. Given the r that Steblay et al. report, the magnitude of the effect is .0256, which means that pretrial publicity can account for approximately 2.5% of the variance in conviction rates. Is this magnitude enough to worry about, or has the laboratory research simply uncovered a statistically significant but trivial finding?

Accounting for 2.5% of the variance is the same as saying that 97.5% of the variance in convictions is accounted for by something other than pretrial publicity. That is *not* the same as saying that 2.5% of the trials conducted when pretrial publicity is present result in faulty convictions or that 2.5 trials in every 100 publicized trials will produce convictions based on the publicity. What the figure means is that jurors exposed to an identical trial can end up having different opinions about whether or not the defendant was guilty, and 2.5% of that difference can be attributed to pretrial publicity. It is easy to imagine a situation where that 2.5% is inconsequential—imagine a jury where six members have seen publicity and six members have not. At the end of the trial, the six unexposed members are ready to vote guilty based on the trial evidence. The six exposed members are also ready to vote guilty, but are 2.5% more certain. The effect of publicity has indeed had a biasing effect on the trial, but one that an appellate judge might call "harmless error" or at least not an error large enough to warrant reversal.

Using this same logic, it is not difficult to identify the sort of trial where pretrial publicity will make a difference. Imagine a situation where the same 12 jurors watched the trial, the case was close, but the 6 unexposed jurors were all convinced of the defendant's guilt at roughly a 51% level, based on the factors that account for the other 97.5% of the decision (different credibility given to witnesses, different life experience, different moral orientations, attention spans, etc.). Meanwhile, the 6 exposed jurors would have been unconvinced by the guilt—presume that they were 49% convinced of guilt—but because of the exposure to pretrial publicity, they all ended up marginally favoring a verdict of guilt. Without the pretrial publicity, an initial poll among the jurors would have resulted in a 6 to 6 split, and it is easy to imagine that the deliberations would result in an outcome favorable to the defendant, because the prosecution did have a burden of proof to fill, determinations of guilt were fragile at the outset, and there was no clear consensus in the room. The same jury exposed to pretrial publicity would have an initial poll of 12 to 0 favoring guilty, and it is easy to imagine the jury deliberating and concluding that although the prosecution's case was not perfect and the defense made some good points, on balance a difficult decision for guilt was probably the best one.

This example is of course a gross simplification and relies on many assumptions about jury deliberation and composition that may not be accurate or even relevant. It makes some assumptions about the dubious task of quantifying what constitutes reasonable doubt. Regardless of these drawbacks, the preceding illustrations show how the findings of current social science might play out in an actual courtroom and how any influence of pretrial publicity might simply be swamped by other trial factors. Given the size of the effect and the phenomenon it represents (a variance in guilt judgments for individual jurors), pretrial publicity is only likely to influence decisions in a way that alters the verdict outcome when, in the minds of the jurors, the case is very close and could go either way. Thus, a second reason pretrial publicity might not show an insidious effect in actual trials is that when it is not corrected by other remedies, it is simply swamped by other factors. Putting this in the context of the laboratory research, it is easy to come to two noncontradictory conclusions. First, as the laboratory research demonstrates, pretrial publicity can sometimes influence a jury, all other things being equal. Second, in the field, all other things are very rarely equal.

This brings us to a crucial point that has to do with the model we use to think about pretrial publicity. Lurking beneath our statistical analyses and our language used to describe the relationships between variables are some largely unexplicated ways of thinking about phenomena. Here we are not referring to a specific statistical model, but instead the more impressionistic motif used to think about the relationship. One way of thinking about the relationship de-

scribed when one hears that there is a "statistically significant relationship between pretrial publicity and trial outcomes," and one that the language of
some commentators seems to suggest, is that of an evil, insidious mist that
floats into the courtroom and colors everything that occurs before the jury,
dooming the poor defendant before the trial even starts. The model makes
pretrial publicity the dominant factor in the outcome of the trial: Unless something else dramatic happens at the trial, the defendant will probably be found
guilty, convicted in the press. This model is not so much specifically advocated
by anyone in particular, but is the sort of commonsense impression that the
non-social scientist can come to when hearing reports of statistical studies,
and indeed is the sort of image it is easy to come away from Studebaker and
Penrod (1997) with.

A second model, perhaps more true to life, is that pretrial publicity is a passive
observer sitting in the back of the courtroom scowling at the defendant. Usually,
this gallery member won't even be noticed and most of the time will simply be
lost in the shuffle of witnesses, motions, and pounding gavels. Usually, the jurors
may notice the scowling observer and be vaguely disquieted, only to retire to the
deliberation chamber, forget the glance, and vote on the evidence. On rare occa-
sions, however, the courtroom will be silent, the evidence inconclusive, the gallery otherwise empty, and the jurors will glance up and, without other
distraction, see the scowl on the face of the observer and think: "Guilty." This
will not happen very often. In this model, pretrial publicity is not the dominant
factor, but the tiebreaker that emerges only in the very closest of situations.

In more traditional academic language, the question "Is there a pretrial
publicity effect at all?" can be answered by saying that there is, at best, a modest
one, often corrected and usually outweighed. But the fact that there is no general, all-encompassing effect for pretrial publicity does not discount that in certain situations pretrial publicity bias might manifest itself. It may occasionally
make a difference. In what cases might this effect emerge? Two themes have
constantly emerged from the body of knowledge collected to date that speak
to the issue, and they seem to have come up in all of the groups of studies reviewed above. First, pretrial publicity is most likely to emerge when trial evidence is inconclusive. Many studies have shown that evidence is the dominant
factor determining the outcome of trials (Dexter et al., 1992; Kramer & Kerr,
1989; Sue et al., 1975; see Visher, 1987), but none more clearly than Otto et al.
(1994). To belabor the point a little, even the study that champions of a strong
pretrial publicity effect point to as conclusively showing a pretrial publicity effect found evidence to be twice as powerful as any other factor in determining
the outcome of trials. Beyond that, studies to date have almost exclusively
studied pretrial publicity in cases that have been pilot tested to produce convictions of 50%, and thus have almost perfectly balanced evidence. Thus, any evidence we have that shows that pretrial publicity can bias the outcome of a case
has been conducted under conditions of very balanced evidence. When evi-

dence is conclusive—for or against the defendant—there is little reason to believe that pretrial publicity will make a difference in the outcome of the trial.

Second, pretrial publicity is most likely to emerge when the pretrial information is especially probative. The knowledge–guilt hypothesis is built on the finding that the more specific information about a trial a juror has the more the juror will presume guilt, suggesting that specific information that speaks to guilt will introduce bias. Additionally, many of the studies that were able to uncover a publicity effect did so with publicity that included specific information that spoke to guilt. This included physical evidence, retracted confessions, fingerprints, and eyewitnesses (see chap. 2). These two factors merge together coherently: If it is true that jurors will try their hardest to base their decisions on the quality of the evidence, pretrial information is most likely to influence trials when it includes really good evidence (and, in the case of the laboratory studies to date, often better evidence than was presented at the trial). Pretrial publicity is most likely to influence the outcomes of trials when there is no conclusive case presented at trial but very important evidence included in the publicity.

A final factor that might make publicity influence the outcome of a trial is the amount of it. Patterns of coverage do not show a steady, linear increase, where levels of coverage intensify predictably and thus pretrial publicity effects should increase steadily with coverage. In fact, some cases tend to dominate all coverage. Surette (1992) observed that some trials become "media trials" and are covered in great detail; most of the cases that are covered at all receive only bare mention. By way of example, in Bruschke and Loges's (1999) examination of all federal murder cases in a 3-year period, the number of articles devoted to the 5 most publicized cases exceeded the number of articles covering the other 67 cases combined. This is the last conclusion this section will draw: A small number of cases receive the vast majority of the coverage.

To put the issue in a nutshell (or at least a short paragraph), pretrial publicity does not always create a bias. Often it will be corrected by one or more of the many remedies that exist, and other times it will simply be outweighed by other factors. However, there are some cases where pretrial publicity might still generate a bias that can alter the outcome of a trial. Pretrial publicity is most likely to bias a trial when the publicity is excessive, it includes probative information, and the evidence at the trial is inconclusive.

FORGING AN APPROPRIATE REMEDY

Accepting at present that there is no insurmountably insidious pretrial publicity effect, and that for the vast majority of cases pretrial publicity will pose no threat, it is still apparent that having effective remedies available for those cases where publicity may still pose a difficulty is a good idea. The point of the cumulative remedy hypothesis is that the legal system should be as vigilant as possible to try to remedy publicity in as many ways as possible. There are three issues that a more careful review of the remedy literature might help illuminate. First, such a review can explore whether the absence of a pretrial publicity effect in the field can be attributed to the effectiveness of current remedies. Second, it can offer proof for the claim, frequently made thus far, that remedies have been studied in isolation. Third, in conjunction with the conclusions of the prior section, it can help provide the basis for imagining new remedies that might fill the gaps left open by the court-imposed and naturally occurring remedies in operation at present.

Extant reviews of remedy effectiveness have been as mixed as those concerning publicity effects themselves. Pember (1984), a legal practitioner, declared that remedies work, a conclusion widely held by those in the legal system (Carroll et al., 1986; Kerr, 1994). Pember also acknowledged that social scientists completely disagreed with his conclusion. It has been common for reviewers to sift through all the potential remedies they can imagine (large numbers in some cases and smaller numbers in others) and find them all to be insufficient. Thus, reviewers have concluded that "normal" remedies are ineffective (Mullin et al., 1996), including instructions (Carroll et al., 1986; Fein, McCloskey, & Tomlinson, 1997; Kaplan & Miller, 1978; Kerr, 1994; Moran & Cutler, 1991; Studebaker & Penrod, 1997; Vidmar & Judson, 1981), deliberation (Carroll et al., 1986; Fein, McCloskey, & Tomlinson, 1997; Moran & Cutler, 1991; Studebaker & Penrod, 1997; Vidmar & Judson, 1981), evidence (Studebaker & Penrod, 1997), and continuance (Kerr, 1994; Studebaker & Penrod, 1997). Change of venue may be the best remedy (Fulero, 1987), but is rarely granted (Pollock, 1977) and may be the most expensive of the possible remedies. Kramer et al. (1990) presented a typical conclusion:

> In light of the general ineffectiveness of the remedies examined (except for continuances for certain types of publicity) and the absence of better evidence for the other commonly used remedy (voir dire), courts may be well advised to make greater use of what are admittedly the most cumbersome and expensive remedies but probably the most effective remedies as well—change of venue and change of venire. (p. 435)

In short, the reviews to date have been fairly damning of most apparent remedies. These conclusions notwithstanding, we believe that an overlooked factor in general has been the quality of the remedy applied, not simply its form. For example, what may matter the most is not whether or not instructions have been issued to a jury but the quality of those instructions. By improving the voir dire process and the instructions given to a jury it might be possible to substantially offset pretrial publicity bias.

The first remedy for which quality might matter is voir dire. Many believe that it fails to eliminate pretrial publicity bias (Dexter et al., 1992; Fein et al., 1997; Kerr et al., 1991; Olczak et al., 1991; Studebaker & Penrod, 1997), some believe that it succeeds (Carroll et al., 1986; Padawer-Singer et al., 1974), and some have suggested that voir dire can be successful but that the questioning must be conducted properly (Vidmar & Melnitzer, 1984; Zeisel & Diamond, 1978). These contrasting findings may suggest a difference that is more ephemeral than real. Those who conclude that voir dire fails have generally studied the process in general, and not whether it can counteract pretrial publicity bias specifically. Those who have studied the question more narrowly have provided some evidence that jury selection can eliminate jurors who have been exposed to publicity, even if it can't produce a prodefense jury, which other reviewers have faulted it for. The only two studies reviewed earlier that examined the ability of voir dire to specifically counteract pretrial publicity came to opposing conclusions about its effectiveness. However, the study concluding that voir dire is effective (Padawer-Singer et al., 1974) is more realistic than the study concluding voir dire is ineffective (Dexter et al., 1992) in two regards: It used a sample of actual jurors rather than college students, and it included deliberation.

There is some disagreement on the point, but there is enough evidence suggesting that voir dire might be effective that examining more carefully how the procedure might best be conducted seems worthwhile, and a more careful review of pertinent research findings might illuminate the processes that are relevant to voir dire effectiveness. First, although voir dire may be effective, lawyers and judges are not especially good at determining who constitutes a good juror. In at least one study, the net effect of voir dire conducted by judges, defense attorneys, and prosecutors was functionally nothing (Kerr et al., 1991), although many of the obviously biased jurors were removed. Despite these findings, the prosecutors, judges, and defense attorneys believed strongly in their own ability to identify biased jurors. In one study, Olczak et al. (1991) found that professional lawyers fared no better than undergraduates at selecting jurors, and that the lawyers tended to use a very limited number of dimensions when selecting jurors. The authors concluded that lawyers tended to rely on lay psychology when assessing possible jurors and largely failed. The obvious implication is that legal practitioners should not rely solely on their own experience to determine juror biases, and some objective criteria should supplement the process.

Second, jurors are largely unaware of or unwilling to admit their own bias (Fein, Morgan, Norton, & Sommers, 1997; Moran & Cutler, 1991; Ogloff & Vidmar, 1994; Studebaker & Penrod, 1997; Vidmar, 2002; Vidmar & Judson, 1981), possibly because the bias exists below conscious awareness (Newman et al., 1997). Thus, the common judicial practice of asking jurors whether they can be unbiased is unlikely to uncover actual bias (Vidmar & Melnitzer, 1984). Again, seeking objective criteria rather than subjective reports of self-bias is more likely to be effective.

Third, despite their inability to recognize their own bias, jurors will take their role very seriously (Davis, 1986; Hoiberg & Stires, 1973; Kaplan & Miller, 1978; Sommers & Kasim, 2001; Thompson et al., 1981; Vidmar & Melnitzer, 1984). Thus, appropriately screened jurors can be expected to carry out their charge with due vigilance.

Fourth, the knowledge–guilt hypothesis reviewed above suggests that simple knowledge of the minimal facts of the case can result in prejudgments of guilt. Although these prejudgments may be counteracted by a number of factors during the trial—ranging from the evidence presented to the judge's admonition to try to ignore preconceptions to the arguments of other, nonexposed jurors during deliberations—there is no good reason to impanel jurors with prejudgements when other potential jurors without them might just as easily serve. Finally, as alluded to earlier and elaborated at some length later in this chapter, it can be expected that jurors will largely base their decision on assessments of the evidence and that probative pretrial information is the most damaging. To the maximum extent possible, therefore, voir dire should guard against evidentiary biases potential jurors may hold.

Put together, the picture that emerges of what may happen at a trial is this: Jurors will come to the trial with various levels of knowledge about the trial. Those that have been biased, however, will not identify themselves as biased and may not even recognize their own bias. Neither will judges or lawyers do an outstanding job of identifying biased jurors. Once the trial starts, jurors will take their job very seriously and try to base their decision on the evidence and their deliberations as much as possible. To the extent that pretrial publicity leads to bias, it will be mediated by perceptions of evidence quality. In other words, biased jurors will *believe* the evidence against the defense to be more conclusive than their unexposed counterparts, but *all* jurors will try to base their decisions on the evidence.

Given these findings, it might be possible to craft a modified voir dire procedure that will be cost-effective, not at all time-consuming, and effective at eliminating bias. Walton (1998), a lawyer by trade, argued that there is a legal basis for a process that includes individual (as opposed to group) voir dire with questions about specific content knowledge. Vidmar (2002), following an excellent review of the ability of jurors to identify their own biases, similarly concluded that the type of voir dire might be a crucial variable. Two impressive field studies (Nietzel & Dillehay, 1982; Nietzel, Dillehay, & Himelein, 1987) showed that in actual, publicized death penalty trials, defense challenges are more effective when jurors are questioned individually (not en masse) and not in front of other jurors (sequestered). The authors conclude: "The robust finding is that defense motions for cause produce more sustained challenges under sequestered conditions, the most probable interpretation of which is that individual questioning of sequestered jurors produces better information on juror bias"

(Nietzel et al., 1987, p. 476). Thus, as a minimum standard of voir dire quality, jurors should be questioned individually about specific content knowledge they might have about a case.

One form this questioning might take is a simple knowledge quiz about the trial. In cases receiving moderate to extensive pretrial publicity, jurors should be given a simple 8- to 10-item quiz about the facts of the case. Based on the knowledge–guilt hypothesis, jurors possessing knowledge of the case before the trial can be assumed to prejudge guilt. The questions for the quiz could be worked out with the lawyers of both parties as well as the judge. They should be objective and neutrally worded, discuss basic facts of the case reported in the media, and include some fictitious items or false statements that potential jurors would have to mark as false to answer correctly. As examples, Constantini and King (1980–1981) asked questions about the number of people arrested, asked respondents to pick the defendant's name in the case from a list of possible names, and then read a list of statements about the defendant concerning confession and prior record, some true and some false, and asked respondents to indicate which were accurate. Moran and Cutler (1991) asked the respondents whether they had heard about the crime, statements the district attorney had made, others pleading guilty in relation to the crime, the amount of money made during the crime, and so on. Moran and Cutler also included fictitious items asking about the defendant. It might also be wise to draw items from specific statements that appeared in the media to determine whether jurors could recall having seen or read about them.

A threshold for unacceptable knowledge must be established, and setting a level at which pretrial knowledge becomes unduly biasing is slightly more difficult. Initially it should be noted that most defense attorneys start in a hole and that jurors seldom assume innocence, with or without pretrial publicity (McConahay et al., 1977). Roughly speaking, Constantini and King (1980–1981) found that bias occurred when jurors could correctly answer four of seven questions about the case. The jump in assumptions of guilt between poorly informed jurors and well-informed jurors was roughly 20 points. For example, in one case assumptions of guilt between uninformed and informed potential jurors jumped from 2% to 22%. Moran and Cutler (1991) studied two different crimes; more than 50% of respondents reported that they believed that there was "a lot of evidence" when they could get 5 of 10 items correct in one case and when they could get 3 of 7 questions correct in the other case. However, the percentage of respondents believing there to be a lot of evidence was never lower than 11%, and the relationship appeared to be roughly linear. To set a conservative figure, jurors able to answer a third or more of the questions correctly should be excluded from the trial. Under no condition should jurors able to answer half or more of the questions correctly be allowed to sit as jurors, because in all likelihood they do not hold a presumption of innocence.

A second remedy that might be applied more effectively is jury instructions. Although early studies generally found judicial admonitions to be ineffective at eliminating bias (Kramer et al., 1990; Padawer-Singer & Barton, 1975; Sue et al., 1974; Thompson et al., 1981), more recent research on instructions has been mixed. Freedman et al. (1997) reported this result:

> There was some indication that the instruction did influence the jurors' opinions. When participants were told to ignore outside information, they were less negative regardless of the information to which they had been exposed. This may be due to what might be called a "bending-over-backward" phenomenon ... they gave the defendant somewhat more benefit of the doubt than those who had not received the admonition. (p. 262)

Sommers and Kassin (2001) found that the rationale jurors are given is crucial; if told to ignore information because it is unreliable, jurors generally comply with the instructions, and they comply to a lesser extent when the rationale for exclusion involves due process. Similar to Freedman et al., the researchers found that a segment of their mock jurors, those high in need for cognition, tended to "overcorrect" and be especially skeptical of prosecution evidence; these findings comported with earlier work the authors had done on juror motivations to reach just verdicts. These studies suggest that jurors will exert considerable effort to reach a just verdict, that given a proper explanation jurors can discount biasing evidence, and that instructions can motivate jurors to go to special lengths to presume innocence.

Other research has shown that jury instructions do generally reduce the bias of inadmissible evidence but can't completely eliminate it. Landsman and Rakos (1994) found that, strangely, instructions that a piece of evidence was inadmissible were effective on juries but not judges. Instructions of inadmissibility lowered conviction rates compared to rulings that evidence was admissible, but conviction rates were still higher than they were in control groups where the evidence had never been presented. Similarly, Bornstein et al. (2002) found that instructions produced a main effect that lowered conviction rates, but they failed to eliminate the effect of pretrial publicity.

Taken together, these two sets of results suggest that, in general, instructions can offset if not always eliminate the bias of inadmissible evidence or exposure to pretrial publicity. Most jurors will try to be vigilant, and there is some evidence that the type of instruction that they receive will have an impact on their decision to consider a given piece of information. Given these factors, improving on jury instructions is likely to be a worthwhile endeavor. Two separate reviews (Lieberman & Arndt, 2000; Wegener, Kerr, Fleming, & Petty, 2000) offered lists of suggestions for improving jury instructions, which are synthesized here:

Instructions should be given early in the trial that emphasize how evidence should be processed and explain legal procedure.

- Rationales should be given along with rules, as jurors are more likely to comply with a rule when they understand why it exists.
- Presenting instructions in narrative form might increase comprehension and adherence; jurors may naturally process trial features in narrative terms anyway, and thus the narrative form is likely to be especially useful.
- Face concerns should be incorporated, so that jurors who identify a bias will not feel foolish for having expressed one.
- Rules should be expressed in "soft sell" terms to avoid reaction effects; instructions should downplay limitations on juror decisional freedom.
- Generally, the presumption of innocence should be emphasized..
- A public pledge to pursue fairness and seek to eliminate bias might help (see also Vidmar, 2002).

This is not the place for a thorough review of all possible improvements to instructions, and interested readers are directed to the reviews already cited. Nonetheless, the list just presented does represent some consistent findings and suggestions, and given the generally incomprehensible state of instructions at present (Wegener et al., 2000), efforts at improving instructions will not be wasted. Better instructions should do an even better job of eliminating any pretrial publicity bias.

In sum, although fears of pretrial publicity biasing trial outcomes may have been overstated, bias remains a cause for concern and there is a constant need to apply effective remedies. There is still justifiable reason to try to begin the case with unbiased minds and to adopt remedies that are both cost-effective and adequate. Individualized, sequestered voir dire has shown to be remarkably effective in field studies. A short quiz constructed by both legal teams and the judge should be sufficient to eliminate most potentially biased jurors, and would be a much cheaper and less time-intensive solution than many other available remedies. A more effectively delivered set of jury instructions might further attenuate pretrial bias. In combination with deliberation and natural and court-imposed delays, these relatively cheap remedies may have much to offer despite published conclusions to the contrary. A series of cheap remedies might serve courts and the body politic better than the frequent use of expensive, time-consuming corrections.

CHAPTER FOUR

Pretrial Publicity and Media Theory: "General" Publicity Revisited

There is a theory that states that if ever anyone discovers exactly what the Universe is and why it is here, it will instantly disappear and be replaced by something even more bizarre and inexplicable. There is another which states that this has already happened. (Douglas Adams, *The Restaurant at the End of the Universe,* p. iv)

MEDIA THEORY: THE INVISIBLE ELEPHANT

It might seem a little obvious to state that if one were looking for a theory that could explain how the media might influence the thoughts and behaviors of jurors, a likely source of information would be media theory. As obvious as it might be, there have been almost no serious attempts to link theories of media influence with pretrial publicity. Invisible elephants have two conspicuous features: They are large, and they can't be seen. Media theory has been the invisible elephant for pretrial publicity research. Here, we seek to paint the elephant to make it a little more visible and, we hope, a little less dangerous.

Our idea is to start from scratch and try to imagine a process described by media theory rather than the disjointed findings of pretrial publicity research that has by and large examined bits and pieces of the process in isolation. For news coverage of a particular crime to influence a jury's verdict, a series of events must occur. Any theory that seeks to account for the effect of pretrial publicity on jury verdicts must account for all of these steps. First, the crime must receive media attention. Second, the nature of that coverage must be prejudicial (either for or against the defendant). Third, future jurors must pay at least some attention to the media coverage, or communicate with someone who has and who shares the news. Fourth, the future jurors must develop a prejudicial attitude for or against the defendant that cannot be put aside for the sake of reaching a fair verdict. Fifth, the future jurors must recall the coverage, or at least recall their attitude, when it comes time to deliberate and vote. Sixth, the future jurors must ignore instructions from the bench and consciously or unconsciously allow their verdict to be influenced by the coverage rather than by the testimony in court and their deliberations. In any given criminal trial, this is an unlikely sequence of events.

Getting Coverage

In the first place, even the initial step is highly unlikely. Most crimes receive no media coverage. It is one thing to argue that there is lots of coverage of crime in the news (a recent study showed that 21% of local news coverage concerned crime or the courts; Brady & Pertilla, 2001), but it is another thing to argue that most crimes receive coverage in the news. Even federal murder cases are unlikely to receive much coverage (Bruschke & Loges, 1999). The news media may have an institutional interest in covering crime because it is attractive to audiences, but they still have limits on how many of the crimes in a given area they have room for in their news hole (i.e., the space left for news around the advertisements). Furthermore, at least some crime coverage involves crimes far away from the audience. Consider the amount of attention to such familiar unsolved murders as JonBenet Ramsey and Chandra Levy. Surely most of the audience members for such news have no prospect of ever being jurors in trials related to those crimes, but coverage of these crimes on local news broadcasts accounts for at least part of their total crime news diet. Pretrial publicity is a relatively rare phenomenon for individual defendants.

What kind of crime is likely to receive coverage? Mayer (1993) noted: "All news items compete for attention with all other news items. The decision on what is 'news' today is therefore a function of the intensity of the competition" (p. 69). He determined that "opinions on the relative salience of different persons and events" (p. 69) are ultimately what get some stories into the news and keep other stories out. Mayer's theory is supported by the work of Pritchard and Hughes (1997), who introduced the concept of "deviance" to capture what Mayer meant by "relative salience."

In a study of a year's worth of homicides in Milwaukee, WI, Pritchard and Hughes (1997) found that the extent to which aspects of the crime deviated from norms predicted the likelihood of that crime receiving coverage. They noted that "journalists have a hard time explaining exactly how they evaluate an event's newsworthiness" (p. 50), and that it may be more fruitful to look at the outcome of journalists' decisions than to consult journalists themselves. They examined all homicides in Milwaukee in 1994 for which a suspect was arrested. One hundred homicide cases involved 104 deaths (i.e., 4 multiple homicides) and led to 160 arrests, and the two daily newspapers in Milwaukee (at the time—they have since merged) published 560 news items regarding these crimes.

Pritchard and Hughes (1997) described four kinds of deviance that they hypothesized would predict the amount of coverage a crime would receive: statistical deviance, status deviance, cultural deviance, and normative deviance. "Statistical deviance is the extent to which something is unusual" (p. 51), and was expected to be positively associated with coverage. Status deviance refers to the social status of the people involved in the crime, "the extent to which a person or group is different, using the well-established benchmarks of high status in U.S. society" (p. 51). Pritchard and Hughes hypothesized that crimes involving people high in status would receive more coverage regardless of what role high status-people played in a crime (e.g., as victims, suspects, or witnesses). "Cultural deviance is the extent to which an act is considered to be unhealthy, unclean, or perverted" (p. 51). Greater cultural deviance was expected to be more newsworthy. Normative deviance is an indication of how severely an act violates social expectations, and Pritchard and Hughes suggested that although by definition all crimes are normatively deviant, society indicates through its sentencing guidelines and practices how various crimes fall along an implied deviance scale. The greater the potential sentence, the more newsworthy a crime was expected to be.

In fact, Pritchard and Hughes (1997) found that coverage of murder in Milwaukee was largely a function of race, gender, and age, and in such a pattern that White males who were children or senior citizens were the most likely to receive coverage. Thus, they argued, a combination of status and cultural deviance contribute to the decisions journalists make with regard to publishing an account of a crime, and then the length of that report. If Whites are considered the most socially privileged ethnic group, and men the more socially privileged sex, then status deviance would be high for White males. As a cultural matter, murdering the very young or the very old would be maximally deviant. In interviews with reporters, Pritchard and Hughes found that White reporters explained the greater coverage given to Whites by its statistical deviance, but when statistical deviance is controlled in the analyses it is insignificant against the basic fact of race alone.

The theory of deviance is compelling because it accounts for factors that reporters readily acknowledge (particularly statistical deviance) while introducing other factors that may be less obvious to reporters as they make hasty judgments in the field, such as how an editor or producer will weigh the relative newsworthiness of a story, given the audience the newspaper or newscast is trying to reach. For instance, Pritchard and Hughes (1997) noted that in a city where newspaper readers are disproportionately White and affluent, news involving affluent Whites (or sympathetic White victims like children and the elderly) may be of more interest to the papers' readers.

Another approach to explaining why some crimes receive coverage, complementary to deviance in many ways, is that of media system dependency (Ball-Rokeach, 1985; Bruschke & Loges, 1999; DeFleur & Ball-Rokeach, 1989;

Loges, 1994; Loges & Ball-Rokeach, 2002). Dependency relations are based on uneven distributions of goals and resources, and in the case of crime coverage the information resources of the criminal justice system are highly prized by reporters. Police and prosecutors have information about most crimes much earlier than defense attorneys do, and their ability to make this information available or withhold it places them in a powerful position vis-à-vis workaday journalists facing deadlines. Pritchard and Hughes (1997) hinted at the importance of this when they noted that the basic pieces of information most easily gathered by reporters about victims and suspects in homicide cases—gender, race, age, and often address (which hints at class)—are those that allow a profile of the cultural and status deviance of the crime to take shape very early in the reporting. Additional details that a defense attorney may choose to make available are likely to come after a decision has been made about the basic newsworthiness of the story, and come from a source that is less powerful from the point of view of reporters (Shapiro, 1994). After all, reporters on the crime beat know they will need a daily relationship with the police and prosecutors, but a given defense attorney may not cross their path again for months. If law-enforcement officials desire coverage of a crime for reasons of their own, they can take advantage of the needs of reporters. To counteract the dependency relations that drive crime coverage, defense attorneys desiring attention to their case may have to play up the deviant nature of the story in order to summon attention, but that strategy hardly seems likely to help the defendant.

A third explanation for crime coverage is the sway of racial attitudes. Dixon and Linz (2000) suggested that structural factors regarding the way news is gathered lead television news to represent non-White ethnic groups as lawbreakers disproportionately. In their study of television news in the Los Angeles area (where the broadcast market includes populous Orange County), they focused on the appearance of African Americans and Latinos in crime stories. In total, 116 local news broadcasts from five stations, randomly chosen from a 20-week period, were examined. Dixon and Linz found that "Blacks and Latinos ... appear as perpetrators at a higher rate than Whites.... When only felons were included in the analysis, Blacks were almost two and a half times more likely to be portrayed as felons than Whites" (p. 142). Moreover, Whites were found to appear as defenders of the law (e.g., as police officers or officers of the court) more often than others.

Dixon and Linz (2000) suggested that crime coverage on television may support an "ethnic blame discourse" by portraying non-Whites as lawbreakers, and that this may be due to stereotypes held by news editors, reporters, and producers (cf. Entman, 1992, 1994). But this is not the only factor they cited to account for the disproportionately negative portrayals they observed. They noted that due to disparate economic opportunity, Blacks and Latinos are more likely to commit "blue-collar" crimes (such as robbery) than "white-collar" crimes (such as tax evasion), and that blue-collar crimes are more attractive to television because they are easy to understand and there is a victim with whom audiences can relate. Second, they noted the dependency relations between reporters and law enforcement officials, and suggested that officials may wish to call more attention to arrests in blue-collar crime cases than in white-collar cases, perhaps because the public fears blue-collar crimes more. Finally, they noted that television in particular "encourages an emphasis on the visual and the dramatic" (p. 149). Thus, crimes may receive coverage on television news that is different in its content and composition than newspapers, but the influence of a combination of audience expectations, law-enforcement interests, and reporters' routines may still account for what makes it on the air.

The findings of Dixon and Linz (2000) may not contradict the deviance theory. First, because Dixon and Linz did not report the ethnicity of the victims of the crimes in the stories they analyzed, it is impossible to fully evaluate the extent to which their findings challenge the theory of deviance in the choice of stories that get on the news. It is also the case that the audience for television news is different from the population of newspaper readers, and that certainly the population of Los Angeles and Orange County differs in its ethnic diversity from that of Milwaukee.

Relatively few crimes receive news coverage. Those that do receive coverage stand out in ways that journalists, law-enforcement officials, and news audiences recognize and react to in somewhat predictable ways. Having decided to give coverage to a crime, journalists invoke (consciously or not) news frames that highlight certain aspects of the story (such as the type of deviance it represents, or the restoration of law and order after an investigation has led to an arrest) that news audiences come to recognize (Entman, 1993; Gans, 1979; Graber, 1980). This suggests that there may be some as-yet-unstudied variable (as least in pretrial publicity research) that accounts for the type of crime that receives coverage. If that variable (deviance, for example) also drives conviction rates, any pretrial publicity influence found in the field might be spurious. Media theory can therefore explain which stories are covered: Stories of high deviance, that foster continuing relations with law enforcement, and that will play to audience expectations (including racial expectations) are the stories most likely to receive coverage. Needless to say, these conclusions pertain to overall patterns of coverage, and may not obtain for all individual stories.

Is Pretrial Publicity Antidefendant?

Partly due to the nature of the relationship between reporters and law enforcement officials, it is true that publicity itself, should it occur, tends to be prejudicial, and moreover it tends to be prejudicial in one direction: against the defendant (Imrich et al., 1995; Tankard et al., 1979). Thus, a defense attorney has reason to be concerned if the defendant's case has received *any* coverage in the media, because chances are that the coverage introduced information that violates American Bar Association guidelines for prejudicial information (such as prior criminal accusations against the defendant and rumors of a confession from the defendant), and that otherwise hurts the defendant's reputation. In other words, if the first step is taken and the crime becomes a news story, odds are that the story is not in the defendant's favor and that it contains information detrimental to the defense.

Imrich et al. (1995), in their "content analysis of 14 American newspapers over an 8-week period" (p. 94), found that "27% of the suspects described in crime stories were associated with at least one of the ABA categories of potentially prejudicial publicity" (p. 110). The authors noted that over 61% of the news stories in which potentially prejudicial information was reported were the initial news accounts of the crime, further demonstrating the influence of the early information provided by law-enforcement personnel described earlier.

Apart from violations of ABA guidelines regarding divulging specific information, the very appearance of a person in the news as a suspect in a crime may be prejudicial in ways that no abstract presumption of innocence can overcome. Apart from the obvious harm done to one's reputation when it becomes known that one has been arrested in the first place, the manner in which people in police custody are shown on television can be damning. Entman (1992, 1994) found that African Americans shown in police custody on local television news were more likely than others to be shown in the grasp of a police officer—for instance, being led into a courtroom or toward a squad car. In 2002, as a large number of White, white-collar crime suspects were arrested, the term "perp walk" was revived to describe their handcuffed, police-escorted steps from a building to a car or from a car to a building (Eichenwald, 2002; Sloan, 2002). Walking a suspected perpetrator publicly, in police custody, is thought to shame him or her, which may be appropriate if the person is guilty but risks prejudicing potential jurors if the person is not. The New York Civil Liberties Union protested that the perp walk "violated a court ruling barring the parading of suspects before the news media and urged prosecutors to stop doing so" ("Group Says," 2002, p. B6).

Robert Shapiro, a criminal defense attorney in Los Angeles who was among the first members of O. J. Simpson's "Dream Team," wrote in the *Columbia Journalism Review* that defense attorneys must assume that press coverage will be biased against their clients, even famous clients (Shapiro, 1994). Citing the dependency relations between journalists and law enforcement officials, Shapiro recommended that defense attorneys do their best to be helpful to reporters by "cultivat[ing] a line of communication with the reporter so the client's point of view can be expressed in the most favorable way" (p. 27), balancing the relationship as much as possible so the reporter is less dependent solely on police and prosecutors.

Do People See the Coverage?

However, for members of the jury to be affected by this coverage, they have to be exposed to it. Crimes that do receive coverage receive relatively little coverage. Much coverage of crime involves activity very early in the case, mostly the discovery of the crime itself and/or capture of a suspect (Imrich et al., 1995). Subsequent events, such as arraignments, pleas, and other pretrial activities, receive less coverage (Randall, See-Sammons, & Hagner, 1988). Thus, the few stories likely to be printed or broadcast about a crime must catch the attention of a citizen who will become a juror down the road. In the unlikely event that a crime receives more than a few stories' worth of pretrial coverage, the odds of one or more story catching a future juror's attention no doubt increases, but it is worth pondering some figures about audiences.

Local news is frequently (and accurately) described as a business driven virtually exclusively by ratings. This truism can be misleading, however. The ratings for local news tend to be in the single digits; that is, fewer than 10% of a television market's households are likely to be watching any one station's newscast, and if a market has four stations broadcasting local news at the same time, collectively somewhere between 15% and 25% of the television sets in the area are tuned to a newscast. The audience for local news has been falling: Of 43 stations studied by the Project for Excellence in Journalism in 2001, 77% reported that their overall ratings trend is downward in the period 1998–2001—a period that included the impeachment of President Clinton, the Florida election debacle of 2000, and heaven knows how many local crimes, car chases, and fires (Gottlieb & Belt, 2001). National news receives single-digit ratings too, so if a local crime receives national coverage it doesn't substantially affect the likelihood that a potential juror will come across it. The existence of a crime story in a given newscast, or in all of an area's newscasts, by no means translates into exposure to that story for any given resident.

Newspaper readership has also been declining. As of 1996, about 60% of American households subscribed to a daily newspaper, a proportion that had been declining for 40 years and was beginning to stabilize (DeFleur & Dennis, 1998). The appearance of a crime story in the local paper thus does not guarantee that the story will be available to every potential juror, but even if it's in the paper, there is no guarantee it will be read.

What Is the Effect on Jurors?

If we assume that a juror was among the audience for a local crime's coverage, we must then ponder the impact of that story on the juror. Two kinds of effects are relevant: remembering specific facts disclosed outside the court-room, and the formation of negative attitudes toward the defendant (or in favor of the prosecutor). Some experiments are interpreted to mean that mock juries don't necessarily remember all the biasing factual information they are given about a defendant, but that they develop enduring negative attitudes nonetheless (Kramer et al., 1990).

One study showed that the frame in which a news story is placed influences people's memory of the story (Valkenburg et al., 1999). A frame is "a particular way in which journalists compose a news story to optimize audience accessibility" (Valkenburg et al., 1999, p. 550). Given limitations of space and time in which to tell their stories, reporters choose frames that allow an audience to recognize familiar themes, types, and storytelling devices and thus understand the story better (Entman, 1993; Graber, 1988). Valkenburg et al. described four common frames in crime news: (1) human interest, (2) conflict, (3) responsibility, and (4) economic consequences. Human-interest frames involve emotional qualities of the crime, such as consequences for victims. In fact, much of the stimulus material typical in laboratory studies of pretrial publicity would fall into the human-interest frame (e.g., Kerr et al., 1991, in whose experiment jurors read of the defendant running over a child with his car). Valkenburg et al. (1999), studying responses of 187 undergraduates in Holland to stories in each of the four frames, found that their subjects remembered less of the human-interest-framed news than news from any of the other categories. That is, the kind of crime news that is most laden with emotions and most emphasizes the consequences of the crime is the kind least likely to encourage recall immediately *after* reading a newspaper article, let alone in a jury room later. (Vidmar's [2002] "Uncle Six" experiment demonstrated something similar.) However, Kramer et al. (1990) showed that even if they don't remember the information itself, mock jurors in an experiment show evidence of bias against a defendant even days after being shown emotionally charged publicity. The facts may fade from memory, but emotion-inducing facts may create lasting negative attitudes. Our concerns about the Kramer et al. study are outlined in chapter 2.

The processes by which news is created and disseminated are designed in part to maximize audience interest in the news. As a result, the news combines surprising stories (statistical deviance) with familiar, consistent themes (frames) that don't challenge an audience's values or assumptions about the world too strongly or too frequently. Pretrial publicity that is most consonant with existing beliefs may have the most lasting effect, not just influencing beliefs about the immediate crime and defendant, but reinforcing more general beliefs about the nature of crime, criminals, and the law enforcement system. People may enter the jury pool holding a variety of beliefs about the cases on the court's docket that day, but if those beliefs were influenced by mainstream news coverage of crime they are likely to be at least mildly antidefendant and supportive of the prosecuting arm of the criminal justice system. People who watch the news with a perspective that is skeptical of the criminal justice system may reject the images of perp-walking defendants and confident prosecutors, but they are still confronted with these images.

The decision of a jury is a small-group task that is often characterized as an attempt to arrive at a collective narrative of the events that is most coherent to the group (Brooks & Gerwitz, 1996; Diamond, 2002; Pennington & Hastie, 1986). This may involve giving more or less credence to some information presented at trial, but it also must involve each juror's notion of what "makes sense" in general. To the extent that information outside the testimony at trial, such as pretrial publicity, enters into the narrative in spite of all attempts to dissuade jurors from considering it, that information may be included in order to help the jurors complete the story. Jurors "fill in gaps in the evidence by drawing inferences based on their understanding of how the world works" (Diamond, 2002, p. 866). Surely a juror exposed to pretrial publicity may find that information helpful in filling in the gaps, and because the news is likely to reinforce existing notions of how the world works, information obtained there may be particularly helpful in rounding out the narrative. The process of deliberation can prevent the introduction of outside information (Kerwin & Shaffer, 1994), and perhaps most effectively when the jurors are able collectively to construct a coherent narrative that they all can accept. But if even their pooled insight into the trial evidence fails to render a story that makes sense, they may relax their guard against inadmissible information for the sake of connecting the dots. As suggested earlier, probative information might be the most critical.

In the end, we believe that most juries are not confronted with pretrial publicity specific to the crime and defendant in their case. But there are circumstances when pretrial publicity is more likely to be available, and more likely to influence jurors no matter what remedies are attempted. Deviant crimes, particularly those that involve unlikely victims or defendants and that represent especially gross violations of the cultural code, are more likely to receive coverage and that coverage will likely reassert the existing norms of status and culture. But it is not the mere amount of coverage that poses a problem for jurors seeking to render an impartial verdict—cases with massive amounts of coverage don't appear to result in more guilty verdicts than cases with very little coverage (Bruschke & Loges, 1999). When the news accounts of the crime offer a coherent narrative that is consistent with a juror's worldview, it may be very difficult for that juror to put that narrative aside, especially if the attorneys fail to offer clear alternative narratives at trial. Crimes that receive a great deal of press coverage may actually make it difficult for a single compelling narrative to emerge such that any given juror, let alone an entire jury, can rely on the pretrial publicity to help when the verdict is being deliberated. When there has been a small amount of publicity but the story that the publicity supports is stable and coherent, when each new piece of news merely adds to the existing narrative instead of forcing reconsideration of the sequence of events and participants, pretrial publicity may be most likely to bias a jury. It could be that moderate levels of publicity introduce more ambiguity, complexity, and incoherence, such that although a juror may recall stray facts that are never presented as evidence, those facts are difficult to integrate into a narrative during deliberations. These comments are attempts to explain the usual pattern of findings where defendants with high and no coverage face identical conviction rates, defendants with moderate publicity face the highest conviction rates, and defendants with low publicity rates have the lowest conviction rates (Bruschke & Loges, 1999).

There is much that can be said about the manner in which pretrial information is processed in the minds of individual jurors once it reaches them, and we discuss the details of those theories in chapter 5. What media theory offers to the mix is a coherent way to explain the type of media content (themes) and the way that such content forms beliefs in the minds of jurors (frames). Speaking most broadly, there are two distinct ways that pretrial publicity can influence a juror's thinking, and those ways are not exclusive. First, media content can form an overall picture of social life variously called a narrative, schema, worldview, or frame. Second, specific pieces of information might be processed through that narrative. It is our belief that theories will improve when they account for both possible influences, and it appears that research at present is not driven by a coherent theoretical explanation for what happens between the introduction of a media message and a final decision (although some studies do have implicit theories; Kovera's [2002] work is a welcome advance on the matter). A trial outcome is likely to be a the complex product of general frames, specific features of the trial, group deliberation dynamics, coverage content and frequency, and juror and lawyer characteristics. It is unlikely that individual media messages will be so all-powerful as to have consistent, pernicious effects in the minds of all (or even a majority) of jurors.

Another Approach: Pretrial Publicity and Cultivation

The importance of people's beliefs about what makes for a coherent narrative in the preceding discussion points to another way that pretrial publicity can influence jurors, apart from introducing specific information or inspiring biased attitudes focused on the defendant or victim involved in the crime at trial. The totality of crime news in the media may cultivate beliefs about the world that in turn make some kinds of narratives sensible and some harder to believe.

Cultivation theory (Gerbner, Gross, Morgan, & Signorielli, 1986) provides an explanation for social level and individual level results of "living with television." As "the source of the most broadly shared images and messages in history" (p. 17), television saturates a society with impressions that encourage some patterns of belief and discourage others. Beliefs that are "cultivated" by television can be quite distorted from reality. For instance, heavy viewers of television, because they see so many dramas about violent crime and law enforcement, tend to believe that they are more likely to encounter violence in their lives than they actually are (Gerbner, Gross, Signorielli, Morgan, & Jackson- Beck, 1979). When television content, considered in its totality instead of in terms of individual programs or news stories, consistently reinforces a belief, television viewers tend to adopt that belief even if it deviates from real life. Heavy viewers of television come to live in a "scary world," where (they believe) others can't be trusted. But even light viewers are susceptible to cultivation if they interact with heavy viewers who share with them a cultivated view of the world. By the same token, however, the cultivation effect is mitigated by interaction with light viewers who provide an alternative source of information, demonstrated in studies of children who have friends and parents who provide alternative information resources (Gross & Morgan, 1985; Rothschild, 1984).

Through cultivation of general beliefs about crime, pretrial publicity about crime in general, not just about the case a juror finds him- or herself deliberating, can make some narratives offered by the prosecution and defense more plausible and some more incredible. Jurors who are heavy viewers of television are the most likely to be exposed to any television coverage the crime in question did receive, but also the most likely to have developed beliefs about the world that are more consistent with the world of television than with reality. This combination may make such jurors more willing to believe that people can't be trusted and that crime is common and ever-threatening. In general, these "scary world" beliefs seem biased against a criminal defendant, although there may be situations in which the defendant might benefit from such beliefs on the part of jurors (e.g., some claims of self-defense might appear more plausible to heavy television viewers).

Some recent research that explores the way cognitive processing strategies affect the cultivation effect shed light on the circumstances under which jury bias may be introduced by television viewing. Shrum (2001), in an experiment involving 122 undergraduates, encouraged one group to respond to questions by thinking carefully (employing central-route cognitive processing; Petty & Cacioppo, 1986) and another group to offer "the first answer that occurs to you, ... off the top of your head" (Shrum, 2001, p. 102; employing peripheral cognitive processing). Students were presented with 40 questions that cultivation researchers have used to measure the degree of cultivation in TV viewers, items that call for respondents to estimate the frequency or prevalence of real-world phenomena (such as the prevalence of crime and the percentage of the workforce engaged in law enforcement).

Shrum (2001) reported that peripheral processing is associated with "TV answers" to the questions, but that students who were encouraged to consider their answers carefully were more accurate in their estimates. He attributed the improved accuracy of the latter group to *source discounting*, which is the tendency to weigh the value of information according to the credibility of its source. When estimating, say, the amount of crime in a neighborhood, a careful thinker might realize that he or she is about to base the estimate on impressions from cop shows or sensational stories on the evening news rather than dispassionate data and thus might temper the estimate. Source discounting may not be easy when one is pressed for the first answer that comes to mind.

If Shrum's theory about the role of source discounting in one's weighing of information from television is correct, it seems important as a consideration about the likelihood of jurors allowing their decisions to be influenced unduly by pretrial publicity or televised violence in general. One presumes that jurors take their task seriously enough to employ central-route cognitive processing rather than a top-of-the-head decision, although Diamond (2002) noted that it is not uncommon for juries to take a vote to open deliberations, which results in the jury "focus[ing] its attention on persuading the minority to join the position initially held by a majority of jurors" (p. 869). An alternative approach to deliberation, "the so-called evidence-driven jury" (p. 869), calls for at least some review of the evidence before any vote is taken. Most juries probably fall between the two extremes Diamond described, which suggests that most deliberations invite some level of careful attention to the evidence, which in turn provides an opportunity for jurors to consider the basis for assumptions they may be making about the crime, the defendant, and the judicial system. As other research has shown, jurors tend to take their job seriously.

Berger (2000, 2001) expressed dismay at the misleading way that quantitative data are frequently presented in the news media, and set out to test the impact of poor or inappropriate presentation of quantities on newspaper readers. Although cultivation theory emphasizes television's importance because of its ubiquity, Berger's results shed more light on the role of cognitive processing in mediating the effects of learning information, including inaccurate information, from the media. Berger (2001) showed through a content analysis of a year's worth of newspaper articles that "there was a distinct proclivity for frequency data to be used to illustrate worsening trends and rate data to be used to characterize improving trends" (p. 673). Frequency data, which deprive the reader of enough mathematical context to know if apparent increases in frequency reflect actual increases in risk, can mislead a reader into overestimating the impact of whatever trend is under discussion. For instance, a story about crime might say that there were 20 more instances of car theft in a city than in the previous year—a simple frequency report—without considering whether there were more cars on the road this year. *Rate* reports account more accurately for the relative significance of changes in frequency by controlling for changes in population size. If negative "trends" are reported without the information necessary to weigh the true impact of such changes on one's community, the result may be further cultivation of needless fear.

In another exploration of the implications of news reports of quantitative information, Berger (1998, 2000) showed that men and women interpret newspaper reports of changes in the frequency of crime and the crime rate per capita differently. Men are more likely to interpret an increase in crime *frequency* that in fact translates into a lower crime *rate* (due to population increase) as a net increase in their safety. Women, however, "showed no reduction in either apprehension or victimization risk after exposure to population data" (Berger, 2000, p. 27). Berger theorized that women, who do not differ from men in their levels of apprehension and risk, process information about threats differently than do men.

> It may be that when confronted with data indicative of an increasing threat, women are more likely than men to focus their attention on the threat, thus reducing the bandwidth of their attention capacity and preventing them from making associations between previous information and data germane to the threat. (p. 47)

Gerbner et al. (1986) found that women are victims of crime on television more often than men. The deviance theory of newsworthiness (Pritchard & Hughes, 1997) would suggest that crimes in which women are victims—particularly in especially vulnerable situations, such as the 1989 Central Park jogger rape case—violate cultural expectations more than when adult men are victims, and are thus more likely to receive news coverage. Thus, Berger's findings may be due to a cultivation effect among women, who interpret reports of increased frequency of crime to indicate greater risk for them than for men.

Shrum also investigated the role of another cultivation concept, *resonance*, in people's thoughts about crime. Shrum and Bischak (2001) reported results of a small survey of a nonrandom sample of 157 adult residents of New Jersey. They find that people whose personal experiences resonate with the scary world depicted on television, in this case people who had been victims of crimes, provided estimates of the prevalence of crime that were more consistent with the world of television than reality. Should these results be generalizable, an available remedy is voir dire, by which attorneys can excuse victims of crime lest their experience (in combination with heavy television viewing) encourage them to perceive the world as scary, lawless, and full of deceit, to the detriment of the defendant.

Conclusion

Jurors find themselves in a unique social role. Thrust into a small group of relative strangers, they are asked to exercise profound power over a defendant's fate and then disband with no expectation that they'll ever assemble again. There are a number of ways they can approach this peculiar task responsibly. It is not surprising if their tendency is to rely on the human desire for coherent narratives to guide their path through the trial and deliberations (Fisher, 1987). But the result of this may be to expose their cognitive processes to biases and distortions, some of which can be traced to their primary storytelling mechanism in day-to-day life—usually some form of mass media. Whether exposure to press coverage of the crime they are called to adjudicate influences their notions of what constitutes a sensible narrative about that specific event, or heavy television viewing has cultivated general beliefs about the way the world works that mitigate against trusting some people's claims of innocence, jurors may find their quest for narrative coherence thwarted by pretrial publicity and other media content.

Despite the potential for pretrial publicity to influence jurors, the actual odds of this happening seem small in most cases. Because most crimes get no press coverage, most jury trials are probably not plagued by the problem of publicity specific to that crime (although cultivation effects remain). When crimes do receive attention in the press, the chances of all members of the jury having been exposed to that coverage seem small in the majority of cases. Deliberation offers the opportunity for inadmissible information to be detected and discounted. Juries may be most prone to effects of pretrial publicity when the press accounts are unambiguous and offer a complete account of the events surrounding the crime.

Such clarity and coherence is not likely to be found in coverage of a "crime of the century" that spawns scores of newspaper stories and hours of TV. The paradigm case of a crime cycle has four consecutive stories in the news: Day 1, a crime occurred; Day 2, police are investigating and have a hypothesis about how the crime was committed; Day 3, police have identified a suspect and described his or her motive; and Day 4, the suspect is apprehended and shown in the grasp of a uniformed officer being led to jail. This pattern may be enough to provide a crystal clear narrative to a community that includes the future jury. The crime may never receive additional news coverage even as it goes to trial, but the story has been told completely already and no one might feel the need to be updated. The professional practices of journalists encourage the use of frames that allow readers and audiences to quickly understand the nature of the story, its characters, and the most likely or appropriate outcome. Most crime reporters also find themselves dependent on the information resources of law-enforcement officials more than on defense attorneys or defendants, so in the course of framing their stories journalists are likely to adopt a point of view distinctly sympathetic to the prosecution's account of events. Such frames may be most consonant with the expectations of news audiences, in part because the audience's worldview has been cultivated by a diet of cop shows and broadcasts of *Die Hard*.

When all of these factors combine, the influence on the outcome of a jury trial may be overwhelming. That may not happen often enough to worry about before other, more profound challenges to the fairness of the criminal justice system are addressed. More complete understanding of the overall pretrial publicity process might allow attorneys, judges, and jurors themselves to consciously fight these effects, using existing judicial remedies more effectively and developing strategies for press relations that break the emerging narrative before it can become too firmly implanted in the community's jury pool. As Robert Shapiro advised his fellow defense attorneys in 1994:

> The initial headlines of the arrest often make the sacred presumption of innocence a myth. In reality, we have the presumption of guilt. This is why dealing with the media is so important. To make inroads into the mind-set that "if the press reported it, it must be true" is the lawyer's most challenging task. (p. 26)

Overall, media theory has introduced (a) some important explanations for why some stories get on the news, as well as what their content is and why it is that way, and (b) some explanation for how that information is processed. Our reading of media theory leads us to suppose that media content tends to cultivate an overall view of what the normal functioning of the criminal justice system is like (including the likelihood of being a victim of a crime, the likelihood that the police have arrested the right suspect, the likelihood of defendant or police misconduct, etc.), but that those images are mediated by cognitive processing and individual differences. Neither the overall worldview perpetuated by the media nor the mediating cognitive processes have been extensively studied in extant pretrial publicity research.

IN SEARCH OF A CULTIVATION EFFECT

Media theory has offered a number of insights into the dynamic between the media and the legal system. The cultivation approach, reviewed earlier and advocated elsewhere as a key to understanding pretrial publicity (Surette, 1992), offers intriguing possibilities. If it cannot supplant individual-level psychological approaches to understanding the processing of media content, it can at least supplement them and add rich new information to scholarly thinking about pretrial publicity at a more macroscopic level. Empirical data on what has been called an "echo" or "general" pretrial publicity effect will make a substantial contribution to media influences at a level of abstraction higher than that of the individual juror.

Methods

To explore the possibility that media coverage of crime might influence trial outcomes by cultivating beliefs about crime, we explored the hypothesis that jurisdictions with higher levels of crime coverage would have conviction rates significantly higher than low crime coverage jurisdictions. An intuitive model suggests that high crime rates drive high crime coverage, and that high crime coverage results in more fear of crime, which results in higher conviction rates. A somewhat less intuitive model might forego the link between the crime rate and the amount of crime coverage and suggest that journalists may choose to cover crime regardless of how much of it there is, and thus cultivate fear of crime regardless of the crime rate. In the world of news, crime may be a perennial topic, sharing the status of war or scandal.

Although there are a number of reasons, based on empirical data, to doubt the veracity of the intuitive model, it did serve to guide us in the selection of variables for analysis. We gathered data from four different sources. First, we obtained actual crime rates from official FBI statistics, which measure in units of crimes reported per 100,000 people. Second, we obtained fear-of-crime data from the results of an academic study placed in the Inter-University Consortium for Political and Social Research (ICPSR) archives (Tjaden & Thoennes, 1998). From the larger data set, we extracted three items measuring General Crime Concern, Violent Crime Concern, and Personal Safety Concern. Third, we obtained coverage data from a Kaiser Foundation report (1998); the Kaiser report measured the amount of crime coverage in local broadcast TV news in 13 different cities over a 3-month period. In general, the number of crime stories broadcast in the sampling period is used as the measure of coverage. Finally, we obtained trial outcome data from official records made publicly available by the Federal Judicial Center. These records include information on all defendants charged at the federal level. The result was a collection of data that included city-level data for crime and crime coverage, respondent-level data for fear of crime, and defendant-level data for conviction rates. The details of the databases and the data extraction strategies are contained in the Appendix.

Our initial analysis examined the intuitive model, and the results indicated that the model was not supported at both the city and individual respondent level. There was no correlation between actual crime levels and crime coverage. Because all data for these comparisons existed at the city level, initial comparisons involved city-level data only. An analytical difficulty is presented by the relatively low n, which can make Pearson's r unstable; an alternative is Spearman's rho rank-order correlation. The latter test is more appropriate to smaller sample sizes but is nonparametric; both tests are reported here. At the city level, Pearson's correlation was low (.043) and not significant, and Spearman's rho was negative (−.16) and not significant.

Another way to look at the same problem is to give each respondent a crime coverage exposure score based on the amount of crime coverage the Kaiser Foundation report found in that respondent's city, and correlate these scores with the respondent's personal fear of crime. This would assign each respondent in a given city the same media exposure score, although scores would vary across the residents of thirteen cities. This maneuver has the advantage of increasing the sample size but at the high cost of assuming identical media exposure for each individual in a given city (an inevitable problem of combining individual- and city-level data). However, cultivation theory provides some justification for this move. Gerbner et al. (1986) argued that the cultivation effect is not limited to those who actually watch large amounts of television. The concept of "mainstreaming" refers to a tendency for the range of public opinion to narrow as television's presentation of events constricts people's points of view of any given issue. Although "heavy" television viewers are shown to be more prone to this effect, Gerbner et al. argued that through interaction with heavy viewers in day-to-day life, even light viewers come to understand the world through the lens of television.

Even with this very liberal analysis, however, there were no significant correlations between any of the three measures of fear of crime and actual crime. Simply eyeballing the data in Figs. A.1 and A.2 (contained in the Appendix), it is apparent that there is no correlation between crime and crime coverage. For example, of the 13 cities included in the study, Minneapolis had the 10th highest crime rate but the lowest crime coverage. New York had the lowest crime rate but the sixth most crime coverage. It is worth noting that Atlanta had both the highest crime rate and the most crime coverage, and that Seattle was ranked ninth in both crime rate and crime coverage.

In addition, there was no correlation between crime coverage and fear of crime. A significant negative relationship existed between coverage and General Crime Concern (Spearman's rho $= -.67$, $p < .05$, $n = 13$), and there were no significant relationships between coverage and the other fear-of-crime measures. Similar results were obtained for Pearson's correlation. When city-level data for crime exposure are entered for each individual in the fear-of-crime data set, a slight but significant relationship emerges for personal safety concern and coverage level ($r = .08$, $p < .05$), whereas the other two fear-of-crime variables exhibit nonsignificant and negative correlations.

Finally, there was no association between actual crime levels and fear of crime. When city crime levels were entered for each individual respondent in the fear-of-crime data set, no measure of fear of crime was correlated with actual crime. At the city level, neither the parametric Pearson nor the nonparametric Spearman's rho measure was statistically significant.

The lack of empirical support for the intuitive model has consequences for the way that any pretrial publicity effect should be conceived. The intuitive model imagines coverage effects in a causal process way, where variables chain together to produce differences in conviction rates. Such a relationship has not been supported here, and our reading of the literature suggests that little support could be found for this model elsewhere. Having cast aside the intuitive model, we formulated a data analysis strategy based on four basic tenets.

First, we sought an alternative to the causal process thinking of the correlation-based analytic approaches. One possible framework for examining the process is a partitioning-of-variance approach, where interactions between variables can be explored but one need not assume any a priori relationships between the variables. The analysis of variance (ANOVA) model is perhaps the most familiar of these approaches. This is not to suggest that there is not a striking similarity between the ANOVA and regression approaches, and there are indeed obvious areas of overlap. However, interaction terms are easier to construct, test, and interpret in the ANOVA approach, and this is especially true when the interactions observed manifest themselves in non-intuitive ways. The ANOVA approach is not without its limitations, however, one of which is the assumption of a normal distribution of each dependent variable. Although all the dependent variables in the subsequent analysis were continuous, none took on the shape of a normal curve. The dependent variables were therefore broken into discrete categories (each described later). When the number of categories is only two, a binary logistic regression is possible. Where the number of categories is greater than two, a multinomial regression is the statistic of choice. One advantage of the binary logistic regression over the multinomial regression is that it produces pseudo-R^2 measures that make magnitude assessments easier.

A second basic component of our analytic strategy was that we need a method sensitive to interpreting the various interactions observed. Essentially, each analysis involved one central question: Does crime coverage influence the dependent variable in question? In addition, it involved a series of interaction questions, all of which stemmed from this concern: Does any influence of pretrial publicity on a case outcome depend on (or shift based on) other variables? Our analytic strategy was to take the most intuitive approach to testing these two questions. To test the central question, the data were analyzed with a simple chi-square test that examined whether there were significant differences in the dependent variable based on the different levels of crime coverage. To test for interactions, the data were entered into a more complex model (either binary logistic regression or multinomial regression). The remaining question was how to interpret the interactions. In a multivariate, categorical model this question is confounded by a number of factors. Often, the comparison points of the significance terms are not those of theoretical interest, are not appropriate to the hypotheses, and are often difficult even to find. Additionally, the basic unit of comparison is the log odds ratio, which is quite useful for many purposes but in a multiway table can be misleading without very careful attention paid to base percentages. For example, a jump from 1% to 3% of variance explained will produce a very impressive odds ratio that correctly shows a 300% effect, an impressively large number that still doesn't account for very much variance overall. Our approach is to use the more complex models to test for significance and then return to the percentages of simple cross-tabulation tables to interpret the interactions.

Our third cornerstone of analysis was an attempt to reduce the three fear of crime measures to a single variable. Although the number of overall defendants in the final data set was large ($n = 7,293$), the number that actually went to trial was fairly modest ($n = 595$). Furthermore, because there were only 13 cities included in the data set any modestly complex crossing of the variables left empty cells. The fewer the variables in the model, the more this problem was minimized, and given the limited size of the data set, selecting a parsimonious measure of fear of crime was paramount. Efforts at combining the fear-of-crime measures into a central index failed; measures of crime and fear-of-crime data did not coalesce into a reliable scale. For this analysis, the Personal Safety Concern scale was retained because it was stable across time but varied across cities; the Overall Crime Concern scale met neither of these criteria. Violent Crime Concern met the criteria but seemed less theoretically relevant, and the use of a single concept was retained to simplify an already complex analysis. It is, however, evident that including a different measure of fear of crime would change the results of any given analysis. Details of these research decisions are contained in the Appendix.

Theoretically, the lack of correlation between the fear of crime measures provides support to the conclusion that the concept of fear of crime is multifaceted. Thus, from the outset we issue the caveat that future analyses should explore the concept of fear of crime in more detail. We further note that the measure we use vastly simplifies the concept, and the choice of measure might produce a different set of results than would have been obtained with other measures included in the same data set.

The final major analytical challenge had to do with selecting the appropriate dependent variable. Two characteristics of our data set have been largely unexplored in laboratory research or even extant field research. First, most defendants (55%) face multiple charges (see Appendix). Second, most defendants plead guilty to at least one count. In our final data set, which included all defendants in the 13 different cities, 60.5% of all charges were pleaded, and 80.0% of criminal defendants pleaded at least one charge. It was thus evident that we had to create a dependent measure that incorporated multiple charges at multiple decision points. After excluding all nonfelony charges from the data, we ended up with a four-measure scheme. The first measure is Percent of Charges Pleaded, and is obtained by dividing the number of charges for which a guilty plea was entered by the total number of charges a defendant faced. The second measure is Average Length of Pleaded Sentence, and is obtained by dividing the total number of pleaded charges by the total length of sentence. In calculating the total sentence length, only the longest concurrent sentence was counted and all consecutive sentences were added together. Death sentences ($n = 2$) were coded as 2,000 months, life sentences ($n = 48$) as

1,999 months, and sealed sentences were excluded. The third measure was Trial Conviction Percentage, and was calculated by dividing the number of charges resulting in convictions at trial by the total number of charges that went to trial. The final measure was Length of Tried Sentence, and was obtained by dividing the total sentence length by the number of charges resulting in guilt at trial. As with the pleaded sentences, only the longest concurrent sentence was counted and all consecutive sentences were included.

There were three independent variables, actual crime, fear of crime, and amount of crime coverage. All variables were dichotomized with simple median splits based on city-level data. Thus, for the final analysis, the defendant was the unit of analysis, and each defendant received a score for actual crime (high or low), fear of crime (high or low), and crime coverage (high or low) based on the city in which the trial was held in. For the trial-level variables a fourth variable was added. In federal courts, defendants may request a trial in front of a judge rather than a jury. In this data set, roughly 7% of defendants elected to be tried in front of a judge. The method of trial (judge or jury) was included as a fourth independent variable in the trial-level analyses.

Results: Percent of Charges Pleaded

The first dependent variable analyzed was Percent of Charges Pleaded. The Percent of Charges Pleaded was neither normal nor dichotomous; instead, a large percentage of defendants either pleaded all their charges (46.4%) or none of them (20.0%). An analysis of the distribution (see Table 4.1) resulted in a four-category scheme, including no charges pleaded (20.0%), 1–49% of charges pleaded (15.3%), 50–99% of charges pleaded (18.2%), and all charges pleaded (46.4%).

For crime coverage, when coverage areas were considered binomially there were differences in the Percent of Charges Pleaded between high and low coverage areas ($\chi^2 = 62.2$, $df = 3$, $p < .001$). In general, more charges were pleaded in high-coverage areas. The cross-tabulation table revealed that in high- as compared to low-coverage areas, a greater percentage of defendants pleaded to all charges (48.0% vs. 43.9%) or a majority of charges (19.4% vs. 16.6%), and a smaller percentage of defendants pleaded to a minority of charges (12.8% vs. 19.3%) or to no charges at all (19.8% vs. 20.3%). The magnitude seems to be 4–5 percentage points, and the nominal-by-interval eta was .047. There is thus a modest relationship such that high-coverage areas tend to have slightly higher levels of plea bargaining.

To test for interactions, all three independent variables (coverage, crime, and Personal Safety Concern) were entered into a multinomial regression. A model with a three-way interaction term was not significant, but a model with two-way interactions revealed significance for both the crime by coverage ($\chi^2 = 1598.39$, $df = 3$, $p < .001$) and Personal Safety Concern by coverage

TABLE 4.1

Distribution of Percent of Charges Pleaded

Proportion of Charges Pleaded	Frequency	Percent	Cumulative Percent
0.0	1460	20.0	20.0
20.0	348	4.8	24.8
25.0	222	3.0	27.8
33.0	403	5.5	33.4
40.0	148	2.0	35.4
50.0	1074	14.7	50.1
60.0	74	1.0	51.1
67.0	127	1.7	52.9
75.0	26	0.4	53.2
80.0	30	0.4	53.6
100.0	3381	46.4	100.0
Total	7293	100.0	

($\chi^2 = 13.76, df = 3, p = .003$) terms. The overall model fitting comparison was significant ($\chi^2 = 332.53, df = 18, p < .001$), and the goodness-of-fit comparison was not (Deviance $\chi^2 = 3.296, df = 3, p = .348$), both indicating a good fit. The Nagelkerke pseudo-R^2 was .048, indicating a modest relationship.

Raw percentages for the crime by coverage interaction are contained in Table 4.2. The table reveals a curvilinear relationship. In high crime areas, a curvilinear relationship emerges between coverage and pleading; in high-coverage areas, a larger percentage of defendants either pleads to all charges (50.2% vs. 42.1%) or to none at all (24.5% vs. 20.1%), with fewer defendants mixing pleas. In low-crime areas there was a more modest tendency for crime coverage to encourage pleas across all categories. Overall, coverage increased pleading in high-crime areas (63.3% vs. 50.8%) but had little effect in low-crime areas (58.5% vs. 56.7%). Thus, coverage is correlated with pleaded outcomes, but in high crime areas the effect becomes slightly curvilinear.

Raw percentages for the Personal Safety Concern by crime coverage interaction are contained in Table 4.3. In high-fear-of-crime areas, coverage is highly and negatively correlated with pleaded outcomes, with a greater percentage of defendants opting against any plea and fewer defendants pleading to all charges. Overall, high amounts of coverage resulted in a lower percentage of pleaded charges in high fear of crime areas (52.4% vs. 61.4%). The pattern reverses in low-fear-of-crime areas, where coverage sharply increases

TABLE 4.2

Crime by Publicity Interaction on Percent of Charges Pleaded

	Actual Crime Low		Actual Crime High	
	Publicity: Low	Publicity: High	Publicity: Low	Publicity: High
0% pleaded	20.5%	18.0%	20.1%	24.5%
1–49% pleaded	17.6%	12.7%	20.9%	12.9%
50–99% pleaded	16.2%	22.1%	16.9%	12.5%
100% pleaded	45.7%	47.2%	42.1%	50.2%

TABLE 4.3

Personal Safety Concern Interaction on Percent of Charges Pleaded

	Fear of Personal Safety Low		Fear of Personal Safety High	
	Publicity Low	Publicity High	Publicity Low	Publicity High
0% pleaded	21.7%	16.0%	19.8%	28.1%
1–49% pleaded	25.8%	11.8%	16.8%	14.9%
50–99% pleaded	19.4%	20.9%	15.5%	16.1%
100% pleaded	33.1%	51.3%	48.0%	40.9%

pleaded outcomes, and a greater percentage of defendants plead to all charges and fewer defendants reject all pleas. Overall, high amounts of coverage resulted in a lower percentage of pleaded charges in low-fear-of-crime areas (67.6% vs. 47.9%), and the effect size was more pronounced than that in high-fear-of-crime areas.

When all main and interaction effects are taken together, this picture emerges: Crime coverage has a general tendency to increase pleading. This influence will be most pronounced when crime is high and fear is low. However, when fear is high, crime coverage actually reduces the amount of pleading activity. The influence of actual crime may be curvilinear, albeit dominated by a tendency to encourage pleaded outcomes. The size of the effect is modest but clearly identifiable, and in the most extreme conditions results in an 18-point swing in the percentage of charges pleaded.

What might cause this pattern of results? There are actually four questions raised here: (a) Why are plea bargains so common in general? (b) Why might media coverage of crime encourage plea bargains? (c) Why does crime coverage in conjunction with higher crime rates encourage more bargains? (d) Why does crime coverage in conjunction with public fear of crime sharply reduce bargained outcomes? As a starting point, it should be remembered that prosecutors control the plea-bargaining process (Pritchard, 1990). Plea bargains offer prosecutors a number of advantages. In general, a plea bargain saves the prosecutor resources and avoids costly trials. It further eliminates any chance that the prosecutor might lose the case; even if the sentence issued is somewhat lower than it would be with a conviction at trial, an alleged criminal is off the streets. Further, criminal defense attorneys are generally aware of the very low defense win rates at trial, which provides the defense an incentive to enter into a plea bargain when the prosecution makes the offer. We believe that these factors serve to explain the generally high plea-bargaining rates.

Why, then, does crime coverage increase plea bargains? The most obvious explanation is that the consequences for a prosecutor losing a case are higher in an area where crime is more highly publicized. If a prosecutor feels there is a chance that a jury might acquit, the prosecutor can avoid losing a case publicly by entering into a plea bargain. Higher crime might exacerbate this tendency by normalizing plea bargains to an even greater extent and by increasing the chances that a prosecutor might lose. High crime rates create higher case loads and strain prosecutorial resources. With more crimes to investigate, research, and prosecute, prosecutors can devote less time to each case and with a lower level of preparation face a greater prospect of defeat. Higher odds of losing any given case, coupled with higher attention to crime in general, may combine to encourage a tendency toward bargaining.

Why, then, might the fear of crime so sharply reduce the tendency of prosecutors to plea bargain? Consider two key elements. First, recall that (somewhat contrary to cultivation theory) crime coverage and fear of crime are uncorrelated. It is always bad for a prosecutor to lose a case, it's always worse in a city where crime is highly publicized, but media attention does not mean that the public cares about the issue or perceives an onslaught of crime. When fear of crime is low, the prosecutor can avoid public losses by entering plea bargains and an unconcerned public won't care, even when the media are covering crime extensively. Second, it is possible that the public may perceive plea bargains to be soft on crime (Pritchard, 1990). This perception may or may not be accurate, but it certainly means that a prosecutor entering plea bargains would suffer in the eyes of the public. When these two possibilities are combined, it could be that a high fear of crime activates the public's attitudes about plea bargains being soft on crime, and thus prosecutors are less likely to entertain plea agreements. When the fear of crime is low, the negative public opinions about plea bargains are not activated, and prosecutors can avoid public losses with plea bargains. Thus, the negative public attitude about plea bargains is relevant only when the public fears crime and crime is well publicized. If crime is publicized but the public doesn't fear it, negative feelings about plea bargains do not plague prosecutors. If the public fears crime but crime isn't covered, the prosecutor still has a relatively free hand to conduct business as he or she sees fit because it will generally be outside of public scrutiny. When, however, the public is concerned about crime and the media cover crime extensively, the prosecutor begins to avoid plea bargains to avoid public disapproval.

When the answers to the four questions just identified are combined, it is possible to produce a short answer to the question: How does crime coverage influence plea bargaining overall? Generally speaking, coverage increases plea bargaining and high crime exacerbates the influence. The fear of crime will create a confounding interaction, however, so that coverage increases pleaded outcomes if fear is low but will reduce pleaded outcomes when fear is high. It should be remembered that these results hinge on a single-item measure of fear of crime, however, and different measures might produce different results.

Results: Average Length of Pleaded Sentence

The second dependent variable examined was the Average Length of Pleaded Sentence, which was obtained by dividing the total number of months of sentence resulting from pleas by the total number of felony counts pleaded. The distribution was not normal (see Table 4.4) but was instead skewed heavily toward zero, with a relatively large number of defendants averaging zero months (21.3%) on pleaded counts. In addition, a small number (1%) of cases were outliers on the extreme right-hand side of the curve with average sentences of 206 months (over 17 years) or more. An ordinal variable was constructed with three levels: zero months (26.7%), 1 to 50 months (46.8%), and more than 50 months (26.5%). Of the 7,293 total defendants analyzed, 5,824 had entered at least one plea and had valid data for analysis.

A chi-square test indicated a significant relationship between coverage and Average Length of Pleaded Sentence ($\chi^2 = 46.734$, $df=2$, $p < .001$). Areas with higher levels of crime coverage had a greater percentage of defendants with pleaded sentences of zero months (29.3% vs. 22.7%) or more than 50 months (27.3% vs. 25.3%) than defendants in areas with lower levels of coverage. Defendants in low-coverage areas had more sentences of 1 to 50 months (52.0% vs. 43.4%; Cramer's $V = .09$). The pattern is roughly curvilinear, with defendants in areas of higher coverage having more extremely long or extremely short sentences and fewer mid-range sentences.

To test for interactions, all three independent variables (coverage, crime, and Personal Safety Concern) were entered into a multinomial regression. A model with a three-way interaction term was significant ($\chi^2 = 9.02$, $df = 2$, $p < .02$). The overall model fitting comparison was significant ($\chi^2 = 214.562$, $df = 14$, $p < .001$), although the goodness-of-fit comparison was not calculated. The Nagelkerke pseudo-R^2 was .041, indicating a modest relationship.

The interaction was relatively powerful and fairly easy to interpret. Overall percentages are contained in Table 4.5, and simple means are reported in Table 4.6. Returning to the use of means when they have been discarded for sig-

TABLE 4.4

Average Length of Pleaded Sentence in 4-Year Increments

		Frequency	Percent	Cumulative Percent
Valid	None	1,553	21.3	26.7
	0 to 4 yrs	3,010	41.3	78.3
	4+ to 8 yrs	850	11.7	92.9
	8+ to 12 yrs	230	3.2	96.9
	12+ to 16 yrs	120	1.6	99.0
	16+ to 20 yrs	35	.5	99.6
	20+ to 24 yrs	9	.1	99.7
	24+ to 28 yrs	3	.0	99.8
	28+ to 32 yrs	4	.1	99.8
	32+ to 36 yrs	1	.0	99.8
	36+ to 40 yrs	1	.0	99.9
	40+ or more	8	.1	100.0
	Total	5,824	79.9	
Missing	System	1,469	20.1	
Total		7,293	100.0	

TABLE 4.5

Average Length of Pleaded Sentence Categories by Fear, Actual Crime, and Publicity

	Low Fear				High Fear			
	Actual Crime Low		Actual Crime High		Actual Crime Low		Actual Crime High	
Sentence (months)	Low Publicity (%)	High Publicity (%)	Low Publicity (%)	High Publicity (%)	Low Publicity (%)	High Publicity (%)	Low Publicity (%)	High Publicity (%)
0	16.8	33.7	16.5	24.1	20.3	21.3	27.9	20.5
1 to 50	56.1	43.3	43.7	55.4	53.0	37.5	50.9	42.1
More than 50	27.2	23.1	39.9	20.5	26.7	41.2	21.2	37.4

nificance testing may seem odd, but we believe it is defensible here. The lack of normality confounds significance calculations but doesn't make the mean any more or less meaningful. This is not to say that the final interpretation is entirely unproblematic, only that as long as it is remembered that the means come from a distribution that is skewed toward zero, comparisons of the relative placement between groups are not without merit.

At any rate, using the results with either the dependent variable broken into categories (Table 4.5) or considered as means (Table 4.6) produces an identical interpretation: Crime coverage produces longer pleaded sentences when the fear of crime is high, but shorter sentences when fear of crime is low. The influence of actual crime is of lesser theoretical concern to the questions addressed here, but it is interesting to note that when fear of crime is high, actual crime reduces pleaded sentence lengths, but when fear of crime is low actual crime increases pleaded sentence lengths. These patterns are represented graphically in Fig. 4.1, which clearly shows a classic crossover interaction effect. It is also interesting to notice that high levels of coverage tend to eliminate differences due to actual crime; in both high and low fear conditions, the means between high and low actual crime areas tend to converge when coverage is high. In the case where fear of crime is low, the influence of actual crime is almost completely eliminated by high amounts of coverage.

The interpretation of the influence of crime coverage is straightforward enough: When fear is high, high levels of coverage result in longer sentences. It is easy to imagine that prosecutors in high-fear areas do not want to appear soft on crime and thus are less likely to make plea deals resulting in lower pleaded sentence lengths. When fear is low, it is especially interesting to notice that high levels of coverage result in lower pleaded sentences. At least two ex-

TABLE 4.6

**Average Length of Pleaded Sentence Means by Fear,
Actual Crime, and Publicity**

| | | Fear: Personal | | |
Actual Crime	Safety	Publicity	Mean	Standard Deviation
Low	Low	Low	25.9	3.16
		High	24.6	1.45
	High	Low	44.7	2.68
		High	47.0	3.69
High	Low	Low	51.8	5.47
		High	25.7	4.12
	High	Low	27.0	2.14
		High	42.9	2.69

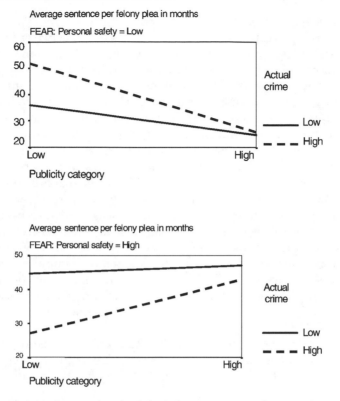

FIG. 4.1. Plots of average length of pleaded sentences versus fear, actual crime, and publicity.

planations come easily to mind. First, if the prosecutor knows that public opinion is not strong, the many advantages to a plea bargain—the reduction of case load, avoiding expensive and difficult trials, eliminating the risk of losing—can be gained without risk of public reprisal. Prosecutors may thus offer better deals to get more of them, or may simply be willing to offer a better deal in the absence of public pressure. Second, if fear of crime is low, it could be that the public is more attuned to civil rights issues and is more likely to evaluate criminal justice issues through a lens of fairness and equity rather than a law and order mentality. If this is the case, the prosecutor could expect more public reprisal from undue harshness or unfairness than from appearing soft on crime (something like this happened after the 11 surviving Branch Davidians were convicted of weapons violations and 5 were given extremely long sentences in June 1994; the jury foreperson publicly chastised the judicially imposed sentence), and thus public focus might serve defendant interests and result in more favorable plea bargains.

It is much harder to interpret the influence of actual crime. The most intuitive relationship to expect is one where higher levels of actual crime result in higher caseloads and more prison overcrowding, resulting in more plea bargains of shorter length. High-crime areas actually have slightly longer average pleaded sentences (33.63 vs. 31.75), and the influence of actual crime seems to depend to a large extent on fear of crime and levels of crime coverage in the media. Of greatest concern here, of course, is how the level of actual crime might alter the effect of coverage, and an intriguing pattern emerges in Table 4.6. One possibility has to do with prison crowding and public opinion. Legal systems must balance the concerns of maintaining a working prison system with maintaining legitimacy in the eyes of the public that prefers harsh sentences. Imagine that less crowded prisons are easier to maintain but public opinion is a greater concern. When fear of crime is low, courts need not fear public disapproval of being soft on crime, and courts in high-crime areas can reduce sentence lengths as a strategy for dealing with prison crowding. When fear of crime is high, courts do fear appearing soft on crime and therefore do not pursue the strategy. In conclusion, high crime tends to encourage lower pleaded sentences where fear is low, tends to encourage longer pleaded sentences where fear is high, and tends to lose its effect altogether when media attention is high.

A snapshot of these findings shows this relationship between coverage and sentence lengths: Pretrial publicity lowers sentences when fear of crime is low, raises sentences when fear of crime is high, and has the greatest affect in high-crime areas.

Results: Trial Conviction Percentage

The distribution of convictions following trial was not normal but was instead skewed heavily toward each pole; 80.2% of defendants were convicted on all counts and 12.4% of defendants were acquitted on all counts. For this analysis the remaining 7.4% of cases were split in half, creating a single dichotomous variable segmented into defendants convicted on fewer than half of the charges they faced (15.6%) and defendants convicted on more than half of the charges (84.4%). Of the 7,293 total defendants analyzed, 595 had taken at least one charge to trial and had valid data for analysis.

A chi-square test indicated a nearly significant relationship between crime coverage and trial conviction percentage ($\chi^2 = 3.813$, $df = 1$, $p = .051$). Defendants in high-coverage areas had lower conviction rates (82.2% of defendants fell in the "more than half" category) than those in low-coverage areas (88.3% in the "more than half" category); Cramer's V was .08.

To test for interactions, all three independent variables (crime coverage, crime rate, and Personal Safety Concern) were entered into a multinomial regression. A model with a three-way interaction term was not significant;

however, a model including two-way interactions was significant ($\chi^2 =$ 18.563, $df = 6$, $p < .005$) and the goodness-of-fit comparison was not significant ($\chi^2 = .34$, $df = 1$, $p = .56$), both indicating a good model fit. The Nagelkerke pseudo-R^2 was .053, indicating a modest relationship. Of the three possible two-way interactions, significance was obtained for the fear by coverage interaction ($\chi^2 = 4.861$, $df = 1$, $p < .05$) and the crime by fear interaction ($\chi^2 = 7.920$, $df = 1$, $p < .005$). No further analysis of the crime by fear interaction was conducted because it did not include crime coverage and thus had no explanatory potential for the questions addressed here.

The results for the coverage by fear interaction are included in Table 4.7. When fear is low, a high level of coverage raises the percentage of defendants in the more-than-half conviction category from 75.8% to 81.0%. When fear is high, high coverage drops percentages in the same category from 90.6% to 84.1%. Thus, fear interacts with crime coverage such that in low fear areas high coverage raises conviction rates, but in high fear areas it lowers conviction rates. This finding is, obviously, counterintuitive.

The reasons that publicity might actually help defendants have already been explored in chapter 2, but the challenge in light of this finding is to explain why publicity might help defendants only when public fear of crime is high. One possibility is that judges are primed to apply remedies only when they perceive trial coverage to create bias against defendants. In areas where crime is generally publicized but the public does not fear crime, judges may not perceive that the publicity poses any special threat to a fair trial, because the public does not appear to have whipped itself into an antidefendant mood. Where coverage is high and the public has a greater fear of crime, however, judges may then perceive a greater need to safeguard defendant interests. This

TABLE 4.7

The Fear by Publicity Interaction for Trial Conviction Percentage

	Fear: Personal Safety							
	Low				High			
	Publicity				Publicity			
	Low		High		Low		High	
	Trial Outcome Percentages		Trial Outcome Percentages		Trial Outcome Percentages		Trial Outcome Percentages	
	Count	%	Count	%	Count	%	Count	%
Less than half conviction	8	24.2%	45	19.0%	17	9.4%	23	15.9%
More than half conviction	25	75.8%	192	81.0%	163	90.6%	122	84.1%

explanation hinges on judges being able to distinguish between publicity levels and public mood, however, and such may be a dubious assumption for a government official who is generally more insulated from public pressure than others.

Alternatively, it is possible that the sorts of cases that go to trial may be different in high-coverage/high-fear areas. Recall that there are fewer cases with plea-bargained outcomes in high-coverage/high-fear areas, and although this may occur for many reasons, at least one is that prosecutors feel they will appear soft on crime by entering a plea bargain (Pritchard, 1990). If this is the case, it may also be true that fewer truly innocent defendants or defendants who can present a strong case will be offered plea deals they are willing to accept, and as a result more defendants will conclude that, relative to the plea deal being offered, the chances at trial are worth it. In other words, harsh plea offers by the prosecutor encourage defendants with a strong case to take the case to trial. If more defendants with strong cases go to trial, defendant win rates should increase, which is in fact the pattern of results observed here.

Regardless of cause, this is now the third examination of actual trial results that has found that heightened levels of coverage or publicity actually lower conviction rates. The implications of this pattern have been discussed earlier and are examined at length in the final chapter, but at this point it is worth mentioning that it seems undeniable that in actual practice publicity helps rather than hinders defendants, at least as conviction rates are concerned. Although we are not confident we have offered a conclusive explanation for why coverage might help defendants, it is clear that these data do not support the conclusion that pretrial publicity is an insidious force that survives all trial remedies. In actual trials, coverage has the influence of lowering conviction rates, and thus an antidefendant influence that survives remedies is not apparent in actual practice.

Results: Length of Sentence at Trial

Finally, the length of tried sentence was analyzed. The distribution of the dependent variable was not normal (see Table 4.8) but was instead skewed heavily toward zero with a notable number of outliers at the extremely high values. To create a workable dependent variable the cases were split roughly into quartiles, with an approximately equal number of defendants in each of four categories: zero to 12 months per convicted count (23.2%), 12.1 to 46 months (26.9%), 46.1 to 121 months (29.0%), and 121.1 months or more (20.9%). Of the 7,293 total defendants analyzed, 521 were convicted on at least one charge at trial and had valid data for analysis.

A chi-square test indicated a significant relationship between coverage and length of tried sentence ($\chi^2 = 9.749$, $df = 3$, $p = .021$). Compared to defendants in low-coverage areas, defendants in high-coverage areas were more likely to

TABLE 4.8

Average Sentence Length per Trial Conviction in 4-Year Increments

		Frequency	Percent	Cumulative Percent
Valid	None	42	.6	8.1
	0 to 4 yrs	227	3.1	51.6
	4+ to 8 yrs	103	1.4	71.4
	8+ to 12 yrs	49	.7	80.8
	12+ to 16 yrs	31	.4	86.8
	16+ to 20 yrs	11	.2	88.9
	20+ to 24 yrs	5	.1	89.8
	24+ to 28 yrs	5	.1	90.8
	28+ to 32 yrs	6	.1	91.9
	32+ to 36 yrs	21	.3	96.0
	40+ or more	21	.3	100.0
	Total	521	7.1	
Missing	System	6772	92.9	
Total		7293	100.0	

fall into the lowest sentence category (27.2% vs. 16.5%), were less likely to fall into either of the mid-range sentence categories (23.9% vs. 32.0% for 12–46 months and 27.5% vs. 31.4% for 46–120 months), and had an almost equal chance of falling into the highest sentence category (21.4% vs. 20.1%). Cramer's V was .137. Generally speaking, defendants in high-coverage areas fell into lower sentence categories in greater proportion than defendants in low-coverage areas.

To test for interactions, all three independent variables (coverage, crime, and Personal Safety Concern) were entered into a multinomial regression. A model with a three-way interaction term was not significant. Neither was a model built on two-way interactions. A model with only main effects was significant ($\chi^2 = 24.839$, $df = 9$, $p = .003$) with a Nagelkerke pseudo-R^2 of .05. Only fear of crime emerged as significant and no further analysis was pursued, as it had no relation to coverage, although higher levels of fear were associated with longer sentence lengths. Thus, the only significant finding in terms of pretrial publicity is the main effect for the level of coverage on sentence length, and an analysis of the categories suggests that greater coverage lowers sentence length.

If categories are not used and instead raw averages are calculated, however, defendants in high-coverage areas actually average longer sentences, although the standard deviations for those averages are quite high. In low-coverage areas, convicted defendants have an average sentence of 94.99 months per count with a standard deviation of 124.8 ($n = 194$), whereas in areas with higher levels of coverage the average sentence per count is 126.6 with a standard deviation of 281.2 ($n = 327$). The difference in averages is not statistically significant ($t = 1.762$, $df = 1/519$, $p = .079$ with equal variances not assumed), due understandably to the large and unequal standard deviations. A small number of cases account for the higher average and standard deviation in the high-coverage areas; low-coverage areas have only 3 cases with average sentences of 666 months and no cases with a higher average. High-coverage areas, by contrast, have 6 cases with average sentences of 666 months and 8 cases with longer average sentences. When all cases with an average sentence per conviction greater than 666 are excluded, the means become closer with lower averages in high-coverage areas (94.99, $n = 194$ in low coverage areas, vs. 89.05, $n = 319$ in high coverage areas), the standard deviations become virtually identical (124.8 vs. 131.6), and the alpha level rises ($t = .51$, $df = 1/511$, $p = .613$ with equal variance assumed).

This pattern of results gets to the heart of how central tendency should be measured in relation to the pattern of results typical in pretrial publicity research. Relying on simple averages, as has been done in the past (e.g., Bruschke & Loges, 1999), may be misleading. Distributions are not normal, and the exclusion of a small number of cases radically changes the pattern of results—differences that appear intuitive and suggestive of significance evaporate entirely when the most extreme instances are removed. At a bare minimum, this phenomenon points to the advantages of selecting a method, such as the multinomial regression, that is free from assumptions about distribution and dispersion. Such an approach is not a panacea, however. The intuitively derived four-category system used here does not do a much better job of dealing with the eight outlying cases, and in fact lumps together sentences of 10 years (120 months), 55 years (666 months), and death sentences. Future research should explore more advanced analytical methods that can better deal with the distributions characterized by a small number of extreme outliers in one condition (high coverage) but not the other (low coverage).

Nonetheless, even without more sophisticated models, taking the data obtained here and adding a healthy dose of common sense it is possible to see striking patterns in the data. In general, areas with higher levels of crime coverage have lower sentences. The four-category scheme reveals that high-coverage areas place a greater percentage of defendants in the lowest sentence category, fewer defendants in the mid-range sentence categories, an equal percentage of defendants in the highest category, and no defendants in the highest end of the highest sentence category. When the highest eight outliers are excluded, defendants in high-coverage areas actually have lower average sentences than those in low-publicity areas (although not to a statistically significant degree). At the same time, it is noteworthy that all eight outlying cases occur in the high-coverage areas, as do all death-penalty cases. The pattern appears to be that, in general, courts in high-coverage areas tend to mete out lower average sentences at trial, but in a very few instances (about 2.5%) will issue their harshest possible sentences.

Each finding deserves its own explanation. The general tendency of crime coverage to produce lower sentences can be explained by the same factors already described in earlier chapters: the tendency of publicity to attract better representation, get a defendant greater attention, and so on. The tendency of coverage to produce extremely harsh sentences in a very few number of cases might be due to a number of factors. It could be that legal practitioners sensitive to public pressure might realize that the public might fear crime but base its collective impression only on those few cases that it chooses to pay attention to. Thus, by handing out extremely harsh sentences to those few defendants the public will be aware of, the legal system can maintain an overall appearance of harshness on crime, even if mean sentences lengths are lower. It may also be that particularly heinous crimes generate both more coverage and higher sentences.

Discussion: How Do General Levels of Crime Coverage Influence Defendants?

The question "Do general levels of crime coverage create bias against defendants?" ends up being three different questions with three different answers. At the pretrial level, a high amount of coverage is good for defendants if fear of crime is low but bad for defendants where fear of crime is high. Generally, high levels of coverage in conjunction with high public fear of crime result in fewer plea bargains being offered and longer average sentences attached to plea deals. Conversely, in low-fear-of-crime areas, defendants in high-coverage areas enter into more plea bargains with shorter average sentences. It is hard to conclude from these data that the coverage alone produces an antidefendant bias, but it does appear that where public fear of crime overlaps with high levels of coverage (a chance occurrence, because we find that coverage is not correlated with public fear), defendants face some disadvantages they would not encounter in areas where crime is less highly publicized.

At the trial conviction stage, the pattern reverses entirely and coverage plus fear of crime actually improves a defendant's chances. This might be due either to increased judicial vigilance to guarantee a fair trial, the sort of case that eventually gets to trial in an area with high amounts of coverage and high fear of crime, or to some reason not imagined here. Regardless of the ultimate explanation, coverage is associated with defendants avoiding conviction in general, and that effect is more pronounced in areas with high fear of crime. This finding, of course, is in direct contradiction to the expectations raised by the findings of laboratory research.

At the trial sentence stage, coverage appears to be good for most defendants but extremely bad for a very few of them. In general, coverage will result in lower sentences, but for a small portion of defendants will result in extremely harsh sentences, including sentences of over 50 years, life imprisonment, and the death penalty.

CONCLUSION: PRETRIAL PUBLICITY IN THE WAKE OF MEDIA THEORY

Whether this pattern of results ultimately speaks to fairness or unfairness for the defendant is a discussion reserved for a later chapter, but a few points are worth dwelling on here. First, this analysis has generally revealed that a cultivation-type approach can be valuable. The patterns of results are interesting and add additional insight into how coverage might influence trials in actual practice. The observed differences are at least as large as those found in controlled laboratory settings and the pattern of results just as intellectually stimulating. In some ways, this analysis highlights some possible distinctions between types of media not recognized in traditional cultivation theory. These data do not support the hypothesis that high coverage of crime produces a public fear of crime. In fact, news coverage of crime and fear of crime are uncorrelated. Thus, fear of crime must be generated by some factor other than news coverage. Entertainment media, personal interactions, culture, and neighborhood characteristics are all vying candidates to explain fear of crime. Because much entertainment television is broadcast nationally, to some extent the nonlocal news portion of the television menu of residents in our study cities is similar. The extent to which television on the whole (including entertainment television) can cultivate fear of crime, and the extent to which such TV-cultivated fear is amplified in personal interaction, are useful hypotheses for cultivation theory to explore, although we cannot directly test such hypotheses with our data. One important conclusion we can offer is that news coverage is not irrelevant, but how it functions is activated by fear of crime. Thus, media theories may benefit by discarding the notion that media work in an all-encompassing system with the power to completely determine public attitudes and experience. Instead, media coverage is one factor that interacts with a host of others to influence social life and, in this particular case, trial outcomes.

Second, the very process of trying to separate out all variables and devise a reasonable strategy of data analysis has highlighted how many features of trial practice are not incorporated into laboratory research designs. Setting aside questions of jury selection, laboratory realism, and deliberation, in actual practice criminal defendants face a process with decisions made at various points, both before and during trials. Most defendants never get to trial, and to focus exclusively on the trial, the least frequently enacted part of the process, is to miss much of the richness of the legal system's functioning. The four-stage dependent variable scheme utilized here—measuring separately plea bargain rates, plea bargain outcomes, trial conviction percentages, and trial sentence outcomes—represents what we feel to be a considerable advance in the ability of our analytical tools to accurately represent the phenomena we wish to understand.

Third, and this may be nothing more than continually whipping the now long-deceased pony, the results of actual trials do not bear out the laboratory conclusion that pretrial publicity is a single, ominous force whose nefarious influence cannot be counteracted by any other factor. The mere fact that areas with the most crime coverage do not exhibit the highest conviction rates points to the conclusion that something other than coverage must be exerting a counterbalancing influence. The fact is that three field studies have now all reported the identical conclusion that high levels of pretrial publicity do not increase and may actually reduce conviction rates. No doubt defenders of laboratory research will make the valid point that in field research, a number of uncontrolled factors might intervene to upset the purity of the test, and that there might be something systematically different in the field that makes the comparisons uneven. Importantly, the comparison of laboratory to field research just suggested is synonymous with saying that laboratory findings do not extrapolate to actual practice. Laboratory research may eventually claim a pretrial influence when all other things are held equal, and the control of the laboratory guarantees the equality of all other things. In the field, things may be unequal. At the very least, these patterns of results present the challenge to researchers of specifying what it is that is unequal. What factor is it that is able to reverse the laboratory influence of pretrial publicity? Focusing on this question may help us move beyond the laboratory versus field debates, improve our understandings of how media systems and communication practices influence our legal system, and perhaps point to more effective remedies than have been currently imagined.

CHAPTER FIVE

Conclusions

"I will bring such a lawsuit against the Brahmin and old Buldeo and the others as shall eat the village to the bone. They shall pay me twice over for my crops untilled and my buffaloes unfed. I will have a great justice." Mowgli laughed. "I do not know what justice is ..." (Rudyard Kipling, *The Jungle Book*, p. 169)

This chapter has three major tasks. First, summaries are in order. The answers to the four main questions of the book, spaced irregularly throughout thus far, are packaged in a neat little section. The three main propositions of the book—the knowledge–guilt hypothesis, the cumulative remedy hypothesis, and the structural paradox—are presented along with the evidence for them. Research findings are summarized. Second, these conclusions will be connected to broader theories. One unsettling facet of pretrial publicity research thus far is its largely atheoretical nature. To be sure, there have been commentators who have suggested theories and theorists who have attempted to apply various rubrics to the findings of empirical research. However, regardless of the research orientation, very little empirical work has *started* with a theoretical orientation, and little of the scholarship is programmatic. Neither have competing theories been compared and contrasted with one another. Given the disparate research findings, lining up the theories that might seek to explain them is work long overdue. Third, this chapter looks to the future and outlines what still needs to be done. As open as many of the questions that pertain to pretrial publicity are, the field will not be wanting for research questions in the coming decades. These three tasks can be summarized as: What do we know? What does it mean? What remains to be done?

IN SUMMARY: WHAT DO WE KNOW NOW?

This book began with four basic questions. The first was whether pretrial publicity biases trial outcomes at all. The first conclusion of this book, and it may be one of the most important, is that current reviews have vastly overstated the case for a pretrial publicity effect. If the number of existing laboratory studies are divided into three groups, including those that demonstrate a pretrial publicity effect, those that fail to demonstrate a pretrial publicity effect, and those that produce mixed results, the groups have an equal number of publications. Other reviews, most notably that of Studebaker and Penrod (1997), have simply not included all extant studies or interpreted them in a more unambiguous light than is warranted. The most impressive meta-analysis to date, completed by Steblay et al. (1999), should be interpreted with two caveats. First, the meta-analytic technique is not especially well suited to the instance where a small number of studies produce contrasting results, a condition that obtains in this instance. Second, it is not directly comparable to the current review because the two efforts, although they did include a number of studies in common, each reviewed a number of studies not considered by the other.

These are, loosely speaking, methodological questions, or at least questions of how current studies should be counted. There are two additional substantive issues that separate the current reviews from those issued previously. First, our review gives little or no credence to studies that did not include trial evidence, whereas each of the reviews identified earlier accepted them as relatively unproblematic. Our reasons for discounting them are straightforward enough: There is no instance in our justice system where a defendant is convicted at trial in the absence of the presentation of evidence, and current research shows that trial evidence is among the most important factors in determining the outcome of a case. The work of Simon (1966), Davis (1986), and Freedman and Burke (1996) has shown that trial evidence can eliminate a publicity effect. Knowing how jurors decide cases in the absence of trial evidence is, at best, trivial.

Second, the cumulative remedy hypothesis is taken seriously here but is by and large not considered in other reviews. Most basically, the idea is that remedies working together can be more effective than remedies applied in isolation. The evidence for this is both empirical and speculative. Empirically, both Kerwin and Shaffer (1994) and London and Nunez (2000) produced results to demonstrate that deliberation and instructions succeed in combination, even when each may fail in isolation. Speculatively, we rely on the commonsense conclusion that if a number of remedies are all attempted in a single trial—for example, juror selection, judicial instructions, trial evidence, deliberation, and natural delays—pretrial publicity must survive all five remedies plus any interaction between combinations of those factors. Thus, pretrial publicity can influence the outcome of a trial only when all remedies and their interactions fail at once. We posit that this might happen less often than is commonly supposed.

Surprisingly, there is even evidence that at least some types of publicity can actually help some defendants in some situations. Davis (1986) found a boomerang effect for sensational publicity, Otto et al. (1994) found that weak inadmissible statements actually increased the chances of acquittal, and Riedel (1993) and Mullin et al. (1996) found that coverage espousing the evils of rape actually makes male jurors more prone to acquittal. Kovera (2002) found that regardless of its slant, media exposure can offset preexisting biases.

When field research is considered, the case for a pretrial publicity effect becomes even more tenuous. The field work of Bruschke and Loges (1999), buttressed by the data offered in chapter 3, suggests that in practice highly publicized trials have conviction rates identical with those of trials that receive no publicity at all. There is anything but a clear, linear influence of pretrial publicity on trial verdicts. When field research proceeds in a theoretical fashion and looks for a cultivation effect, as we have done in chapter 4, the influence of pretrial publicity interacts with public fear of crime in a series of nonintuitive ways. Generally, high levels of publicity plus high fear of crime are bad for defendants at the pretrial stage, but good for defendants at the trial stage. At any rate, areas with the highest amounts of crime coverage do not exhibit the highest criminal conviction rates, as might be expected if the biasing influence of pretrial publicity were pernicious, resistant to remedy, and of a meaningful magnitude.

In short, there is not a pretrial publicity effect that is powerful and able to survive all remedies. There is even some evidence that pretrial publicity might help defendants. There may yet exist a pretrial publicity effect that can be detected with strict control in laboratory conditions, and we interpret this to mean that there may be a pretrial publicity effect that emerges in some very specific conditions in actual courtrooms. This directs us to our second question.

If publicity might plausibly influence the opinion of jurors, how and when might it do so? Many possible factors and limitations have been discussed throughout the book, but here we focus on four basic conditions that we believe must be met before pretrial publicity can materially damage the interests of the defense. First, the jurors must be exposed to the publicity. The knowledge–guilt hypothesis suggests that the more the jurors know about the case, the more they will presume guilt. This hypothesis is borne out by the research that shows that jurors exposed to pretrial information will, at least in the absence of trial evidence, presume defendant guilt to a greater degree than jurors without any information. The level of publicity that is damaging is a more open question. The work of Pritchard and Hughes (1997) and Surette (1992) suggests that a very few cases will garner the most publicity, and thus it is in those especially well-publicized trials that concern is most warranted. On the other hand, some field research has shown that those cases with the lowest amount of coverage (but some level of coverage greater than zero) actually display the highest defendant conviction rates. There is an additional question about the number of jurors who must be exposed to publicity before it can survive deliberation. Because a single juror holding out for the defense can result in a hung jury, it is hard to imagine that pretrial publicity can bias a final jury decision if only a few jurors have ever seen it. Deliberation does appear to be able to weed out bad information, at least a decent chunk of the time.

Second, pretrial publicity can only have an influence when all remedies fail at the same time. If voir dire does a good job of finding jurors who have not been exposed to publicity, there is little chance of a direct influence. Natural and court-imposed delays, judicial admonitions, trial evidence, and deliberations are all hedges against publicity successfully biasing the final decision. If any remedy works in isolation, or in combination with some other remedy, the influence of pretrial publicity can be corrected. This is perhaps one of the most crucial conclusions that we have to offer: *We believe that pretrial publicity does not usually bias decisions in actual cases because of the care courts take to apply remedies, and nothing we have to say here should be taken as a reason that pretrial publicity need not be remedied.*

Third, for pretrial publicity to alter the outcome of a trial, the evidence must be close. Virtually all of the laboratory research has studied the instance where the evidence is very close and where conviction and acquittal are equally likely outcomes. If the laboratory research is taken as fully consistent and at face value, it can still only be taken to mean that pretrial publicity can alter juror opinions when the evidence is exceedingly close. Furthermore, the research evidence is quite conclusive on the importance of trial evidence on the final jury outcome. Given that jurors will try their best to come to a fair conclusion based on trial evidence (the research evidence suggests rather powerfully that they do), if there is a means by which pretrial publicity can muddle a jury's decision it is likely to be through a distortion of evidence interpretation. The ability of pretrial information to color the interpretation of the evidence is most nefarious when the evidence is close enough that coloring will make a difference.

Fourth, the more probative the pretrial information is, the more likely the jury is to be persuaded by it. The research rather unanimously demonstrates that what jurors want to do is to come to a just decision, take their task seriously, and behave as optimal decision makers (see Bornstein & Rajki, 1994; London & Nunez, 2000; Sommers & Kassin, 2001). It is easy to imagine that in the case where a juror is trying hard to come to a just decision, *and* the information presented at trial does not clearly point to a just conclusion, *and* information presented outside the trial materially points to guilt or innocence, a juror will rely on the best information that they have at their disposal, regardless of its source.

These four conditions speak to situations where trial evidence might upset jury verdicts at trial. There are other stages of the process, most notably the pretrial and sentencing phases, where pretrial publicity might produce bias independent of these four states of affairs. Those possibilities are considered later.

The third major question is: Given that there may be some conditions under which publicity is damaging, what remedies are appropriate? Contrary to opinions published elsewhere (e.g., Fulero, 1987; Studebaker & Penrod, 1997), we believe that it is not generally necessary to pursue the most expensive and time-consuming remedies, notably a change of venue. Instead, there are three relatively cheap and useful remedies that should do much to eliminate pretrial bias. First, voir dire should include a short quiz about factual items that have been presented in the media. If jurors can answer a third or more of the questions correctly, they should not be allowed to hear the trial. Second, even if the quiz procedure is maintained, individual and sequestered voir dire is likely to be more effective in eliminating juror bias. Third and finally, attention to improving jury instructions can make them more effective. Needless to say, trial evidence should be presented and jurors should deliberate.

The fourth and final major question is how pretrial publicity relates to the overall question of trial fairness. The answer is to be found in the structural paradox, the unwelcome condition for a defendant where something that is quite bad from the perspective of juror psychology might be perversely useful in formulating an overall strategy. The structural paradox stems from legal-economic theory, and is explored in full depth at the end of the next section.

ADDING THEORY: WHAT DOES IT ALL MEAN?

Theories are unusual things. They are undoubtedly abstract, although some are much more directly related to concrete practice than others. They are informed by and inform research results, although they undoubtedly enjoy a privileged place in the academy. It is not uncommon to find snooty theorists who presume themselves superior to the doggerel researchers, or the theorist who grates at having ideas put to empirical test. One can almost see the ephemeral specter of Albert Einstein floating through university halls, repeating for all eternity, "If the facts don't fit the theory, so much worse for the facts." But the truly unusual thing about theories is how often they contradict one another and how noncomparable they can be. Different theories often have different starting points, and this makes them difficult to reconcile.

There are at least three major theoretical orientations that bear on the issue of pretrial publicity. The first, and certainly the most dominant, is the psychological perspective. Of the articles reviewed in chapter 2, 9 in 10 were either written by psychologists or published in psychology journals. The second, and less prominent, is media theory that has largely developed in the communication field. Where the psychological theories are primarily concerned with how individuals process pretrial information, the communication theories tend to be concerned with how characteristics of the mass media influence social thought in general terms, although individual processing of media messages is certainly an important variable. Most of what we have to say about this is in chapter 4, although it bears repeating that those immersed in the study of mass media have generally decided that if there is anything to be found in the way of a mass media effect it is in studying the multiple, repeated messages on a large group of people rather than studying the influence an individual message has on an individual recipient. There is very little in contemporary media theory to suggest that a pretrial publicity effect of the sort supposed by the psychological theories exists in a way likely to contaminate an entire jury pool.

The third and largely unaddressed theory is economic-legal theory, or a theory of how the legal system works. A point we have made earlier is how silly communication researchers might look trying to delve into case law, but we believe that it is possible for those trained in communication to be reasonably intelligent on the issue of system functioning. We are not arrogant enough to believe we can accomplish this without relying heavily on the work of those employed by law schools. At any rate, if the account of the legal formalists is taken as more normative than descriptive, and the legal realists have a decent point about the importance of extralegal factors on the outcomes of the legal system, it becomes possible to explain why, even if pretrial publicity might create a degree of bias in the minds of some individual jurors, even negative publicity might be a good thing for a defendant overall. The first and third of these approaches to theory are fleshed out in more detail later; the second approach was explored earlier.

PSYCHOLOGICAL THEORIES

A much-made point is that the work on pretrial publicity thus far has proceeded in the absence of theorizing (Lieberman & Arndt, 2000). Because the biasing influence of pretrial publicity is such an applied question, little work has gone into the underlying processes that might activate it. What theoretical work has been done seems to focus more on the type of reaction that publicity produces—a biasing effect, halo or reverse halo effect, reactance, and so forth. We do not correct this shortcoming in its entirety here; the question is indeed applied enough that very specific and practical answers are important in their own right. Nonetheless, we wish to point out the sort of psychological theory that will be necessary to explain the issue at hand.

To our thinking, although research that seeks to explain underlying psychological mechanisms has much to add to the discussion, there is a more central question that deserves focus: If most people can't remember the coverage they view in the media, how can it influence a trial decision? A baseline issue, before questions of content processing become relevant, is whether messages perceived unconsciously influence later attitudes and decisions, and even more importantly how messages perceived unconsciously fare when they contradict messages perceived consciously. It is evident that at present there is a schism between how most people encounter the media in their daily lives and the way publicity has been manipulated in pretrial publicity research. That schism is spelled out in earlier chapters. To summarize a lot of research in a single sentence, most people encounter the media casually, attend to very little of it, and remember even less.

We take as a starting point the premise that not much media content is recollected by the average media consumer. Vidmar's (2002) account of the "Uncle Six" experiment is quite telling in this regard. Even when presented with news coverage with massive publicity about "Uncle Six," none of 109 people could spontaneously link the defendant to the coverage a relatively short time later. If those results are typical of media consumers, then for pretrial publicity to influence the outcome of a trial it must be possible for jurors to have experienced perception and attitude change beneath the level of their conscious awareness. Broadly speaking, two conditions are possible (Gass & Seiter, 1999). "Subliminal" persuasion occurs when individuals have their later attitudes influence by stimuli that they experienced beneath the level of human perception. A picture flashed so quickly the human mind could not explicitly process the image is an example of subliminal persuasion. "Supraliminal" persuasion, on the other hand, involves images or messages that can be seen and heard but gather little attention. Product placement in movies, where a manufacturer might have a billboard in an action scene that advertises a particular product, is an example of supraliminal persuasion.

Gass and Seiter (1999) had this to say about subliminal persuasion:

> We believe much of the information published in the popular press about subliminal persuasion can be dismissed as 'junk science.' Popular reports of subliminal effects typically haven't used control groups.... None to our knowledge have employed a *double-blind procedure* [italics in original] ... nor have they been published in reputable scholarly journals ... the few studies that have reported positive results haven't been successfully replicated. (p. 297)

This rather dim view is not the only one. Experts in the area contend that subliminal effects can be demonstrated, but only under very carefully controlled conditions and with proper experimental techniques. One reviewer counted 61 supportive studies, 22 with mixed results, and 14 that were nonconfirming (Masling, 1992, p. 268). Masling wrote:

> Obtaining mixed results, however, is another matter and usually occurs for one of two reasons: (1) The subliminal condition produces an effect, but so does the supraliminal, eliminating unconscious processing as a necessary condition; and (2) the experimental subjects respond as predicted, but so do the controls, ruling out the message employed as unique to the experimental results. (p. 268)

Thus, the disconfirming results of the subliminal research might actually show that both subliminal and supraliminal messages are effective. However, in the context of pretrial publicity, for us to fear that pretrial publicity would survive the influence of trial evidence it would need to be the case that the subconscious supraliminal message (pretrial publicity) was more powerful than the consciously perceived supraliminal message (the trial evidence). There is little in the subliminal research to date that suggests this is the case, as Masling's interpretations demonstrate.

But the story does not end there. Even if we can perceive and be persuaded by messages that we are not consciously aware of, there are three possibilities that confound a simple relationship between perception and attitude change. First is the question of which stimuli we perceive. We can't possibly perceive everything. At any given moment we are bombarded by a series of images and sounds. If something as simple as "color" can have even a supraliminal effect, at any given moment a normal human can probably identify eight distinct colors in his or her line of vision. As I type this, my central focus is on the screen, but I can also see a gray keyboard, an orange Winnie-the-pooh sticker on that keyboard, a blue Zip drive, a green can of Silly String, a black brush for my cat, a red box with an amber scorpion in it, yellow tape, and a purple insignia on my mouse. Which of those would be the one to persuade me? Which do I perceive? Masling put it this way:

> We know little about effective parameters for dosage, exposure time of the stimulus, intervals between exposures, number of words and letters that can be understood at rapid exposure times, and magnitude of the stimuli. Nor do we have reliable information about the duration of the effect after a subject is exposed to a subliminal stimulus. (p. 272)

The second question involves what happens when contradictory supraliminal messages are received. What happens if a juror sees one supraliminal message that speaks to defendant guilt (an accusing glance cast by the judge) but another that speaks to innocence (a smile directed at the defendant by a prosecution witness, or nice clothes on the defendant)? This may be one of the many mysteries about subliminal and supraliminal persuasion we have yet to unwrangle. Yet it is only if pretrial publicity messages are both pernicious and more powerful than all other possible explicit and implicit stimuli that they might be expected to exert a meaningful influence on trial outcomes.

Third, as Masling (1992, pp. 282–283) indicated, a subliminal message can activate several underlying psychological processes simultaneously, such as fluency, affective, and cognitive processes, and there is no reason to expect that these underlying processes will be consistent. Sensational coverage might, for example, cue attitudes about both defendant guilt and media misrepresentation, or cue emotional feelings of sympathy for the victim and a desire to block the image out to reduce fear.

Research findings make it seem possible that some (if not all) unconsciously perceived messages might make a difference to some audience members. The research does not show that such unconscious predispositions are powerful enough to determine an individual's attitudes, much less a person's decision making on a cognitively involving task. What would be especially useful is a theory that could compare the relative influence of conscious and unconscious persuasion.

One theory that can disentangle these contradictory tendencies is the Elaboration Likelihood Model (Petty & Cacioppo, 1986). At its core, the theory contends that there are two routes to persuasion, labeled the central and the peripheral. Although it is possible to process a message via both channels, one will tend to predominate. Messages that are processed centrally are more carefully considered and scrutinized. The more that an individual feels involved in a message, the more likely he or she is to process the message centrally. Messages that are processed centrally and accepted tend to be held more firmly, to have a longer duration, and to be less resistant to counterpersuasion. In short, the research evidence mustered for the Elaboration Likelihood Model makes it apparent that a clash between a centrally processed and a peripherally processed message is no contest: The centrally processed message will win the day. Similar predictions are offered by the Heuristic Systematic Model (Chaiken, Liberman, & Eagly, 1989). The application to the pretrial publicity question is straightforward. A subconsciously perceived message cannot be processed other than peripherally. It does not exist in conscious awareness to be analyzed. There is every reason to expect that trial evidence will be processed centrally. Jurors take their task seriously and try hard to come up with a good decision; they are highly involved decision makers. Research also confirms that the most dominant factor at the trial is, by far, the quality of the evidence. If the predictions of the Elaboration Likelihood Model are correct, supraliminal bias encountered by jurors and processed peripherally would not be expected to dominate centrally processed messages presented at trial. Shrum (2001) demonstrated that cultivation effects tend to be moderated by central processing.

This brief review is, of course, not intended to be a thorough review of all psychological theory. It is intended to make one central point, which is to identify what sort of psychological theory would be necessary to confirm the view that pretrial publicity is an important factor that survives all remedies. Such a theory cannot rest solely on the underlying explanatory mechanism, such as the halo effect, or some other approach. Currently psychological theorizing has seemed to have just such an emphasis. What is needed instead is a theory that can explain how unconsciously perceived messages interact with consciously perceived messages, and especially how individuals process contradictory information from the two different levels. To be sure, there is much work to be done in this area, but the theories that do the best job of this at present seem to indicate that consciously processed information will win out.

ECONOMIC-LEGAL THEORY

"If wishes were lawyers, doubtless the poor would be well represented"
(Rob Atkinson, 2001, p. 135).

The traditional or "received" view of the court system is often labeled *formalism*. Burns (2001) adapted Leiter's account of the formalist view of law this way:

(1) Law is rationally determinate in that the class of legal reasons justifies one and only one outcome to a legal dispute; (2) judging is mechanical in that judges exercise no discretion and that they do not render decisions by reasoning in ways that are not sanctioned by legal reasons or reach judgments that legal reasons do not justify; and, as a corollary to (1), (3) legal "reasoning" is autonomous in that legal reasons determine a unique result without recourse to non-legal reasons. (pp. 226–227)

Put in slightly different terms, the law and nothing but the law determines the outcome of a case. Criticism of the received view has come from many fronts, most notably from the critical legal studies (CLS) movement and the legal realist approach, and although here is not the place to review in detail the contrasting legal theories and their various permutations, one reasonable conclusion about the debate is that one need not accept the more radical claims of the CLS and realist thinkers to recognize that there are a number of factors other than the law that have been empirically linked to trial outcomes. A nonexhaustive review includes the race, gender, age, education, status, jury experience, personality characteristics, and occupation of the jury, as well as lawyer and witness message style, similarity to the jury, confidence, nonverbal behavior, proxemic behavior, social power, attractiveness, and physical appearance (see Rieke & Stutman, 1990). In the end, it remains possible to debate about whether the formalist view provides a useful prescription for the way that court decisions should be made (Burns thought it did not), but it is increasingly difficult to argue that it provides an accurate and complete description of the legal system.

Of the various nonlegal factors that contribute to trial outcomes, one rather powerful factor is a defendant's economic status. Two strands of research have documented the point; the first is social science, and the second is legal commentary about pro bono work. Social science has repeatedly demonstrated that economic status relates to trial outcomes. In one sample of 2,760 offenders randomly selected from the Florida Department of Corrections, a defendant's socioeconomic status was linked to the sentence received depending on the offense type (D'Alessio & Stolzenberg, 1993). Socioeconomic status and other extralegal factors figured more prominently in the sentencing of violent and moral order offenders, and prior record was more important when sentencing property offenders. There are two explanations for findings of this type. The first is that juries form a bias against defendants at trial. A meta-analytic review of mock trial research found that "low SES defendants were more likely to be found guilty than high SES defendants" (Mazzella & Feingold, 1994). The second explanation for the lower success rates of less wealthy litigants is the quality of representation that they can afford. Field research has shown that lawyer quality is related to sentence length such that defendants who were able to pay a private attorney had shorter sentence lengths (Daudistel et al., 1999). At the appellate level, defendants who have powerful groups offer to support their causes fare better, undoubtedly due to increased resource access before and during the trial. Although one study found that the NAACP-sponsored Legal Defense Fund was ineffective (Tauber, 1998), it also found that the fund's sponsorship was thwarted by a number of other extralegal variables. Subsequent research demonstrated that amicus curiae support did indeed improve a less wealthy litigant's chances, and the contrary findings (such as those of Tauber) were due to a failure to account for the normally high win percentages of wealthy litigants. Songer et al. (2000) wrote:

> The first phase of analysis in this study provided yet another confirmation of the basic thrust of a long series of studies providing support for the insight of Galanter that the "haves" come out ahead in American courts.... While one-shot litigants like individuals with relatively low levels of resources generally have low rates of success in state supreme courts, their chances of victory can be dramatically increased by the intervention of interest groups who will support their position with the filing of an *amicus curiae* brief. (p. 552)

The work of Black (1976) and Emmelman (1994) is especially useful in describing the processes that work against defendants. Studying court-appointed defense attorneys, Emmelman concluded that the social class of criminal defendants related to defense attorneys' interpretive procedures in a way that worked contrary to defense interests. Essentially, Emmelman found that the court system was organized so that persons of middle and upper classes applied their experience and values to judge persons of lower classes. Because they come from deviate knowledge systems, poor defendants do not portray the persona of a virtuous person. Because they associate with others in the lower class, such defendants are also generally unable to call witnesses on their behalf who appear virtuous to decision makers. As a result, even their own court-appointed defense attorneys tend not to presume their innocence, especially the innocence of indigent defendants, and this influences a number of defense tactics and strategies during the pretrial release phase, motions made concerning evidence, plea bargaining, trial practice, and sentencing. Importantly, the social class of the defendants altered the manner in which defense attorneys perceived the strength of evidence against their clients. Emmelman offered two conclusions that are relevant here:

> Because typical indigent defendants are likely to have less credible witnesses (or by the same token, less convincing "facts" to present) than the prosecution or other types of defendants, they tend to have weaker evidence to present on their behalf. ... [T]he cards are generally stacked against such defendants. (p. 13)

In a way that confounds the legal/extralegal distinction of the formalist view, Emmelman concluded that "this study also indicates that social class influences adjudication outcomes not only as an extralegal variable but also as a component of legal variables" (p. 15).

In short, social science research has demonstrated that less wealthy defendants fare more poorly than wealthy defendants, and that this occurs both because they are discriminated against at trial and because they are treated differently prior to the start of the trial. In both legal and extralegal ways, resource-poor defendants do not receive equal treatment from our legal system.

Legal commentary on these matters is generally consistent with the conclusions of the social scientists. For example, one law review article has examined Paula Jones's sexual harassment suit against Bill Clinton and noted that the case brings up two crucial issues, one of which is sexual harassment, and the other equally important question is the chance for fairness given the tremendous imbalance in the access to legal resources in a case that is basically the "low-life-sleazy big-haired-trailer park girl v. The President" (Palmer, Baer, Jasperson, & DeLaat, 2001). Others have taken a broader view. The adversarial system is the key to justice and equal treatment in court; judges and prosecutors are employees of the state, and historical experience has demonstrated that inquisitorial systems with supposedly neutral fact finders have a tremendous antidefendant bias (Freedman, 1998). As such, it is crucial that each side in a legal dispute have the ability to serve as effective adversaries. In many ways, access to a good lawyer is the key to all other rights. As Stephen Bright (1997) put it:

> The right to counsel is clearly the most fundamental constitutional right for a poor person charged with a crime. An attorney is needed to protect the client's rights and marshal the evidence necessary for a fair and reliable determination of guilt or innocence and, if guilty, a proper sentence. (p. 793)

Rights that can't be exercised or enforced have no material meaning in the praxis of life, and the ability to enforce rights is synonymous with being able to win their enforcement in court. Without a good lawyer it is virtually impossible to win in court. Atkinson (2001) put it like this:

Our system of legally regulated market capitalism, for all its manifest virtues, has undeniable short-comings. The most salient, for present purposes, is this: Without careful attention to the distribution of its bounties, the rich tend to get richer and the poor, poorer. Indeed, unless the poor have lawyers, the rich will get the poor themselves, or at least all of theirs that's worth having. (p. 159)

Atkinson concluded that public financing of legal services is essential, and that current pro bono systems are not adequate.

An especially telling account of the state of legal advocacy for poor clients was offered by Bright (1997). Horace Dunkins, an indigent defendant in Alabama, was sentenced to death even though the jury was never told that he was mentally retarded. A second example, the case of Gregory Wilson, is worth quoting at length:

Wilson had no counsel because the state public defender program would not handle the case and the local indigent defense program could not find a lawyer because compensation for defense counsel in capital cases at that time was limited by statute to $2500. When the head of the local indigent defense program urged the judge to order compensation beyond the statutory limit in order to secure a lawyer qualified for such a serious case, the judge refused and suggested that the indigent defense program rent a river boat and sponsor a cruise down the Ohio River to raise money for the defense. The judge eventually obtained counsel by posting a letter in the courthouse asking any member of the bar to take the case with the plea "PLEASE HELP. DESPERATE." ... Not surprisingly, this method of selecting counsel did not produce a "dream team." The lead counsel, William Hagedorn, can charitably be described as well past his prime. He did not have an office or support staff, but practiced out of his home, where a large flashing Budweiser beer sign was prominently displayed. He had never previously handled a death penalty case.... Hagedorn "manifested all the signs of a burned-out alcoholic.... He would ramble and digress. At times he appeared disoriented. He did not make sense.... He seemed incapable of having any meaningful discussion about the case." ... Wilson became even more concerned upon learning that the police had recently executed a search warrant and recovered stolen property in garbage bags from beneath Hagedorn's floor; that Hagedorn had engaged in unethical conduct, including forging a client's name to a check; and that Hagedorn was a "heavy drinker," who had appeared in court drunk on occasion, and was consistently to be found at a bar known as "Kelly's Keg." Mr. Hagedorn had even given the name and telephone number of Kelly's Keg as his business address and telephone number.... But, unlike those with resources, Wilson could not afford another lawyer. Wilson repeatedly objected to being represented by the lawyers appointed by the court. He asked the judge that he be provided with a lawyer who was capable of defending a capital case. The judge refused and proceeded to conduct a trial that was a travesty of justice.

Hagedorn was not even present for parts of the trial. He cross-examined only a few witnesses, including one witness whose direct testimony he missed because he was out of the courtroom. Wilson was sentenced to death. (pp. 793–796)

One additional example is that of George McFarland:

The *Houston Chronicle* described the following spectacle in one of the cases:

Seated beside his client—a convicted capital murderer—defense attorney John Benn spent much of Thursday afternoon's trial in apparent deep sleep.

His mouth kept falling open and his head lolled back on his shoulders, and then he awakened just long enough to catch himself and sit upright. Then it happened again. And again. And again.

Every time he opened his eyes, a different prosecution witness was on the stand describing another aspect of the Nov. 19, 1991, arrest of George McFarland in the robbery-killing of grocer Kenneth Kwan.

When state District Judge Doug Shaver finally called a recess, Benn was asked if he truly had fallen asleep during a capital murder trial.

"It's boring," the 72-year-old longtime Houston lawyer explained…. Court observers said Benn seems to have slept his way through virtually the entire trial.

Attorney Benn's sleeping did not offend the Sixth Amendment, the trial judge explained, because, "the Constitution doesn't say the lawyer has to be awake." (Bright, 1997, p. 829)

Bright took great effort to prove that this example is not an isolated one or limited to a few jurisdictions or geographical regions. The general trend has been inadequate funding for indigent defense (Bright, 1997; Freedman, 1998; Gerber, 2001). Compensation for court-appointed attorneys is such that "lawyers assigned cases are required to choose between working hundreds of hours without compensation or not providing competent representation" (Bright, 1997, p. 827). The point is clear: Although the right to counsel is supposed to exist, criminal defendants have a hard time getting a good attorney to represent them. As Bright put it, "The Supreme Court held in *Gideon* that a poor person facing felony charges 'cannot be assured a fair trial unless counsel is provided for him.' But in the years since, the courts have held that the lawyer need not be aware of the governing law, sober, or even awake" (pp. 786–787).

The point here is not to rant about the failings of the legal system but to theorize about them. As a description of the legal system, the legal realists have a point, and research shows that nonlegal factors can alter the outcome of trials. Empirical evidence and legal commentary seem to agree that one of the crucial factors that comes into play is the economic status of the defendant. Poor defendants face the triple disadvantage of being unable to present a solid case (by virtue of being unable pay for investigation and unable to produce credible witnesses and evidence on their behalf), being presumed guilty by jurors at trial even when the evidence is equal, and being unable to find an effective law-yer who can offset these other disadvantages. Defendants thus enter a system interested in clearing dockets (Bright, 1997), maintaining positive public opin-ions for political purposes (Pritchard, 1990), and controlling costs (Bright, 1997; Gerber, 2001) as much as it is interested in dispensing justice. This view of the legal system is fully consistent with the incredibly high plea-bargaining rates and notably lopsided criminal conviction rates.

Viewed this way, the most onerous burden criminal defendants face is not proving their innocence but mustering the resources to prove their innocence. This provides the key to the structural paradox—criminal defendants must, before all other things, muster the resources to present a defense, and those who can't do so find themselves in the lamentable condition of those defen-dants Bright documented. A defendant in a publicized case has one resource other poor defendants do not—attention. This attention can garner the sup-port of an amicus curiae, better attorneys, or legal defense funds. Interest groups dedicated to crucial legal issues and public opinion have things to gain in publicized cases they do not have in other cases. A public defender faced with a massive caseload must make choices about how to focus limited time and research energy; it is easy to imagine a right-meaning attorney spending more time and effort on the case that he or she knows everyone is watching than on the cases that nobody will ever notice. Additionally, a defendant in a publicized case has at least one issue that other defendants do not have—the publicity itself, which can be cause for a host of pretrial motions and posttrial appeals. The paradox is this: By drawing even negative attention to them-selves, criminal defendants gain the resources they otherwise would not have. If those resources are more important than the potential bias created by the press attention, a defendant has little to lose with publicity. The paradox can also explain, to some extent, the disparate findings of field and laboratory re-search. The point has been made by now that laboratory research can set all other things to equal. In the field, things seem to be ridiculously unequal. Pre-trial publicity equalizes that which is otherwise unequal, and such an influence can offset bias introduced in the minds of jurors.

The structural paradox has two important implications. The first is that less focus should be given to pretrial publicity than to resource equalization. For all the case law and research and trial time devoted to the issue of pretrial public-ity, it may not be the most important, or even a major, factor in the overall cause of justice. What is far, far, more important is defendant access to the le-gal resources necessary to make the adversary system function as it should. The recent revelations about the number of people wrongly convicted of cap-ital offenses are reminder enough that the stakes are high. In short, those interested in reforming the system to make it more fair to defendants would do well to focus their energies on reducing economic inequalities primarily and focus on relatively minor issues of procedure (such as pretrial publicity) as second-tier issues.

The second implication is related to the first, and it is a point taken up by Atkinson (2001) in his advocacy for publicly funded legal defense: The good can be the enemy of the best if it drains resources that are more effectively used elsewhere. A very narrow question is whether pretrial publicity biases trials against defendants; a broader question is how the issue of pretrial publicity fits into the overall scheme of justice. Atkinson took the broad view of socio-economic issues in relation to legal defense in this comment:

> Increasing legal aid to the poor, particularly certain kinds of legal aid, may well be counterproductive. Resources may be diverted from programs that would benefit the poor more; political backlashes or economic dislocates [sic] may reduce the share of the poor rather than expand it; publicly subsidized ideological advocacy on behalf of the poor may unacceptably compromise core liberal values. On these points, we need to listen carefully to the opposition, especially those who can plausibly claim to have the interests of the poor at heart. (p. 167)

In relation to pretrial publicity, we run the risk that focusing so much attention on the question of whether there is a publicity bias to correct for directs attention and resources away from other possible issues. Put differently, the issue of pretrial publicity does not arise in a vacuum but in a political system with multiple interconnections and complex interactions with other issues.

What is most necessary, it seems, is an approach to reform that is not issue driven but that is instead system aware. It seems fruitless to debate the minutiae of legal doctrine when the overall system has fatal flaws, or, in Biblical terms, it seems better to remove the plank in our eye before we worry too much about the splinters. This is, of course, not the way that the system works now. Judge Rudolph Gerber (2001), at the conclusion of 22 years on the bench in Arizona, described that state's approach in a way that seems sadly descriptive nationally: "This state's crime policy has been driven over the past quarter-century by exaggerated fears, political ideology, and electoral opportunism rather than by criminological data. Indeed, no other field of endeavor shows such a chasm between government policy and scholarly research" (pp. 167–168). He concluded that

> this state's lawmakers have linked political success to polishing a tough-on-crime image that translates, first and foremost, into the emphasis on unprincipled legal procedures and draconian severity of punishment that in turn translates into prison as the paradigm of severity. This penchant for severe prison sentences at all costs, including taxes and human lives, obstructs

more realistic, less expensive, more effective, and more just crime policies. (pp. 170–171)

These thoughts do not present an encouraging picture for legal reform, but we add our voices to that of Judge Gerber and call, primarily, for reasoned reactions based on empirical evidence rather than short-term, politically driven solutions.

In fact, this all creates a rather complex politics for this book. It would certainly be possible to read our conclusions to mean that pretrial publicity has no effect, and as a consequence come away with the view that courts need not be vigilant in protecting defendant rights. We sincerely hope that such an interpretation will not be given to our findings. Instead, we offer two other policy prescriptions. First, based on the premise that the absence of pretrial publicity effects is due in large measure to the success of current remedies, we recommend their continued vigilant application, especially in regard to improved voir dire techniques and more effectively devised judicial instructions. We are reluctant to recommend expensive solutions, such as change of venue, both because they are costly and because that cost can further drain resources from an already impoverished system. Second, we heartily endorse efforts to reformulate the justice system in a way that makes resource access a less crucial factor in the outcome of the trial. Part of this solution will require reorienting decision making about the justice system, but part of it will involve greater heed to empirical research as part of the search for a more cost-effective and just system. There seems little reason not to pursue procedures that are both more just and more cost-effective. Until we are, as a society, ready to tackle the broad questions of fairness and resource equity in our legal system, winning small victories for cost-efficiency may not be wasted effort. We hope that the suggestions offered here are steps in that direction.

LOOKING FORWARD: WHAT DO WE STILL NEED TO KNOW?

By any account, we have only begun to scratch the surface of what there is to be known about pretrial publicity. The total number of studies done is less than 50, even with a liberal counting. In comparison to other areas of study, like research on IQ, this number is tiny. Research in this area needs to improve in both quantity and quality, and there are both methodological and substantive issues to improve on.

Thinking first of the methodological issues we need to confront, at least five have been raised in this volume. The first of these is the possibility, introduced by Freedman et al. (1998), that asking jurors for their pretrial opinions is a research artifact that might skew results. It is of course true that unless jurors are asked for their pretrial opinions it will be very difficult to measure attitude shifts caused by the trial, and it is almost impossible to measure jurors' opinions without asking them. The research procedure does differ markedly from an actual trial, however. If jurors are asked during an actual trial whether they have yet formed an opinion it is because they will be excused if they answer in the affirmative. Jurors are frequently admonished not to come to a decision before they have heard all the evidence and are asked to keep an open mind. It is worth pondering what is to be gained by asking jurors their opinion before the start of the trial. Although such information makes it possible to gauge the influence of trial evidence on the outcome, such information is largely arcane. We have often made the point that all actual defendants are disposed of after trial evidence, and thus measuring juror opinions after the presentation of the trial will speak to the only situations defendants will ever face. A little later, we offer this suggestion in more depth, but rather than study whether trial presentations alter juror opinions—there is little reason to keep our legal system if they do not—we may do well to explore what type of trial presentation can offset pretrial biases. What is really needed is some way of classifying the quality of trial evidence. At any rate, continuing the procedure of asking jurors for their opinions prior to the introduction of trial evidence is likely to inflate research results and introduce the possibility of Type I error, that is, false positives.

A second issue, raised by the work of Kerwin and Shaffer (1986) and London and Nunez (2000), is the possibility of interactions between remedies. The work of these scholars has shown that remedies that might fail in isolation can work when used in combination. The particular remedies that were invoked by these scholars were jury instructions and deliberations, but there are many other remedies and many possible combinations. Research will improve vastly if designs include not only the use of remedies but the use of remedies in combinations that allow a testing of interaction effects. Once again, failure to consider such possibilities introduces the possibility of inflating effect sizes.

Third, research should conceptualize all phases of a legal case and not simply the trial. Important decisions are made during at least three distinct phases of the case: the pretrial plea stage, the trial itself, and the posttrial sentencing phase. Most laboratory research concerns itself with the trial phase although some research does seek sentencing recommendations. No research has treated sentencing as a completely separate phase of the trial as many courts are required by law to do. At any rate, virtually no research has been done in the laboratory on the pretrial plea phase. This oversight is enormous because the vast, vast majority of cases are settled rather than tried, and there are good reasons to suspect that pretrial publicity might be more influential with the decision makers at the pretrial phase (prosecutors, defense attorneys, etc.) than with decision makers at the trial phase (the jury). Among other things, people in the latter group are supposed to shun publicity and ignore what they hear whereas people in the former group can watch and hear whatever they want to.

A related question is just what the dependent variable should be. As we have just suggested, there may be four dependent variables (plea bargain rate, plea bargain sentence, trial verdict, and trial sentence) and not simply one. Reviews of current research have not been especially careful about separating out a pretrial publicity effect on the sentence rather than verdict; either is generally taken as supportive of a pretrial publicity effect. Steblay et al. (1999), for example, made no distinction in their excellent meta-analysis. Even at the trial phase, however, "guilt" has been measured differently. Some studies ask for a dichotomous verdict (guilty/not guilty), whereas others ask for a guilt rating on a continuous scale, and some use still other measures. The concern is whether continuous-type data can speak at all to how jurors will make a forced-choice verdict, especially in the context of deliberations. There may indeed be some relation between a continuous rating of guilt and a dichotomous verdict choice, but that relationship is all but completely unexplored at present. At any rate, researchers and especially reviewers will do well to specify what their dependent variable is, and more research needs to be done on the issue of how continuous ratings relate to verdict choices. Finally, individual jurors' verdicts, reported in the majority of studies of pretrial publicity, do not necessarily predict the verdicts of whole juries.

Fourth, and this concern relates more to the sentencing dependent variable, there is the question of what to do with outliers. One common methodological suggestion, often contained in advanced research texts, is to exclude them. The methods used to analyze individual cases that deviate from central tendencies of a data set are less well known than those that compare amalgamations of data. If our suspicions about the sentencing effects are true, however, it may be that the most damaging pretrial publicity effect is not publicity that has a composite effect on a large number of cases but instead is publicity that influences a very small number of defendants very profoundly. Working out a methodological scheme to explore such an influence will substantially advance research on this subject.

A fifth and final methodological direction is to make a more definitive test of laboratory against field research. Although we believe that the research at present generally suggests that laboratory work does not replicate in the field, we also believe that there are substantial gaps on our knowledge. Kerr's (1994) call has largely gone unheeded. Although we have attempted to examine a large number of cases in our various studies, because pretrial publicity is so rare we fear that in very few of the cases we have researched has any juror seen any of the pretrial coverage. It is relatively easy to find cases for which there is no publicity at all, but by sampling all the cases within a given charge over a given time period we have failed to uncover a very large sample of cases receiving coverage, or at least not enough that we are convinced that our tests are definitive. Future research might usefully explore methodological questions of sampling. Although matched-case sampling is generally discouraged in research texts, given the infrequency of highly publicized trials, future research might seek to gather a reasonable sample of highly publicized cases and then randomly select an equal number of nonpublicized cases. Because systemwide conviction rates are known, it might also be possible to conduct z-score tests. At any rate, research that delves more deeply into those few cases that are highly publicized, or at least that uncovers more of them, might prove fruitful and allow for more meaningful comparisons to be conducted between laboratory and field research.

In addition to these methodological concerns, there are a series of substantive questions that future research can seek to answer. The first has to do with measuring the probative value of publicity. Currently, the most elaborate scheme for measuring pretrial publicity is the nine-category system posited by the American Bar Association. Although the system certainly has its advantages, it tends to focus on information that is irrelevant to the trial or inadmissible but still potentially biasing. If, as we suspect, the crucial feature of pretrial information is not whether it is legally permissible but instead whether it has probative value, a new coding scheme is needed. Using either the logic tables of philosophy or the argument schemes of the communication field (a Toulmin-type system, for example), it ought to be possible to construct a reasonably accurate manipulation that can distinguish probative negative pretrial information from pretrial information that is simply negative. For the purposes of field research, a coding scheme that can reliably differentiate accurate from inaccurate pretrial publicity would be especially useful. As Freedman and Burke (1996) noted, a large amount of the media coverage in the Bernardo trial was simply inaccurate. At any rate, we remain ambivalent about current ways of categorizing pretrial publicity. The basic hypothesis—that some sorts of publicity will produce bias whereas others will not—does not seem to deal very well with the basic facts of pretrial publicity, namely, that virtually all of it is antidefendant, very few jurors see any of it, and those that see it can't remember it. We suspect that if there is some content variable that will make a difference in the jury room, it is a content characteristic that truly stands out against the general din of hard-on-crime media messages. Highly probative information might well fit this description. In general, we recommend less focus on coverage content and, when content is examined, it be examined for its probative value.

A second question has to do with audience retention of news coverage. Current research does demonstrate that very little news coverage is remembered for very long. Despite this rather clear finding, it would be useful to identify thresholds of coverage before there is widespread knowledge about a trial. The work of Vidmar (2002) is quite intriguing, but much more research could be done. One basic question is the number of news stories that need to appear before a sizeable group of the public has seen any of them. Even coverage of a high-speed chase, simultaneously broadcast on three networks and covered in all major newspapers the next day, will not be viewed by more than half the eligible jury pool. How many times does a story have to be broadcast on television or printed in the papers before most potential jurors will have seen it? At present, we simply don't know. A second basic question is how often a viewer has to see a story to remember it. Seeing a story once, against the barrage of other news stories and media images a media consumer encounters, could easily be forgotten over the course of several weeks or months before a trial begins. Undoubtedly, the vividness or unusualness of a story will influence this figure. At any rate, we need research that can identify how often a story has to be seen before a juror is likely to remember it, as well as what features a story might have that will make it more memorable. At present we have little more than informed guesses.

Third, if we accept that little news coverage is remembered, it might still be possible for perception to occur beneath consciousness in a subliminal or supraliminal way. However, as noted previously, not all subconscious persuasion can be influential, if for no other reason than the sheer number of stimuli that we encounter daily. Is it reasonable to expect that, if a juror has seen a news story about a defendant in passing, has no explicit memory of the defendant a month later when called as a juror, and is then exposed to trial evidence, a bias against the defendant will still exist? Our current research is inadequate to answer the question. If unconscious psychological mechanisms are at work and are the ways that researchers suspect that pretrial publicity is biasing a trial, more work is necessary to theorize these unconscious mechanisms.

A fourth need, and possibly the most urgent one, is a way to categorize the evidence at trial. At present, of course, laboratory research studies only those cases where the evidence is very close. If, as we suspect, pretrial publicity can't overcome strong trial evidence but may shade interpretations of evidence in a close call, there is an immediate need to conduct research that involves pretrial publicity on cases with various evidence strength. Manipulations of evidence strength are available and readily used in other research; it should be an easy task for a laboratory experiment to manipulate the evidence strength at a trial. At its base, there is every reason to expect that if pretrial publicity does have an effect, it is one that interacts with trial evidence. Research that examines that interaction effect more closely will surely advance our understanding of the phenomenon.

Related to this is the question of what sort of case typically goes to trial and receives coverage. One way to explain our field finding that low-publicity cases have the highest conviction rates but moderate-publicity cases have the lowest is that the type of case that receives low coverage tends to be different from the case that receives moderate coverage. In other words, it might be the type of case driving both the coverage and the publicity rates. This, of course, would reverse the causal chain of the laboratory that assumes that publicity drives conviction rates. At a minimum, a very meaningful interaction between the case type and the pretrial publicity is suggested. It tells us little that publicity can drive conviction rates in the laboratory when case evidence is close if the only cases that receive coverage in actual practice are those cases where the evidence is not close. If, for example, the heinousness of the crime drives coverage in actual cases, we need to know how pretrial publicity influences juror decision making in heinous crimes, and not traffic infractions (as some prior research has studied). At any rate, categorizing case types would go a long way toward placing boundary conditions on a pretrial publicity effect.

Fifth, studies on resources would be useful. In this book we have pieced together evidence about the influence of economic standing on defendant chances. Our basic thesis that adequate legal representation can compensate for pretrial publicity bias remains untested, however. A field comparison of publicized trials with poor representation (say, a public defender with a high caseload) against publicized trials with higher quality representation (say, a private attorney who conducted an independent investigation) is the sort of thing that could validate or disprove the hypothesis. Related to this would be research that explored trial strategies that might compensate for pretrial publicity bias. Current research has shown that some types of pretrial publicity can backfire (e.g., antirape coverage in a rape trial) and that some defense strategies can offset publicity bias and perhaps make it work in favor of the defense (e.g., casting racial motives on the coverage and the prosecution). A common understanding in the legal system is that not all issues need to be dealt with before the trial. For example, if the prosecution was going to present a witness of dubious credibility, a court would not exclude the testimony but rather would rely on the defense to expose the shady nature of the information. In a similar vein, if proper defense strategy can counteract preexisting bias (the defense must counteract a number of preexisting biases as it is), the issue of pretrial publicity is best dealt with at trial rather than with pretrial remedies. This, of course, returns to the question of adequate representation. Perhaps the most effective remedy for a defendant, and one that is largely unavailable now, is a good lawyer. Research that can confirm this relationship will improve understandings of pretrial publicity and, perhaps, prod the legal system to provide less wealthy defendants with better counsel.

The ideal study would be complex and as a result expensive. If, in a laboratory study, pretrial publicity is varied in only three ways, trial evidence in three more, and only three remedies are varied in their use (much less their effectiveness), the study would already have a 27-cell design. If jury verdicts are used rather than individual judgments, the number of jurors needed exceeds a thousand, and if those jurors should be representatives of the jury population and not simply undergraduate college students finding them would be difficult. Such a study would be a massive methodological advance over what is currently known but also quite resource intensive. The phenomena we study are under no obligation to make themselves easy to understand, however, and valid knowledge demands its own price. Either funding will be provided for probing and inclusive research, or our knowledge will continue to be a patch-work of separate findings that may or may not produce a coherent picture when combined.

That having been said, a broader prioritization of societal resources is in order. We believe that expensive pretrial publicity research should not be conducted at the expense of quality defense representation. It ought to be a little embarrassing for everyone that the millions of dollars are spent each year for social science legal research whereas public defense programs are so desperately underfunded. In the end, we believe that a trade-off is not necessary but a reprioritization is. To the extent that we stop pursing cost-ineffective policies contrary to empirical data, we can free up more resources to spend effectively. We should not have to sacrifice intellectual progress in order to fund our constitutional rights. If our conclusions are correct, social science research in this case points to a way to free up system resources by spending less on expensive remedies and utilizing instead more effective and cheaper approaches. Let us hope that our system has the wisdom to enact these changes and the foresight to spend the savings judiciously.

Appendix:
Detailed Discussion
of City-Level Data

This analysis involved combining data from three different data sets to provide information about publicity, crime, fear of crime, and conviction rates. The coverage data were obtained from a report published by the Kaiser Family Foundation (1998). Essentially, data were collected from 13 different cities over a 3-month period. Cities were selected to include geographic diversity and to include markets of different sizes. The cities selected were Seattle, San Francisco, Los Angeles, and Phoenix in the West, Denver, Minneapolis, Chicago, and St. Louis in the Midwest, New York, Philadelphia, and Baltimore in the Northeast, and Houston and Atlanta in the South. In each market, the top-ranked news program was sampled, with the exception of San Francisco, where the second-ranked station was selected to get a better distribution of network affiliations (ABC affiliates were heavily represented in the sample, and thus a CBS affiliate was selected in San Francisco). Shows in each market were taped by residents from October to December 1996; weekends were excluded due to concerns about preemption by sporting events. The final sampling frame was 66 days. Of 858 taped broadcasts, 833 were usable; the other tapes were lost to errors in taping and other technical difficulties. Broadcasts were content analyzed utilizing a 19-category scheme. The "news story" was the unit of analysis, and each story was placed into one of the 19 categories. From those data, we extracted only the number of crime stories. Other technical details and reliability estimates are available in the report (Kaiser Family Foundation, 1998). Atlanta had the most crime stories (494 for an average of 7.5 stories per broadcast) and Minneapolis had the fewest (117 crime stories for an average of 1.8 per broadcast). A bar chart of crime coverage by city is included in Fig. A.1.

All estimates of crime were taken from official FBI statistics (Federal Bureau of Investigation, 1996). The FBI calculates a "crime index" to measure

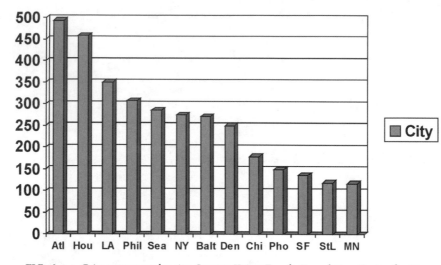

FIG. A.1. Crime coverage by city. Source: Kaiser Family Foundation Center for Media and Public Affairs. Copyright © 1997. Assessing Local Television News Coverage of Health Issues.

crime in each city; the crime index includes the total count of seven different crimes (murder, rape, robbery, aggravated assault, burglary, larceny, and motor vehicle theft). Crime totals for each city are divided by the city's population and standardized in units of 100,000. The result is the number of crimes per 100,000 people. The only difficulty in calculation was that for the city of Chicago rapes were not reported in 1996. In order to obtain a crime index score, we estimated the number of rapes in Chicago based on the national average and the population size of Chicago (we substituted the national average of rapes per 100,000 people, 36.1, and multiplied it by the number of units of 100,000 people in the city of Chicago, or the population divided by 100,000). Substituting the average for Chicago, we obtained crime index estimates for each city. It is important to note that the crime estimates we adopted came from Table 8 of the FBI report, which uses the population within the city limits proper, rather than Table 6, which relies on the population of an entire metropolitan statistical areas. We did this because Table 6 was missing data for three different cities, which would have required a number of different estimations, whereas Table 8 was missing only the rape data for Chicago. Atlanta had the most crime per capita, while New York had the least. Figure A.2 is a bar chart of crime by city.

Data on fear of crime were obtained from Tjaden and Thoennes (1998) via the Inter-University Consortium for Political and Social Research (ICPSR). The researchers sampled 8,000 men and 8,000 women over the age of 18 years between November 1995 and May 1996. The lengthy survey queried many issues, one of which was general fear of violence and the ways that fears were

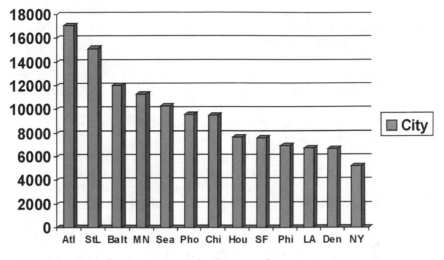

FIG. A.2.   Crime by city. Source: Federal Bureau of Investigation (1996).

managed. Three items from the survey were extracted for the present analysis: (a) "Would you say that personal safety for [women / men] in this country has improved since you were a child, gotten worse since you were a child, or stayed about the same?" (b) "Do you think the following things are more of a problem for [women / men] today, less of a problem, or about the same? Do you think violent crime is…?" (c) "How concerned are you about your own personal safety?" The first variable is called Overall Crime Concern, the second variable Violent Crime Concern, and the third variable Personal Safety Concern. ZIP code data were included, and ZIP codes were matched with the 13 cities included in the Kaiser data set. ZIP code information was obtained from the Langenberg web site (Langenberg.com, 2001), and ZIP codes were utilized only for the city proper and not the metropolitan statistical area, to make them consistent with the FBI crime data. Data that were not from one of the cities in the Kaiser data were excluded from subsequent analysis.

Correlations between the three fear of crime variables were low (Overall / Violent $r = .21$, $p < .01$, $n = 832$; Overall / Personal $r = .06$, ns, $n = 832$; Violent / Personal $r = .09$, $p < .01$, $n = 858$), and they did not form a reliable scale (alpha = .21, $n = 832$; excluding Personal Safety Concern raised alpha to a maximum of only .31). With individual respondents in the fear-of-crime data set as the unit of analysis and city averages of crime entered for each respondent, none of the three measures of fear of crime exhibited a statistically significant correlation with actual crime levels ($n = 832$). At the city level ($n = 13$) with averages of fear of crime for each city and FBI crime levels for each city entered, no fear-of-crime measure demonstrated a significant relationship with actual crime either for traditional Pearson tests or for nonparametric Spearman rho tests. Neither did any of the fear of crime measures produce statistically significant correlations with one another at the city level.

To see whether fear of crime measures varied by city and across time, a multivariate analysis of variance (MANOVA) with city and month of sampling (excluding data from November 1995) as the independent measures and the three fear-of-crime dependent measures was performed. At the multivariate level, significance was obtained for both city (Pillai's trace $= .033$, $F = 2.11$, $12/2301$, $p < .014$) and month (Pillai's trace $= .106$, $F = 2.33$, $36/2301$, $p < .001$), but not the interaction between the two. The tests of between-subjects effects revealed significance by month for the Overall Crime Concern variable ($F = 3.98$, $4/831$, $p = .003$) but not the other two, and significance by city for Violent Crime Concern ($F = 4.44$, $12/767$, $p = .004$) and Personal Safety Concern ($F = 3.75$, $12/767$, $p < .001$) but not for Overall Crime Concern. Thus, Overall Crime Concern seemed sensitive to time but did not vary by city, whereas Violent Crime Concern and Personal Safety Concern did not vary across time but did vary by city.

In order to determine whether measures of actual crime and fear of crime were independent, we explored the possibility that fear of crime might be linked to actual crime. If such an association existed, it would be possible to covary actual crime victimization with fear of crime, and after removing the influence of actual crime on fear of crime get a measure of fear of crime that was independent of actual crime. Items measuring violence victimization were extracted from the Tjaden and Thoennes (1998) data set to create separate measures of victimization as a child and victimization as an adult. No significant differences were found between different levels of either adult victimization or childhood victimization and either Violent Crime Concern or Personal Safety Concern. It should be noted that significant differences were observed for Overall Crime Concern and both measures of victimhood, but because Overall Crime Concern was not retained for any subsequent analysis, those differences were not explored, and in any event the variance explained was so small (eta squared was never as high as .01 for any comparison) that covariance adjustments seemed unnecessary.

At the city level, a significant negative relationship existed between coverage and General Crime Concern analyzed nonparametrically with Spearman's rho rank-order correlation ($-.67$, $p < .05$, $n = 13$). No other significant differences were obtained between the coverage measure and the other two fear-of-crime measures. Similar results were obtained for the more traditional Pearson's correlation. Based on these results and for reasons explained in the text, the Personal Safety Concern variable was retained for the analysis.

Finally, conviction rates were obtained from official federal court records stored in the ICPSR (Federal Judicial Center, 2001). Yearly additions are made to the data set that include all cases sentenced between October of the preceding year and the end of September of the year of the data file. Each separate year of criminal terminations data is referred to as a "part." Because our research questions concerned the outcomes of trials at the disposition date rather than the sentencing date, we drew data from all parts, 1996–2000, and selected from those parts cases that reached disposition between July 1, 1996, and June 30, 1997. The unit of analysis in the data set is the individual defendant, and each record includes up to five charges against the defendant. All criminal defendants who were not charged with a felony count were excluded. Over 55% of defendants faced at least two felony charges. Of those facing two or more felony charges, 24.4% faced two felony charges, 11.5% faced three felony charges, 6.9% faced four felony charges, and 12.6% faced five felony charges. Data were included only for those defendants tried in one of the 13 cities under consideration. In total, 7,293 defendants were included. Five hundred and eighty-seven defendants went to trial (8.0%); the remainder pleaded guilty on all counts (92.0%). Of those cases that went to trial, 39 were tried in front of judges (7.1%) and 548 (92.9%) were tried in front of juries. An index of outcomes can be created by calculating the percentage of counts on which the defendant was found guilty. To a statistically significant degree ($t = 2.33$, $df = 40.42$, $p < .05$; equal variances not assumed), defendants were convicted on a lower percentage of charges in front of judges (69%) as compared to juries (87%).

Two issues related to the data bear special consideration. First, the choice to focus only on the area of a city proper rather than its metropolitan statistical area does have consequences. Fear-of-crime and crime data were obtained only for respondents living within city limits, whereas stories were broadcast to an entire viewing area. The choice was made in order to get more complete data on actual crime rates; data for citizens living within the city limits proper were available for 12 of the 13 cities, whereas data for citizens living in the metropolitan statistical area were available for only 10 of 13 cities. However, in doing so, potential respondents living outside city limits were not included. It is true that all respondents living in the city limits had an equal opportunity to view the crime coverage, and thus any conclusions about relationships between coverage and conviction rates seem warranted. It is possible, however, that city dwellers differ in their reaction to crime coverage when compared with nonurban media users, and any such differences are not examined in this study. All conclusions are therefore properly restricted to city dwellers only.

A second issue of considerable consequence has to do with the time frame of the various data sets. Frustratingly, the data on the fear of crime were drawn from the first 5 months of 1996 (and also November 1995), whereas the data on coverage were drawn from the last 3 months of 1996. Crime data span the entire year, and trial data cover the period of July 1996 through June 1997. Obviously, the overlap is incomplete and there is nothing that can be done analytically to correct this shortcoming of the data. The analysis must proceed on the assumption that the measures obtained represent general trends in the cities studied and that these values remain fairly constant over time. The most crucial issue is whether the relationships between the variables under study remain constant over time, or, in other words, whether there are interactions between the various independent variables (the measure of crime, coverage, and the three measures of fear of crime) and the four dependent variables (percent of charges pleaded, average length of pleaded sentence, percent conviction at trial, and average sentence length per trial conviction; see main text for discussion) and a time variable. If the relationships between the variables remain constant in the periods for which we do have data, it provides some evidence that lack of data overlap does not so distort these results so that they become meaningless.

To test whether the relationship between the variables was constant across time, we divided the data between October 1996 and June 1997 into four quarters and conducted four separate univariate ANOVAs, one for each dependent variable, specifying a model that tested five separate two-way interactions between each independent variable and the quarter of time. The results are contained in Table A.1. As the table reveals, no significant time by independent variable interactions were present for any independent variable for percent of trial convictions or length of trial sentence. Four significant differences were obtained for the five independent variables for percentage of charges pleaded, and three significant differences were obtained for length of pleaded sentence. On the one hand, this pattern of results gives reason to conclude that time in-

TABLE A.1
Significance Tests for Time Interactions

	Percent of Trial Convictions		Percentage of Charges Pleaded		Length of Pleaded Sentence		Length of Trial Sentence	
	F, p [a]	Power	F, p [b]	Power	F, p [c]	Power	F, p [d]	Power
Crime	.59, [ns]	.20	3.38^{f}	.85	5.92^{g}	.99	1.32, [ns]	.41
Fear 1	.43, [ns]	.15	5.06^{g}	.97	3.23^{e}	.93	.11, [ns]	.07
Fear 2	.92, [ns]	.29	19.98^{g}	1.0	1.98, [ns]	.60	2.23, [ns]	.65
Fear 3	1.92, [ns]	.58	1.29, [ns]	.41	6.44^{g}	.99	.36, [ns]	.13
Publicity	.73, [ns]	.24	7.92^{g}	.99	1.90, [ns]	.58	2.15, [ns]	.64

[a] All tests in for conviction percentage have 4/571 degrees of freedom.
[b] All tests in for percentage of charges pleaded have 4/7269 degrees of freedom.
[c] All tests in for length of pleaded sentence have 4/5800 degrees of freedom.
[d] All tests in for length of trial sentence have 4/497 degrees of freedom.
[e] Significant at $p < .05$.
[f] Significant at $p < .01$.
[g] Significant at $p < .001$.

fluences pleaded outcomes but not trial outcomes; however, the table also raises the question of whether this pattern may be an artifact of different power levels for the different dependent variables. The overall n was much higher for the pleaded outcomes, because more charges are pleaded than come to trial, and the corresponding power is much higher. Based on the issue of power, two elements of the data argue against the conclusion that the variables influence plea bargaining but not trials. First, the magnitude estimates for the pleaded variables ($R^2 = .02$ for percentage of charges pleaded and .02 for length of pleaded sentence) are actually smaller than those for the trial outcomes ($R^2 = .06$ for average length of trial sentence and .05 for percentage of charges resulting in conviction). This pattern gives the impression that the significance obtained for the pleaded outcome variables is present because the large n results in the detection of small differences, a condition Hays (1981) described as the detection of significant but trivial differences. Second, even where power estimates are fairly high for the trial outcome variables, for example, Violent Crime Concern (.65) and Coverage Level (.64) for length of trial sentence, nonsignificance is still obtained. Thus, the relationship between the variables does appear to remain stable across time, as no time by independent variable differences are observed for trial outcomes across time and those that do emerge for pleaded sentences are of exceedingly small magnitude.

An analysis of the means for the significant differences observed in the pleaded outcome variables further supports the conclusion that relationships are stable across time. The means for average length of felony plea are contained in Table A.2 and the means for percentage of charges pleaded guilty are contained in Table A.3. As the data in the tables reveal, any interactions are or-

TABLE A.2

Average Sentence Length per Felony Plea by Time Period for All Five Independent Variables

Time	Actual Crime[a]		Fear: General Crime Worse		Fear: Violent Crime Worse		Fear: Personal Safety[a]		Publicity Category	
	Low	High	Low	High	Low	High	Low	High	Low	High
July–Sept. 1996	37.62	35.91	28.94	48.11	31.06	41.13	29.04	48.59	47.11	30.63
Oct.–Dec. 1996	28.97	32.30	26.33	34.65	32.62	29.04	25.03	35.55	32.12	28.83
Jan.–Mar. 1997	28.40	34.25	27.48	34.75	31.66	29.70	28.90	32.34	32.22	29.37
April–June 1997	31.45	32.15	29.94	34.51	31.00	32.32	28.07	35.82	30.38	32.44

[a]Statistically significant difference.

TABLE A.3

Percentage of Charges Pleaded per Felony Plea by Time Period for All Five Independent Variables

	Actual Crime[a]		Fear: General Crime Worse[a]		Fear: Violent Crime Worse[a]		Fear: Personal Safety		Publicity Category[a]	
	Low	High	Low	High	Low	High	Low	High	Low	High
July–Sept. 1996	.64	.57	.63	.59	.59	.63	.64	.58	.57	.64
Oct.–Dec. 1996	.62	.58	.62	.59	.55	.64	.64	.58	.59	.61
Jan.–March 1997	.58	.56	.60	.54	.54	.60	.59	.57	.56	.59
April–June 1997	.62	.63	.64	.60	.62	.63	.64	.60	.59	.65

[a]Statistically significant difference.

dinal—that is, the differences observed are more pronounced for some time periods and not for others. For example, the percentage of charges pleaded is always higher in the high- rather than low-coverage category, although the differences are more stark in the July–September 1996 quarter when compared to the October–December 1996 quarter. Any instances where the overall pattern of results is different are trivial. For example, the percentage of pleaded sentences is higher in areas where actual crime is low, with the exception of the April–June 1997 quarter, where the order of the means reverses, but only to very small degree (.64 vs. .63).

In short, the relationships between the independent and dependent variables do seem to be stable across time. For the trial outcome variables, time does not interact with the independent and dependent variables. For the pleaded outcome variables, significant interactions are present, but these appear to be the result of unusually high power and are of minimal magnitude. An analysis of the means reveals that any interactions that do exist for the pleaded variables do not reverse the direction of the overall relationship.

References

Adams, D. (1980). *The restaurant at the end of the universe*. New York: Pocket Books.

Arkin, R., Cooper, H., & Kolditz, T. (1980). A statistical review of the literature concerning the self-serving bias in interpersonal influence situations. *Journal of Personality, 48*, 435–448.

Atkinson, R. (2001). Historical perspectives on pro bono lawyering: A social-democratic critique of pro bono publico representation of the poor: The good as the enemy of the best. *American University Journal of Gender, Social Policy, and the Law, 9*, 129–170.

Ball-Rokeach, S. J. (1985). The origins of individual media system dependency: A sociological framework. *Communication Research, 12*, 485–510.

Bauer, W. J. (1976). Newspapers under fire. In *Problems in journalism* (pp. 226–227). American Society of Newspaper Editors. Washington, DC.

Berger, C. R. (1998). Processing quantitative data about risk and threat in news reports. *Journal of Communication, 48*(3), 87–106.

Berger, C. R. (2000). Quantitative depictions of threatening phenomena in news reports: The scary world of frequency data. *Human Communication Research, 26*(1), 27–52.

Berger, C. R. (2001). Making it worse than it is: Quantitative depictions of threatening trends in the news. *Journal of Communication, 51*(4), 655–677.

Black, D. (1976). *The behavior of law*. New York: Academic Press.

Bornstein, B. H. (1999). The ecological validity of jury simulations: Is the jury still out? *Law and Human Behavior, 23*, 75–91.

Bornstein, B. H., & Rajki, M. (1994). Extra-legal factors and product liability: The influence of mock jurors' demographic characteristics and intuitions about the cause of an injury. *Behavioral Sciences and the Law, 12*, 127–147.

Bornstein, B. H., Whisenhunt, B. L., Nemeth, R. J., & Dunaway, D. L. (2002). Pretrial publicity and civil cases: A two-way street? *Law and Human Behavior, 26*, 3–17.

Brady, L. A., & Pertilla, A. (2001, Nov./Dec.). The look of local news. *Columbia Journalism Review* (Suppl. to the Nov./Dec. issue [Gambling with the future: Local newsrooms beset by sponsor interference, budget cuts, layoffs, and added programming]), pp. 11–12.

Bright, S. B. (1997). Neither equal nor just: The rationing and denial of legal services to the poor when life and liberty are at stake. *Annual Survey of American Law, 1997*, 783–836.

Brooks, P., & Gewirtz, P. D. (Eds.). (1996). *Law's stories: Narrative and rhetoric in the law*. New Haven, CT: Yale University Press.

Bruschke, J. C. (1994). Law, politics, and communication: An argument based model of legal decision-making. *Dissertation Abstracts International, 56*(01A).

Bruschke, J. C., & Loges, W. E. (1999). The relationship between pretrial publicity and trial outcomes. *Journal of Communication, 49*(4), 104–120.

Burns, R. P. (2001). The lawfulness of the American trial. *American Criminal Law Review, 38*, 205–239.

Carroll, J. S., Kerr, N. L., Alfini, J. J., Weaver, F. M., MacCoun, R. J., & Feldman, V. (1986). Free press and fair trial: The role of behavioral research. *Law and Human Behavior, 100*, 187–201.

Chaiken, S., Liberman, A., & Eagly, A. H. (1989). Heuristic and systematic information processing within and beyond the persuasion context. In J. S. Uleman & J. A. Bargh (Eds.), *Unintended thought* (pp. 212–252). New York: Guilford Press.

Constantini, E., & King, J. (1980–1981). The partial juror: Correlates and causes of prejudgment. *Law and Society Review, 15*, 9–40.

Cook, T. D., & Leviton, L. C. (1980). Reviewing the literature: A comparison of traditional methods with meta-analysis. *Journal of Personality, 48*, 449–472.

D'Allessio, S. J., & Stolzenberg, L. (1993). Socioeconomic status and the sentencing of traditional offenders. *Journal of Criminal Justice, 21*, 61–77.

Daudistel, H. C., Hosch, H. M., Holmes, M. D., & Graves, J. B. (1999). Effects of defendant ethnicity on juries' disposition of felony cases. *Journal of Applied Psychology, 29*, 317–336.

Davis, R. W. (1986). Pretrial publicity, the timing of the trial, and mock jurors' decision processes. *Journal of Applied Psychology, 16*, 590–607.

Davidson, W. P. (1982). The third-person effect of communication. *Public Opinion Quarterly, 46*, 1–15.

DeFleur, M. L., & Ball-Rokeach, S. J. (1989). *Theories of mass communication* (5th ed.). New York: Longman.

DeFleur, M. L., & Dennis, E. E. (1998). *Understanding mass communication: A liberal arts perspective* (6th ed.). Boston: Houghton Mifflin.

Detroit newspaper strike ends. (1997, February 27). *Facts on File World News Digest*, p. 123D3.

Dexter, H. R., Cutler, B. L., & Moran, G. (1992). A test of voir dire as a remedy for the prejudicial effects of pretrial publicity. *Journal of Applied Psychology, 22*, 819–832.

Diamond, S. S. (2002). Juries: Behavioral aspects. In J. Dressler (Ed.), *Encyclopedia of Crime & Justice* (2nd ed., pp. 865–870). New York: MacMillan.

Dixon, T. L., & Linz, D. (2000). Overrepresentation and underrepresentation of African Americans and Latinos as lawbreakers on television news. *Journal of Communication, 50*(2), 131–154.

Eichenwald, K. (2002, August 4). Economy; Perp walk. *The New York Times*, Section 4, p. 2.

Emmelman, D. S. (1994). The effect of social class on the adjudication of criminal cases: Class-linked behavior tendencies, common sense, and the interpretive procedures of court-appointed defense attorneys. *Symbolic Interaction, 17*, 1–20.

Entman, R. (1992). Blacks in the news: Television, modern racism, and cultural change. *Journalism Quarterly, 69*, 341–361.

Entman, R. (1993). Framing: Toward clarification of a fractured paradigm. *Journal of Communication, 43*(4), 51–58.

Entman, R. (1994). Representation and reality in the portrayal of Blacks on network television news. *Journalism Quarterly, 71*, 509–520.

Fairchild, H. H., & Cowan, G. (1997). The O. J. Simpson trial: Challenges to science and society. *Journal of Social Issues, 53*, 583–591.

Federal Bureau of Investigation. (1996). *Uniform Crime Reports 1996*. Retrieved May 20, 2001: http://www.fbi.gov/ucr/Cius_97/96CRIME/96crime2.pdf

Federal Judicial Center. (1997). *Federal court cases: Integrated database, 1970–1994* (Parts 1–14; 29–33, 58–60, 67–69: criminal data, 1970–1991) [computer file]. 3rd ICPSR version. Washington, DC: Federal Judicial Center [producer], 1992. Ann Arbor, MI: Inter-University Consortium for Political and Social Research [distributor].

Federal Judicial Center. (2001). *Federal court cases: Integrated database, 1970–2000* (Parts 109–114: criminal data, 1996–2000) [computer file]. ICPSR version. Washington, DC: Federal Judicial Center [producer], 2000. Ann Arbor, MI: Inter-University Consortium for Political and Social Research [distributor].

Fein, S., McCloskey, A. L., & Tomlinson, T. M. (1997). Can the jury disregard that information? The use of suspicion to reduce the prejudicial effects of pretrial publicity and inadmissible testimony. *Personality and Social Psychology Bulletin, 23,* 1215–1226.

Fein, S., Morgan, S. J., Norton, M. I., & Sommers, S. R. (1997). Hype and suspicion: The effects of pretrial publicity, race, and suspicion on jurors' verdicts. *Journal of Social Issues, 53,* 487–502.

Fisher, W. L. (1987). *Human communication as narration: Toward a philosophy of reason, value, and action.* Columbia: University of South Carolina Press.

Frasca, R. (1988). Estimating the occurrence of trials prejudiced by press coverage. *Judicature, 27*(3), 162–170.

Freedman, J. L., & Burke, T. M. (1996). The effect of pretrial publicity: The Bernardo case. *Canadian Journal of Criminology, 38,* 253–270.

Freedman, J. L., Martin, C. K., & Mota, V. L. (1998). Pretrial publicity: Effects of admonition and expressing pretrial opinions. *Legal and Criminological Psychology, 3,* 255–270.

Freedman, M. H. (1998). Our constitutionalized adversary system. *Chapman Law Review, 1,* 57–90.

Fulero, S. M. (1987). The role of behavioral research in the free press/fair trial controversy. *Law and Human Behavior, 11,* 259–264.

Fulero, S. M. (2002). Afterword: The past, present, and future of applied pretrial publicity research. *Law and Human Behavior, 26,* 127–133.

Fulero, S. M., & Penrod, S. D. (1990). Attorney jury selection folklore: What do they think and how can psychologists help? *Forensic Reports, 3,* 233–259.

Gans, H. J. (1979). *Deciding what's news: A study of* CBS Evening News, NBC Nightly News, Newsweek, *and* Time. New York: Pantheon Books.

Gass, R. H., & Seiter, J. S. (1999). *Persuasion, social influence, and compliance gaining.* Boston: Allyn and Bacon.

George, T. E., & Epstein, L. (1992). On the nature of Supreme Court decision making. *American Political Science Review, 86,* 323–337.

Gerber, R. J. (2001). Essay: On dispensing justice. *Arizona Law Review, 43,* 135–172.

Gerbner, G., Gross, L., Morgan, M., & Signorielli, N. (1986). Living with television: The dynamics of the cultivation process. In J. Bryant & D. Zillmann (Eds.), *Perspectives on media effects* (pp. 17–40). Hillsdale, NJ: Lawrence Erlbaum Associates.

Gerbner, G., Gross, L., Signorielli, N., Morgan, M., & Jackson-Beeck, M. (1979). The demonstration of power: Violence profile no. 10. *Journal of Communication, 29*(3), 177–196.

Gibson, D. C., & Padilla, M. (1998, November). *Litigation public relations problems and limits.* Paper presented to the Commission on Communication & Law of the National Communication Association, New York.

Gottlieb, C., & Belt, T. (2001, Nov./Dec.). Where have all the viewers gone? *Columbia Journalism Review.* (Suppl. to the Nov./Dec. issue [Gambling with the future: Local newsrooms beset by sponsor interference, budget cuts, layoffs, and added programming]), pp. 11–12.

Graber, D. A. (1980). *Crime news and the public.* New York: Praeger.

Graber, D. A. (1988). *Processing the news: How people tame the information tide.* New York: Longman.

Greene, E., & Loftus, E. F. (1984). What's new in the news? The influence of well-publicized news events on psychological research and courtroom trials. *Basic and Applied Social Psychology, 5,* 211–221.

Greene, E., & Wade, R. (1988). Of private talk and public print: General pre-trial publicity and juror decision-making. *Applied Cognitive Psychology, 2*, 123–135.

Gross, L., & Morgan, M. (1985). Television and enculturation. In J. Dominick & J. Fletcher (Eds.), *Broadcasting research methods* (pp. 221–234). Boston: Allyn & Bacon.

Group says "perp walks" violate the law. (2002, August 14). *The New York Times*, p. B6.

Hans, V. P., & Doob, A. N. (1976). Section 12 of the Canada Evidence Act and the deliberations of simulated juries. *Criminal Law Quarterly, 18*, 235–253.

Hays, W. L. (1981). *Statistics* (4th ed.). New York: Harcourt Brace.

Hedges, L. V. (1990). Directions for future methodology. In K. W. Wachter & M. L. Straf (Eds.), *The future of meta-analysis* (pp. 11–26). New York: Russell Sage Foundation.

Hoiberg, B. C., & Stires, L. K. (1973). The effect of several types of pretrial publicity on the guilt attributions of simulated jurors. *Journal of Applied Social Psychology, 3*, 267–275.

Hough, G. A. (1970). Felonies, jury trial, and news reports. In C. R. Bush (Ed.), *Free press and fair trial: Some dimensions of the problem* (pp. 36–48). Atlanta: University of Georgia Press.

Hvistendahl, J. K. (1979). The effect of placement of biasing information. *Journalism Quarterly, 56*, 863–865.

Imrich, D. J., Mullin, C., & Linz, D. (1995). Measuring the extent of prejudicial pretrial publicity in major American newspapers: A content analysis. *Journal of Communication, 45*, 94–117.

Infante, D. A., Rancer, A. S., & Womack, D. F. (1997). *Building communication theory* (3rd ed.). Prospect Heights, IL: Waveland Press.

Jaccard, J., Turrisi, R., & Wan, C. K. (1990). *Interaction effects in multiple regression*. Newbury Park, CA: Sage.

Jones, R. M. (1991). The latest empirical studies on pretrial publicity, jury bias, and judicial remedies—not enough to overcome the first amendment right of access to pretrial hearings. *American University Law Review, 40*, 841–848.

Kaiser Family Foundation. (1998). *Assessing local television news coverage of health issues*. Menlo Park, CA: Henry J. Kaiser Family Foundation/Center for Media and Public Affairs.

Kaplan, M. F., & Miller, L. E. (1978). Reducing the effects of juror bias. *Journal of Personality and Social Psychology, 36*, 1443–1455.

Kelman, M. (1987). *A guide to critical legal studies*. Cambridge, MA: Harvard University Press.

Kerr, N. L. (1994). The effects of pretrial publicity on jurors. *Judicature, 78*, 120–127.

Kerr, N. L., Kramer, G. P., Carroll, J. S., & Alfini, J. J. (1991). On the effectiveness of voir dire in criminal cases with prejudicial pretrial publicity: An empirical study. *American University Law Review, 40*, 665–693.

Kerr, N. L., Nerenz, D. R., & Herrick, D. (1979). Role playing and the study of jury behavior. *Sociological Methods and Research, 7*, 337–355.

Kerwin, J., & Shaffer, D. R. (1994). Mock jurors versus mock juries: The role of deliberations in reactions to inadmissible testimony. *Personality and Social Psychology Bulletin, 20*, 153–162.

Kipling, R. (1948). *The jungle book*. New York: Doubleday & Company.

Kline, F. G., & Jess, P. H. (1966). Pretrial publicity: Its effect on law school mock juries. *Journalism Quarterly, 43*, 113–116.

Kotiaho, J. S., & Tomkins, J. L. (2002). Meta-analysis, can it ever fail? *Oikos, 96*, 551–553.

Kovera, M. B. (2002). The effects of general pretrial publicity on juror decisions: An examination of the moderators and mediating mechanisms. *Law and Human Behavior, 26*, 43–72.

Kramer, G. P., & Kerr, N. L. (1989). Laboratory simulation and bias in the study of juror behavior: A methodological note. *Law and Human Behavior, 13*, 89–99.

Kramer, G. P., Kerr, N. L., & Carroll, J. S. (1990). Pretrial publicity, judicial remedies, and jury bias. *Law and Human Behavior, 14*, 409–437.

Kulish, M. (1998). The public's right of access to pretrial proceedings versus the accused's right to a fair trial. *Army Law, 1998*, 1–15.

Langenberg.com. (n.d.). *ZIP code, area code, city, county & time zone cross refs—ZIP code maps & surrounding ZIPs*. Retrieved December 2001 from http://zip.langenberg.com

Landsman, S., & Rakos, R. F. (1994). A preliminary inquiry into the effect of potentially biasing information on judges and jurors in civil litigation. *Behavioral Sciences and the Law, 12,* 113–126.

Lieberman, J. D., & Arndt, J. (2000). Understanding the limits of limiting instructions: Social psychological explanations for the failures of instructions to disregard pretrial publicity and other inadmissible evidence. *Psychology, Public Policy, and Law, 6,* 677–711.

Lindman, R. (1989). Sources of judicial mistrust of social science evidence: A comparison of social science and jurisprudence. *Indiana Law Journal, 64,* 755–768.

Lofton, J. (1966). *Justice and the Press.* Boston: Beacon Press.

Loges, W. E. (1994). Canaries in the coal mine: Perceptions of threat and media system dependency relations. *Communication Research, 21*(1), 5–23.

Loges, W. E., & Ball-Rokeach, S. J. (2002). Mass media and crime. In J. Dressler (Ed.), *Encyclopedia of Crime & Justice* (2nd ed., pp. 988–995). New York: Macmillan.

London, K., & Nunez, N. (2000). The effect of jury deliberations on jurors' propensity to disregard inadmissible evidence. *Journal of Applied Psychology, 85,* 932–939.

MacCoun, R. J., & Kerr, N. L. (1988). Asymmetric influence in mock jury deliberation: Jurors' bias for leniency. *Journal of Personality and Social Psychology, 54,* 21–33.

Masling, J. M. (1992). What does it all mean? In R. F. Bornstein & T. S. Pittman (Eds.), *Perception without awareness* (pp. 259–276). New York: Guilford Press.

Mayer, M. (1993). *Making news.* Boston: Harvard Business School Press.

Mazzella, R., & Feingold, A. (1994). The effects of physical attractiveness, race, socioeconomic status, and gender of defendants and victims on judgments of mock jurors: A meta-analysis. *Journal of Applied Social Psychology, 24,* 1315–1344.

McConahay, J. B., Mullin, C. J., & Frederick, J. (1977). The uses of social science in trials with political and racial overtones: The trial of Joan Little. *Law and Contemporary Problems, 41,* 205–229.

Medina, H. R. (1967). *Freedom of the press and fair trial: Final report with recommendations.* New York: Columbia University Press.

Melton, G. B. (1987). Bringing psychology to the legal system: Opportunities, obstacles, and efficacy. *American Psychologist, 42,* 488–495.

Miller, G. R. (1975). Jurors' responses to videotaped trial materials: Some recent findings. *Personality and Social Psychology Bulletin, 1,* 561–569.

Moran, G., & Cutler, B. L. (1991). The prejudicial impact of pretrial publicity. *Journal of Applied Social Psychology, 21,* 345–367.

Mullin, C., Imrich, D. J., & Linz, D. (1996). The impact of acquaintance rape stories and case-specific pretrial publicity on juror decision-making. *Communication Research, 23,* 100–135.

Newman, L. S., Duff, K., Schnopp-Wyatt, N., Brock, B., & Hoffman, Y. (1997). Reactions to the O. J. Simpson verdict: "Mindless tribalism" or motivated inference processes. *Journal of Social Issues, 53,* 547–562.

Newsom, A. (2000). Pretrial publicity and individual voir dire: What has the Florida Supreme Court done to the jury selection process? *Florida Law Review, 52,* 1039–1072.

Nietzel, M. T., & Dillehay, R. C. (1982). The effects of variations in voir dire procedures in capital murder trials. *Law and Human Behavior, 6,* 1–13.

Nietzel, M. T., & Dillehay, R. C. (1983). Psychologists as consultants for changes of venue. *Law and Human Behavior, 7,* 309–335.

Nietzel, M. T., Dillehay, R. C., & Himelein, M. J. (1987). Effects of voir dire variations in capital trials: A replication and extension. *Behavioral Sciences and the Law, 5,* 467–477.

Ogloff, J. R. P. (2002). Two steps forward and one step backward: The law and psychology movement(s) in the 20th century. *Law and Human Behavior, 24,* 457–483.

Ogloff, J. R. P., & Vidmar, N. (1994). The impact of pretrial publicity on jurors: A study to compare the relative effects of television and print media in a child sex abuse case. *Law and Human Behavior, 18,* 507–525.

Olczak, P. V., Kaplan, M. R., & Penrod, S. (1991). Attorneys' lay psychology and its effectiveness in selecting jurors: Three empirical studies. *Journal of Social Behavior and Personality, 6,* 431–452.

Olkin, I. (1990). History and goals. In K. Wachter & M. Straf (Eds.), *The future of meta-analysis* (pp. 3–10). New York: Russell Sage.

Ostrom, T. M., Werner, C. M., & Saks, M. J. (1978). An integration theory analysis of jurors' presumptions of guilt or innocence. *Journal of Personality and Social Psychology, 36,* 436–450.

Otto, A. L., Penrod, S. D., & Dexter, H. R. (1994). The biasing impact of pretrial publicity on juror judgements. *Law and Human Behavior, 18,* 453–469.

Padawer-Singer, A. M., & Barton, A. H. (1975). The impact of pretrial publicity on jurors' verdicts. In J. Simon (Ed.), *The jury system in America: A critical overview* (pp. 125–139). Beverly Hills, CA: Sage.

Padawer-Singer, A. M., Singer, A., & Singer, R. (1974). Voir dire by two lawyers: An essential safeguard. *Judicature, 57,* 386–391.

Padawer-Singer, A. M., Singer, A. N., & Singer, R. L. J. (1977). Legal and social-psychological research in the effects of pretrial publicity on juries, numerical makeup of juries, non-unanimous verdict requirements. *Law and Psychology Review, 3,* 71–79.

Palmer, B., Baer, J., Jasperson, A., & DeLaat, J. (2001). Low-life-sleazy big-haired-trailer-park girl v. the President: The Paula Jones case and the law of sexual harassment. *American University Journal of Gender, Social Policy, and Law, 9,* 283–304.

Peacock, M. J., Cowan, G., Bommersbach, M., Smith, S. Y., & Stahly, G. (1997). Pretrial predictors of judgments in the O. J. Simpson case. *Journal of Social Issues, 53,* 441–454.

Pember, D. R. (1984). Does pretrial publicity really hurt? *Columbia Journalism Review, 23*(3), 16–20.

Pember, D. R. (1990). *Mass media law.* Dubuque, IA: William C. Brown.

Pennington, N., & Hastie, R. (1986). Evidence evaluation in complex decision making. *Journal of Personality & Social Psychology, 51*(2), 242–258.

Petty, R. E., & Cacioppo, J. T. (1986). *Communication and persuasion: Central and peripheral routes to attitude change.* New York: Springer-Verlag.

Pollock, A. J. (1977). The use of public opinion polls to obtain changes of venue and continuances in criminal trials. *Criminal Justice Journal, 1,* 269–288.

Posey, A. J., & Dahl, L. M. (2002). Beyond pretrial publicity: Legal and ethical issues associated with change of venue surveys. *Law and Human Behavior, 26,* 107–125.

Pritchard, D. (1990). Homicide and bargained justice. In R. Surette (Ed.), *The media and criminal justice policy: Recent research and social effects* (pp. 143–152). Springfield, IL: Charles C. Thomas.

Pritchard, D., & Hughes, K. D. (1997). Patterns of deviance in crime news. *Journal of Communication, 47*(3), 49–67.

Randall, D. M., Lee-Sammons, L., & Hagner, P. R. (1988). Common versus elite crime coverage in network news. *Social Science Quarterly, 69,* 910–929.

Reskin, B. F., & Visher, C. A. (1986). The impacts of evidence and extralegal factors in jurors' decisions. *Law and Society Review, 20,* 423–438.

Riedel, R. G. (1993). Effects of pretrial publicity on male and female jurors and judges in a mock rape trial case. *Psychological Reports, 73,* 819–832.

Rieke, R. D., & Stutman, R. K. (1990). *Communication in legal advocacy.* Columbia: University of South Carolina Press.

Riley, S. G. (1973). Pretrial publicity: A field study. *Journalism Quarterly, 50,* 17–23.

Robinson, J. P., & Levy, M. R. (1996). News media use and the informed public: A 1990s update. *Journal of Communication, 46,* 129–137.

Rollings, H. E., & Blascovich, J. (1977). The case of Patricia Hearst: Pretrial publicity and opinion. *Journal of Communication, 27,* 58–65.

Roth, P. A. (1987). *Meaning and method in the social sciences: A case for methodological pluralism.* Ithaca, NY: Cornell University Press.

Rothschild, N. (1984). Small group affiliation as a mediating factor in the cultivation process. In G. Melischek, E. R. Rosengren, J. Stappers, et al. (Eds.), *Cultural indicators: An international symposium* (pp. 377–388). Vienna: Osterreichischen Akademie der Wissenschaften.

Rouse, J. (1987). *Knowledge and power: Toward a political philosophy of science.* Ithaca, NY: Cornell University Press.

Saks, M. J., & Hastie, R. (1978). *Social psychology in court.* New York: Van Nostrand.

Schlag, P. (1997). *Laying down the law: Mysticism, fetishism, and the American legal mind.* New York: New York University Press.

Shaffer, R. A. (1986). Pretrial publicity: Media coverage and guilt attribution. *Communication Quarterly, 34,* 154–169.

Shapiro, R. (1994). Secrets of a celebrity lawyer: How O.J.'s chief strategist works the press. *Columbia Journalism Review, 33*(3), 25–29.

Sheppard v. Maxwell, 384 U.S. 333 (1966).

Sherard, R. G. (1987). Fair press or trial prejudice?: Perceptions of criminal defendants. *Journalism Quarterly, 64,* 337–340.

Shrum, L. J. (2001). Processing strategy moderates the cultivation effect. *Human Communication Research, 27*(1), 94–120.

Shrum, L. J., & Bischak, V. D. (2001). Mainstreaming, resonance, and impersonal impact: Testing moderators of the cultivation effect for estimates of crime risk. *Human Communication Research, 27*(2), 187–215.

Simon, R. J. (1966). Murder, juries, and the press. *Trans-Action, 3*(4), 40–42.

Simon, R. J. (1977). Does the Court's decision in *Nebraska Press Association* fit the research evidence on the impact on jurors of news coverage? *Stanford Law Review, 29,* 515–528.

Simon, R. J., & Eimermann, T. (1971). The jury finds not guilty: Another look at media influence on the jury. *Journalism Quarterly, 48,* 343–344.

Skolnick, P., & Shaw, J. I. (1997). The O.J. Simpson criminal trial verdict: Racism or status shield. *Journal of Social Issues, 53,* 503–516.

Slaughter, J. (1997, April 14). Business as usual unionism in Detroit; Failed strike against the *Detroit News* and *Detroit Free Press. The Nation, 264*(14), 10.

Sloan, A. (2002, August 12). How to look like a good guy. *Newsweek,* p. 32.

Sohn, A. B. (1976). Determining guilt or innocence of accused from pretrial news stories. *Journalism Quarterly, 53,* 100–105.

Sommers, S. R., & Ellsworth, P. C. (2001). White juror bias: An investigation of prejudice against black defendants in the American Courtroom. *Psychology, Public Policy, and Law, 7,* 201–229.

Sommers, S. R., & Kassin, S. M. (2001). On the many impacts of inadmissible testimony: Selective compliance, need for cognition, and overcorrection bias. *Personality and Social Psychology Bulletin, 27,* 1368–1377.

Songer, D. R., & Kuersten, A. (1995). The success of amici in state supreme courts. *Political Research Quarterly, 48,* 31–42.

Songer, D., Kuersten, A., & Kaheny, E. (2000). Why the haves don't always come out ahead: Repeat players meet amici curiae for the disadvantaged. *Political Research Quarterly, 53,* 537–556.

Spencer, D. (1982). Coverage seldom cause for conviction reversal. *Presstime,* 8–10.

Spiegel, M. R. (1990). *Statistics* (2nd ed.). New York: McGraw-Hill.

Steblay, N. M., Besirevic, J., Fulero, S. M., & Jimenez-Lorente, B. (1999). The effects of pretrial publicity on juror verdicts: A meta-analytic review. *Law and Human Behavior, 23,* 219–235.

Strauss, D. A. (1998). Why it's not free speech versus fair trial. *University of Chicago Legal Forum, 1998,* 109–123.

Studebaker, C. A., & Penrod, S. D. (1997). Pretrial publicity: The media, the law, and common sense. *Psychology, Public Policy, & Law, 3,* 428–460.

Studebaker, C. A., Robbennolt, J. K., Pathak-Sharma, M. K., & Penrod, S. D. (2000). Assessing pretrial publicity effects: Integrating content analytic results. *Law and Human Behavior, 24,* 317–336.

Studebaker, C. A., Robbennolt, J. K., Penrod, S. D., Pathak-Sharma, M. K., Groscup, J. L., & Davenport, J. L. (2002). Studying pretrial publicity effects: New methods for improving ecological validity and testing external validity. *Law and Human Behavior, 26,* 19–41.

Sue, S., Smith, R. E., & Gilbert, R. (1974). Biasing effects of pretrial publicity on judicial decisions. *Journal of Criminal Justice, 2,* 163–171.

Sue, S., Smith, R. E., & Pedroza, G. (1975). Authoritarianism, pretrial publicity, and awareness of bias in simulated jurors. *Psychological Reports, 37,* 1299–1302.

Surette, R. (1992). Media trials and echo effects. In R. Surette (Ed.), *The media and criminal justice policy: Recent research and social effects* (pp. 177–192). Springfield, IL: C. C. Thomas.

Tanford, S., & Penrod, S. (1982). Biases in trial involving defendants charged with multiple offenses. *Journal of Applied Social Psychology, 12,* 453–480.

Tankard, J. W., Middleton, K., & Rimmer, T. (1979). Compliance with American Bar Association fair trial-free press guidelines. *Journalism Quarterly, 56,* 464–468.

Tans, M. D., & Chaffee, S. H. (1966). Pretrial publicity and juror prejudice. *Journalism Quarterly, 43,* 647–654.

Tauber, S. C. (1998). On behalf of the condemned? The impact of the NAACP Legal Defense Fund on capital punishment decision making in the U.S. Courts of Appeals. *Political Research Quarterly, 51,* 191–219.

Thompson, W. C., Fong, G. T., & Rosenhan, D. L. (1981). Inadmissible evidence and juror verdicts. *Journal of Personality and Social Psychology, 3,* 453–463.

Tjaden, P., & Thoennes, N. (1998). *Role of stalking in domestic violence crime reports generated by the Colorado Springs Police Department, 1998* [computer file]. ICPSR version. Denver, CO: Center for Policy Research [producer], 2001. Ann Arbor, MI: Inter-University Consortium for Political and Social Research [distributor], 2001.

Valkenburg, P. M., Semetko, H. A., & de Vreese, C. H. (1999). The effects of news frames on readers' thoughts and recall. *Communication Research, 26*(5), 550–569.

VanDyke, J. M. (1977). *Jury selection procedures: Our uncertain commitment to representative panels.* Cambridge, MA: Ballinger.

Vidmar, N. (2002). Case studies of pre- and midtrial prejudice in criminal and civil litigation. *Law and Human Behavior, 26,* 73–105.

Vidmar, N., & Judson, J. T. (1981). The use of social science data in a change of venue application: A case study. *La Revue Du Barreau Canadien, 59,* 76–102.

Vidmar, N., & Melnitzer, J. (1984). Juror prejudice: An empirical study of challenge for cause. *Osgoode Hall Law Journal, 22,* 487–511.

Visher, C. A. (1987). Juror decision making: The importance of evidence. *Law and Human Behavior, 11,* 1–17.

Wachter, K. W., & Straf, M. L. (1990). *The future of meta-analysis.* New York: Russell Sage Foundation.

Walton, J. A. (1998). From O.J. to Tim McVeigh and beyond: The Supreme Court's totality of circumstances test as ringmaster in the expanding media circus. *Denver University Law Review, 75,* 549–593.

Wegener, D. T., Kerr, N. L., Fleming, M. A., & Petty, R. E. (2000). Flexible corrections of juror judgments: Implications for jury instructions. *Psychology, Public Policy, and Law, 6*, 629–654.

Wilcox, W. (1970). The press, the jury, and the behavioral sciences. In C. R. Bush (Ed.), *Free press and fair trial: Some dimensions of the problem* (pp. 49–106). Atlanta: University of Georgia Press.

Wilcox, W., & McCombs, M. (1967). *Crime story elements and fair trial/free press.* Unpublished report, University of California at Los Angeles. Reported in Wilcox (1970).

Wilson, J. R., & Bornstein, B. H. (1998). Methodological considerations in pretrial publicity research: Is the medium the message. *Law and Human Behavior, 22*, 585

Wolf, F. M. (1986). *Meta-analysis: Quantitative methods for research synthesis.* Beverly Hills, CA: Sage.

Zeisel, H., & Diamond, S. S. (1978). The effect of peremptory challenges on jury and verdict: An experiment in a federal district court. *Stanford Law Review, 30*, 491–531.

Zuckerman, M. (1979). Attribution success and failure revisited, or: The motivational bias is alive and well in attribution theory. *Journal of Personality, 47*, 245–287.

Author Index

A

Adams, D., 99, 165
Alfini, J. J., 4, 6, 9, 14, 49, 93, 94, 106, 166, 168
Arkin, R., 68, 165
Arndt, J., 97, 139, 169
Atkinson, R., 143, 145, 149, 165

B

Baer, J., 24, 145, 170
Ball-Rokeach, S. J., 101, 102, 165, 166, 169
Barton, A. H., 4, 6, 8, 9, 28, 33, 40, 46, 96, 170
Bauer, W. J., 29, 165
Belt, T., 105, 167
Berger, C. R., 110, 111, 165
Besirevic, J., 7, 9, 20, 23, 24, 29, 66, 67, 68, 69, 70, 71, 74, 77, 88, 89, 135, 152, 172
Bischak, V. D., 111, 171
Black, D., 144, 165
Blascovich, J., 4, 6, 8, 30, 50, 171
Bommersbach, M., 24, 170
Bornstein, B. H., 6, 9, 23, 24, 25, 30, 41, 43, 45, 46, 47, 97, 137, 165, 173
Brady, L. A., 100, 165
Bright, S. B., 76, 145, 146, 147, 148, 165
Brock, B., 23, 94, 169
Brooks, P., 107, 165
Bruschke, J. C., 4, 5, 8, 11, 27, 76, 85, 87, 92, 100, 101, 107, 108, 130, 136, 165
Burke, T. M., 9, 58, 61, 65, 66, 87, 135, 152, 167
Burns, R. P., 143, 166

C

Cacioppo, J. T., 109, 142, 170
Carroll, J. S., 4, 5, 6, 9, 10, 14, 27, 28, 38, 45, 46, 49, 93, 94, 96, 106, 166, 168
Chaffee, S. H., 30, 31, 77, 172
Chaiken, S., 142, 166
Constantini, E., 4, 29, 30, 96, 166
Cook, T. D., 25, 67, 68, 70, 71, 72, 166
Cooper, H., 68, 165
Cowan, G., 23, 24, 166, 170
Cutler, B. L., 4, 6, 8, 9, 29, 30, 42, 46, 47, 49, 91, 93, 94, 96, 166, 169

D

Dahl, L. M., 6, 170
D'Allessio, S. J., 143, 166
Daudistel, H. C., 11, 24, 144, 166
Davenport, J. L., 6, 9, 23, 24, 26, 55, 172
Davidson, W. P., 31, 166
Davis, R. W., 6, 28, 40, 59, 61, 65, 66, 94, 135, 166
DeFleur, M. L., 101, 105, 166
DeLaat, J., 24, 145, 170
Dennis, E. E., 105, 166
de Vreese, C. H., 41, 106, 172
Dexter, H. R., 8, 9, 28, 42, 46, 47, 49, 51, 54, 57, 65, 66, 74, 88, 91, 93, 94, 136, 166, 170
Diamond, S. S., 9, 94, 107, 110, 166, 173
Dillehay, R. C., 4, 5, 6, 87, 95, 169
Dixon, T. L., 102, 103, 166
Doob, A. N., 8, 9, 28, 168

Duff, K., 23, 94, 169
Dunaway, D. L., 45, 46, 47, 97, 165

E

Eagly, A. H., 142, 166
Eichenwald, K., 104, 166
Eimermann, T., 30, 171
Ellsworth, P. C., 25, 171
Emmelman, D. S., 144, 166
Entman, R., 102, 103, 104, 106, 166
Epstein, L., 11, 167
Espie, R. H. M., 166

F

Fairchild, H. H., 23, 166
Federal Bureau of Investigation, 157, 159,
      166
Federal Judicial Center, 12, 25, 77–78, 79,
      160, 166, 167
Fein, S., 27, 49, 54, 55, 93, 94, 167
Feingold, A., 144, 169
Feldman, V., 4, 6, 9, 14, 93, 166
Fisher, W. L., 112, 167
Fleming, M. A., 97, 98, 173
Fong, G. T., 28, 94, 97, 172
Frasca, R., 4, 5, 167
Frederick, J., 6, 96, 169
Freedman, J. L., 8, 9, 23, 28, 36, 43, 46, 47,
      53, 58, 61, 65, 66, 70, 71, 87, 97,
      135, 150, 152, 167
Freedman, M. H., 145, 147, 167
Fulero, S. M., 7, 9, 14, 20, 23, 24, 29, 66, 67,
      68, 69, 70, 71, 74, 77, 88, 89, 93,
      135, 138, 152, 167, 172

G

Gans, H. J., 103, 167
Gass, R. H., 140, 167
George, T. E., 11, 167
Gerber, R. J., 147, 148, 149, 167
Gerbner, G., 108, 109, 111, 115, 167
Gewirtz, P. D., 107, 165
Gibson, D. C., 66, 167
Gilbert, R., 9, 33, 46, 47, 97, 172
Gottlieb, C., 105, 167
Graber, D. A., 103, 106, 167
Graves, J. B., 11, 24, 144, 166
Greene, E., 28, 29, 31, 50, 167, 168

Groscup, J. L., 6, 9, 23, 24, 26, 55, 172
Gross, L., 108, 109, 111, 115, 167, 168

H

Hagner, P. R., 105, 170
Hans, V. P., 8, 9, 28, 168
Hastie, R., 47, 107, 170, 171
Hays, W. L., 163, 168
Hedges, L. V., 23, 67, 68, 70, 71, 168
Herrick, D., 73, 168
Himelein, M. J., 95, 169
Hoffman, Y., 23, 94, 169
Hoiberg, B. C., 48, 94, 168
Holmes, M. D., 11, 24, 144, 166
Hosch, H. M., 11, 24, 144, 166
Hough, G. A., 5, 168
Hughes, K. D., 100, 101, 102, 111, 136, 170
Hvistendahl, J. K., 28, 29, 30, 168

I

Imrich, D. J., 1, 4, 28, 44, 60, 65, 66, 86, 93,
      104, 105, 136, 168, 169
Infante, D. A., 28, 168

J

Jaccard, J., 83, 168
Jackson-Beeck, M., 109, 167
James, P. C., 166
Jasperson, A., 24, 145, 170
Jess, P. H., 4, 28, 48, 168
Jimenez-Lorente, B., 7, 9, 20, 23, 24, 29, 66,
      67, 68, 69, 70, 71, 74, 77, 88, 89,
      135, 152, 172
Jones, R. M., 4, 6, 8, 9, 10, 22, 168
Judson, J. T., 6, 30, 93, 94, 172

K

Kaheny, E., 11, 144, 171
Kaiser Family Foundation, 114, 157, 158, 168
Kaplan, M. F., 26, 28, 93, 94, 168
Kaplan, M. R., 24, 93, 94, 170
Kassin, S. M., 94, 97, 136, 171
Kelman, M., 14, 168
Kerr, N. L., 4, 5, 6, 8, 9, 10, 14, 27, 28, 37, 38,
      39, 45, 46, 47, 49, 66, 73, 76, 78,
      91, 93, 94, 96, 97, 98, 106, 152,
      166, 168, 169, 173

Kerwin, J., 10, 23, 26, 28, 107, 135, 151, 168
King, J., 4, 29, 30, 96, 166
Kipling, R., 134, 168
Kline, F. G., 4, 28, 48, 168
Kolditz, T., 68, 165
Kotiaho, J. S., 69, 168
Kovera, M. B., 4, 8, 9, 17, 26, 63, 65, 66, 108,
    136, 168
Kramer, G. P., 4, 5, 9, 10, 27, 28, 37, 38, 39,
    45, 46, 47, 49, 73, 91, 93, 94, 96,
    106, 168
Kuersten, A., 11, 144, 171
Kulish, M., 14, 27, 168

L

Landsman, S., 97, 169
Langenberg,com, 159, 169
Lee-Sammons, L., 105, 170
Leviton, L. C., 25, 67, 68, 70, 71, 72, 166
Levy, M. R., 29, 171
Liberman, A., 142, 166
Lieberman, J. D., 97, 139, 169
Lindman, R., 6, 169
Linz, D., 1, 4, 28, 44, 60, 65, 66, 86, 93, 102,
    103, 104, 105, 136, 166, 168, 169
Lofton, J., 1, 169
Loftus, E. F., 29, 31, 167
Loges, W. E., 4, 5, 8, 27, 76, 85, 87, 92, 100,
    101, 107, 108, 130, 136, 165
Loges, W. E., 102, 169
London, K., 11, 23, 28, 40, 71, 73, 135, 137,
    151, 169

M

MacCoun, R. J., 4, 6, 9, 14, 73, 93, 166, 169
Martin, C. K., 8, 9, 23, 28, 36, 43, 46, 47, 53,
    61, 66, 70, 71, 97, 150, 167
Masling, J. M., 140, 141, 169
Mayer, M., 100, 169
Mazzella, R., 144, 169
McCloskey, A. L., 27, 49, 54, 55, 93, 167
McCombs, M., 9, 173
McConahay, J. B., 6, 96, 169
Medina, H. R., 2, 169
Melnitzer, J., 6, 9, 94, 94, 172
Melton, G. B., 6, 169
Middleton, K., 4, 104, 172
Miller, G. R., 73, 169
Miller, L. E., 26, 28, 93, 94, 168

Moran, G., 4, 6, 8, 9, 29, 30, 42, 46, 47, 49,
    91, 93, 94, 96, 166, 169
Morgan, M., 108, 109, 111, 115, 167, 168
Morgan, S. J., 54, 94, 167
Mota, V. L., 8, 9, 23, 28, 36, 43, 46, 47, 53, 61,
    66, 70, 71, 97, 150, 167
Mullin, C., 1, 4, 28, 44, 60, 65, 66, 86, 93,
    104, 105, 136, 168, 169
Mullin, C. J., 6, 96, 169

N

Nemeth, R. J., 45, 46, 47, 97, 165
Nerenz, D. R., 73, 168
Newman, L. S., 23, 94, 169
Newsom, A., 4, 14, 169
Nietzel, M. T., 4, 5, 6, 87, 95, 169
Norton, M. I., 54, 94, 167
Nunez, N., 11, 23, 28, 40, 71, 73, 135, 137,
    151, 169

O

Ogloff, J. R. P., 4, 6, 29, 30, 94, 170
Olczak, P. V., 24, 93, 94, 170
Olkin, I., 19, 170
Ostrom, T. M., 47, 170
Otto, A. L., 8, 9, 28, 51, 54, 57, 65, 66, 74, 88,
    91, 136, 170

P

Padawer-Singer, A. M., 4, 6, 8, 9, 23, 28, 33,
    35, 40, 46, 49, 93, 94, 96, 170
Padilla, M., 66, 167
Palmer, B., 24, 145, 170
Pathak-Sharma, M. K., 4, 6, 7, 8, 9, 23, 24,
    26, 55, 172
Peacock, M. J., 24, 170
Pedroza, G., 3, 35, 46, 47, 91, 172
Pember, D. R., 6, 9, 28, 29, 93, 170
Pennington, N., 107, 170
Penrod, S., 24, 36, 41, 47, 77, 93, 94, 170, 172
Penrod, S. D., 4, 6, 7, 8, 9, 10, 14, 23, 24, 26,
    28, 49, 51, 54, 55, 57, 58, 64, 65,
    66, 73, 74, 76, 88, 91, 93, 94, 135,
    136, 138, 167, 170, 172
Pertilla, A., 100, 165
Petty, R. E., 97, 98, 109, 142, 170, 173
Pollock, A. J., 93, 170
Posey, A. J., 6, 170

Pritchard, D., 78, 100, 101, 102, 111, 121, 128, 136, 148, 170

R

Rajki, M., 23, 24, 30, 137, 165
Rakos, R. F., 97, 169
Rancer, A. S., 28, 168
Randall, D M., 105, 170
Reskin, B. F., 47, 170
Riedel, R. G., 50, 60, 65, 66, 85, 86, 136, 170
Rieke, R. D., 36, 143, 170
Riley, S. G., 4, 6, 9, 29, 30, 171
Rimmer, T., 4, 104, 172
Robbennolt, J. K., 4, 6, 7, 8, 9, 23, 24, 26, 55, 172
Robinson, J. P., 29, 171
Rollings, H. E., 4, 6, 8, 29, 30, 50, 171
Rosenhan, D. L., 28, 94, 97, 172
Roth, P. A., 16, 171
Rothschild, N., 109, 171
Rouse, J., 13, 171

S

Saks, M. J., 47, 170, 171
Schlag, P., 15, 171
Schnopp-Wyatt, N., 23, 94, 169
Seiter, J. S., 140, 167
Semetko, H. A., 41, 106, 172
Shaffer, D. R., 10, 23, 26, 28, 107, 135, 151, 168
Shaffer, R. A., 30, 171
Shapiro, R., 1, 102, 104, 113, 171
Shaw, J. I., 23, 171
Sheppard v. Maxwell, 2, 5, 171
Sherard, R. G., 28, 171
Shrum, L. J., 109, 111, 142, 171
Signorielli, N., 108, 109, 111, 115, 167
Simon, R. J., 2, 4, 6, 14, 30, 58, 61, 65, 66, 135, 171
Singer, A., 9, 23, 35, 49, 93, 94, 170
Singer, A. N., 6, 8, 23, 170
Singer, R., 9, 23, 35, 49, 93, 94, 170
Singer, R. L. J., 6, 8, 23, 170
Skolnick, P., 23, 171
Slaughter, J., 80, 171
Sloan, A., 104, 171
Smith, R. E., 3, 9, 33, 35, 46, 47, 91, 97, 172
Smith, S. Y., 24, 170
Sohn, A. B., 30, 171

Sommers, S. R., 25, 54, 94, 97, 136, 167, 171
Songer, D., 11, 144, 171
Songer, D. R., 11, 171
Spencer, D., 4, 171
Spiegel, M. R., 23, 33, 172
Stahly G., 24, 170
Steblay, N. M., 7, 9, 20, 23, 24, 29, 66, 67, 68, 69, 70, 71, 74, 77, 88, 89, 135, 152, 172
Stires, L. K., 48, 94, 168
Stolzenberg, L., 143, 166
Straf, M. L., 69, 71, 172
Strauss, D. A., 4, 14, 172
Studebaker, C. A., 4, 6, 7, 8, 9, 10, 14, 23, 24, 26, 28, 49, 55, 58, 64, 66, 73, 76, 91, 93, 94, 135, 138, 172
Stutman, R. K., 36, 143, 170
Sue, S., 3, 9, 33, 35, 46, 47, 91, 97, 172
Surette, R., 5, 92, 113, 136, 172

T

Tanford, S., 36, 41, 47, 77, 172
Tankard, J. W., 4, 104, 172
Tans, M. D., 30, 31, 77, 172
Tauber, S. C., 144, 172
Thoennes, N., 114, 158, 160, 172
Thompson, W. C., 28, 94, 97, 172
Tjaden, P., 114, 158, 160, 172
Tomkins, J. L., 69, 168
Tomlinson, T. M., 27, 49, 54, 55, 93, 167
Turrisi, R., 83, 168

V

Valkenburg, P. M., 41, 106, 172
VanDyke, J. M., 49, 172
Vidmar, N., 4, 6, 7, 8, 9, 23, 27, 28, 29, 30, 73, 87, 93, 94, 95, 98, 106, 140, 152, 170, 172
Visher, C. A., 36, 47, 91, 170, 172

W

Wachter, K. W., 69, 71, 172
Wade, R., 28, 50, 168
Walton, J. A., 1, 6, 27, 95, 172
Wan, C. K., 83, 168
Weaver, F. M., 4, 6, 9, 14, 93, 166
Wegener, D. T., 97, 98, 173
Werner, C. M., 47, 170

Whisenhunt, B. L., 45, 46, 47, 97, 165
Wilcox, W., 8, 28, 173
Wilson, J. R., 9, 41, 43, 46, 47, 173
Wolf, F. M., 67, 68, 69, 70, 173
Womack, D. F., 28, 168

Z

Zeisel, H., 9, 94, 173
Zuckerman, M., 68, 173

Subject Index

A

"Acquittal by court," 82
"Acquittal by jury," 82
African Americans, media crime coverage and, 102
Age, media crime coverage and, 101
Aggravated assault, 158
America's Most Dangerous Car Chases, 4
American Bar Association
    Standards / Model Rules on pretrial publicity, 4, 32, 104
    system to measure pretrial publicity, 153
American Justice, 4
Ames, Fisher, 1
Amicus curiae, 144
Analysis
    city-level, 157–164
    meta-, 7, 67–72, 135
    path, 51
    statistical, 114–116, 119, 122, 126, 127, 129, 130, 160
Analysis of variance (ANOVA) model, 116
Antidefendant pretrial publicity, 4, 50, 99, 103–105
Appeals, publicity as grounds for, 5
Appellate courts
    interest groups and, 144
    wealth and decisions of, 11
Assault, aggravated, 158
Atlanta
    analysis of court cases in, 78, 81, 157–159
    relation between crime coverage and crime rate in, 115, 158

Attitude change, perception and, 140–141
Attitudinal variables, mock jurors and, 24, 25
Attorneys
    defense, 102, 104–105, 144–147
    on pretrial publicity, 1
    quality of representation, 144, 155
Audience retention, of media coverage, 153–154
Authoritarianism, 36

B

Bailey, F. Lee, 11
Baltimore, analysis of court cases in, 157–159
Bank robberies, 78, 79
    sentence length and coverage of, 83–84, 85, 86
Bar of the City of New York, on pretrial publicity, 2
Beliefs about crime, *see* Cultivation effect study
Benn, John, 147
Bernardo (Paul) trial, 61, 153
Bias
    juror willingness to admit, 94
    meta-analysis and, 68–72
    pretrial publicity and preexisting, 63–64
    publication, 69–70
    Type I error and, 78
Binary logistic regression, 116
Blue-collar crime, coverage of, 102–103
Bobbitt, Lorena, 2
Burglary, 158
Burr (Aaron) treason trial, 1

C

Case law, on pretrial publicity, 5–7
Cell size equalization, 87
Central-route cognitive processing, 109, 110, 142
Central tendency, measuring, 130
Change of jurors, 8
Change of venue, 3, 6, 8, 93, 138
Charges pleaded, *see* Plea bargaining
Chicago, analysis of court cases in, 157–159
Chi-square test, 122, 126, 128
Civil trials, 45–46
Clinton, William Jefferson (Bill), 145
CLS, *see* Critical legal studies
Cochrane, Johnny, 11
Coding, in meta-analysis, 70
Cognitive processing, 109–110, 142
Columbia Journalism Review, 104
Combs, Sean "Puffy," 2
Conflict frame, 106
Connally, John, 2
Context, science and, 13
Continuance
    pretrial publicity and, 39
    as remedy for pretrial publicity, 8, 9–10, 93
    retrials and, 34, *see also* Delays
"Conviction by court," 82
"Conviction by jury," 82
Conviction rates
    criminal, 4
    in city-level analysis, 157, 162, 163
    in laboratory studies, 25–26
    pretrial publicity and, 8, 108, 136–137
    trial length and, 37–38
    see also Trial outcomes; Verdicts
Court-appointed defense attorneys, 144–147
Court records, 79, 160–161
Court TV, 4
Crime
    concern for overall, 159, 160–164
    fear of, *see* Fear of crime
    fear of violent, 114, 117, 158–159, 160–164
    media coverage of, *see* Media coverage of crime; Pretrial publicity
    sentence length and type of, 83–84, 85
    types of, 158
Crime coverage, *see* Media coverage of crime
Crime cycle, 112

Crime index, 157–158
Crime rate, 114
    crime coverage and, 114, 115
    fear of crime and, 115
    length of pleaded sentence and, 123, 124, 125, 126
    length of tried sentences and, 130–131
    plea bargaining, crime coverage, and, 119, 120–121
Criminal cases, 77
Criminal convictions, 4, *see also* Conviction rates; Trial outcomes; Verdicts
Critical legal studies (CLS), 13–14, 143
Crossover interaction effect, 124
Cultivation effect study, 113–132
    average length of pleaded sentence, 122–126
    crime coverage effect on defendants, 131–132
    length of sentence at trial, 128–131
    methods, 113–118
    percent of charges pleaded, 118–122
    trial conviction percentage, 126–128
Cultivation theory, 108–109
    central processing and, 109, 110, 142
    mainstreaming and, 115
    pretrial publicity and, 108–111, 132–133
Cultural deviance, 101, 102, *see also* Deviance
Cumulative remedy hypothesis, 17, 18, 57, 92–98, 135–136
    evidence for, 74
    field research support for, 89
    laboratory evidence for, 61, 65
    meta-analysis and, 70–71

D

Davis, Angela, 2
Death penalty, 117, 131, 132
Defendant(s)
    benefits from pretrial publicity, 11–12
    bias against, 144
    characteristics of, 30
    level of crime coverage and, 131–132
    likeability of, 51
    persuasiveness of, 51
    pretrial publicity when fear of crime is low and, 127–128
    socioeconomic status and trial outcomes for, 143–148
    sympathy for, 51, 52

Defense attorneys
  court-appointed, 144–147
  cultivating, relations with media,
      104–105
  media system dependency and, 102, 104
  see also Attorneys
Defense strategies
  plea bargaining and, 86
  as remedy for pretrial publicity, 54–55,
      57, 89, 155
Delays
  natural, 59, 65, 89, 135, 137
  as remedy for pretrial publicity, 28–29,
      135, 137, 148
  see also Continuance
Deliberation
  alternative to, 110
  in laboratory studies, 27–28, 33
  mock jurors and, 24, 39–40
  pretrial publicity and, 49–50
  process of, 107
  prodefendant shift and, 59
  as remedy for pretrial publicity, 9, 10, 11,
      61–62, 65, 89, 93, 135, 137, 151
  trial outcomes and, 58
Demographic variables, mock jurors and,
      23–24, 25
Denver, analysis of court cases in, 157–159
Dependent variables, 116–117, 151–152
Detroit, analysis of court cases in, 78, 80, 81
Deviance, media coverage and, 100–101,
      103, 107–108, 111
"Dismissed," 82
"Dismissed without prejudice," 82
Dunkins, Horace, 146

E

Echo effect, 113
Ecological validity, Internet and, 55–57
Economic consequences frame, 106
Economic-legal theory, pretrial publicity
      and, 139, 143–150, *see also* Realist
      movement in law
Education, trial outcomes and juror, 143
Einstein, Albert, 138
Elaboration Likelihood Model, 142
Emotional publicity, 37, 41, 43–45, 106
Evidence
  categorizing, 154
  classifying quality of, 151

cognitive processing of, 142
crime coverage and juror processing of,
      64
defendant socioeconomic status and,
      145–148
in laboratory studies, 32–47
laboratory studies without, 135–136
as natural remedy, 29
pretrial publicity and, 36, 95, 137
as remedy for pretrial publicity, 34,
      61–62, 65, 93
supraliminal persuasion and, 141
trial outcome and, 25, 26, 35–37, 38, 43,
      47, 52–53, 57, 58
weak inadmissible, 50–51, 53, 57, 65, 136
Evidence-driven jury, 110

F

Face concerns, 98
Factual publicity, 34–35, 37, 41, 43–45
Fair trial, 85, 138
False positives, 151
FBI statistics, 157–158
Fear of crime, 114
  city-level analysis of, 157, 159–164
  crime coverage and, 115
  crime coverage, defendants, and, 131–132
  crime rate and, 115
  cultivation theory and, 132
  length of pleaded sentence and, 123,
      124–125
  length of tried sentences and, 129
  plea bargaining, crime coverage, and,
      119–120, 121
  pretrial publicity and, 126, 136
  trial conviction percentage and, 127–128
  variables, 117
Fear of violence, 114, 117, 158–159, 160–161
Federal court records, 79, 160–161
Federal Judicial Center (FJC), 79, 82, 114
Federal-level offenses, 87
Field studies
  conclusions regarding pretrial publicity
      effect, 7, 12, 88–92, 136
  forging remedy based on, 92–98
  vs. laboratory, 17, 21–23, 66, 72, 152–153
  literature review, 76–77
  new research, 77–88
First Amendment, 4, 19
FJC, *see* Federal Judicial Center

Florida Department of Corrections, 143–144
Florida Supreme Court, 14
Formalism, legal, 139, 143
Frames, 106, 108, 112
Free speech issues, 4, 19
Frequency data, 110–111

G

Gazette and Daily Advertiser, 1
Gender
    pretrial publicity and, 48, 101
    quantitative data and, 111
    rape cases and, 60, 65
    trial outcomes and juror, 143
Generalization, of laboratory studies on
        pretrial publicity, 7–9, 23, 26, 72–74
Gerber, Rudolph, 149–150
Gideon v. Wainwright, 147
Guilt
    determination of, 82
    measuring, 152
    presumption of, 113
Guilt rating, 152
"Guilty but insane," 82
Guilty plea, 82

H

Hagedorn, William, 146–147
Halo effect, 139
Hauptmann (Bruno) trial, 1
Hearst (Patty) trial, 30–31
Heuristic Systematic Model, 142
Hiss (Alger) trial, 1
Houston, analysis of court cases in, 157–159
Houston Chronicle, 147
Human interest frame, 106
Hung juries, 34, 39, 40–42, 59

I

ICPSR, *see* Inter-University Consortium for
        Political and Social Research
Inadmissible evidence in pretrial publicity,
        50–51, 53, 57, 65, 136
Independent tests, 68
Indigent defense, 146–147
Individual verdicts, 54, 59
Individual voir dire, 14, 95, 138
Injustice, stories of, 32

Innocence, presumption of, 98, 113
Interest groups, defendants and, 144, 148
Internet, ecological validity and, 55–57
Inter-University Consortium for Political
        and Social Research (ICPSR), 79,
        114, 158, 160
Ito, Lance, 19

J

Joined-charge effect, 41
Jones, Paula, 145
Judges, response to pretrial publicity when
        fear of crime is low, 127–128
Judge trial, 118
Juries
    evidence-driven, 110
    hung, 34, 39, 40–42, 59
    simulated, 10–11, 23–25, 73–74, *see also*
            Laboratory studies
Jurors, 93–96
    bias and, 94, 95–96
    change of, 8
    cultivation effect and, 109
    effect of pretrial publicity on, 17–18,
            105–108, 136–137
    mock, 10–11, 23–25, 73–74
    narrative coherence and, 112
    research focus on individual, 40–41
    role of, 111–112
    selection of, 9, 89, 94, 135, 137, *see also*
            Voir dire
Jury instructions, 57
    evidence and, 36
    improving, 97–98
    including rationale in, 97
    mock jurors and, 24
    as remedy for pretrial publicity, 8, 9, 10,
            17, 28, 45, 62, 93, 96–98, 135,
            137, 138, 150–151
Jury trial, 118
Justice, pretrial publicity and, 149

K

Kaiser Family Foundation, 114, 157
King, Rodney, 2
Knowledge-guilt hypothesis, 16–17, 75, 95,
        136
    defendant persuasiveness and, 51
    laboratory study and, 36

laboratory studies without trial evidence and, 30–32
McVeigh case and, 56–57
support for, 92
Kuhn, Thomas, 12
Kwan, Kenneth, 147

L

Laboratory studies
  categorizing, 20–21
  conviction rates in, 25–26
  delay between publicity exposure and presentation of evidence and, 28–29
  deliberation in, 27–28, 33
  demographic variables and, 23–24, 25
  disproving pretrial publicity effect, 58–65
    Davis, 59–60
    Freedman and Burke, 61
    Freedman, Martin, and Mota, 61–62
    Kovera, 63–64
    Mullin, Imrich, and Linz, 60–61
    Riedel, 60
    Simon, 58, 66
  evaluation criteria, 21, 23–29
  features of trial practice and design of, 132–133
  vs. field studies, 17, 21–23, 66, 152–153
  level of publicity exposure in, 26–27
  meta-analysis and, 67–72
  methodological studies, 72–74
  partially supporting pretrial publicity effect, 47–57
    Fein, McCloskey, and Tomlinson, 54–55
    Fein, Morgan, Norton, and Sommers, 54
    Greene and Wade, 50
    Hoiberg and Stires, 48
    Kline and Jess, 48
    Otto, Penrod, and Dexter, 50–54, 66–67
    Padawer-Singer, Singer, and Singer, 49–50
    Studebaker, Robbennolt, Penrod, Pathak-Sharma, Groscup, and Davenport, 55–57
  pretrial publicity and, 7–12, 74–75, 133
  on remedies, 9–10
  without trial evidence, 29–32, 70, 71, 135–136

with trial evidence and pretrial publicity effect, 32–47
    Bornstein, Whisenhunt, Nemeth, and Dunaway, 45–46
    Dexter, Cutler, and Moran, 42–43
    Kramer and Kerr, 37–38
    Kramer, Kerr, and Carroll, 38–42
    Padawer-Singer and Barton, 33–35
    Sue, Smith, and Gilbert, 33
    Sue, Smith, and Pedroza, 35–37
    Wilson and Bornstein, 43–45
  use of probative information in publicity manipulation, 46–47
LA Cops, 4
Langenberg web site, 159
Larceny, 158
Latinos, media crime coverage and, 102
Law, as theoretical base, 13–15
Law enforcement, information resources of, 102, 103, 104, 112
Law reviews, social science and, 14–15
Lawyers, see Attorneys
Legal case
  criminal, 77
  media coverage and types of, 154–155
  phases of, 151
Legal defense, publicly funded, 149
Legal doctrine, on pretrial publicity, 5–7
Legal reform, 149–150
Legal resources, access to, 11–12, 15–16, 17, 145–149
Leopold and Loeb conviction, 1
Levy, Chandra, 100
Lexis/Nexis database, 79–80
Life sentence, 117–118, 132
Lindberg prosecution, 1
Litigants, on pretrial publicity, 1
Local television news, 105, 114
Log odds ratio, 116
Los Angeles, analysis of court cases in, 78, 81, 157–159

M

Mainstreaming, 115
MANOVA, see Multivariate analysis of variance
Mass media effect, 139
Matched-case sampling, 152
McFarland, George, 147
McVeigh (Timothy) trial, 8, 55–57

Media
   on pretrial publicity, 1
   use of quantitative data, 110–111
Media coverage of crime, 100–103
   audience retention of, 153–154
   of blue-collar crime, 102–103
   crime rate and, 114, 115
   exposure of jurors to, 105
   fear of crime and, 115
   influence on defendants, 131–132
   juror processing of evidence and, 64
   length of pleaded sentence and, 122,
      123, 124, 125
   length of tried sentence and, 128–131
   plea bargaining and, 118–122
   trial conviction percentage and, 126–128
   types of crime and, 100–101
   of white-collar crime, 102–103
Media studies, pretrial publicity and, 2
Media system dependency, 101–103
Media theory, 99–113
   antidefendant slant of pretrial publicity
      and, 99, 103–105
   cultivation theory and, 108–111
   effect of crime coverage on jurors, 99,
      105–108
   pretrial publicity and, 99, 100–103,
      138–139
   viewership/readership of crime cover-
      age, 99, 105
Media trial, 75, 92
Men
   interpretation of quantitative data, 111
   pretrial publicity in rape cases and, 60,
      65, 136, *see also* Gender
Meta-analysis, 7, 67–72, 135
Meta-theories, 12–13
Methodological artifact, 24, 28
Methodological issues/questions, 72–74,
      150–153
Minneapolis
   analysis of court cases in, 157–159
   crime rate and crime coverage in, 115
Mistrial, 82
Mitchell, John, 2
Mock jurors, 10–11, 23–25, 73–74
Moral order offenders, 144
Motor vehicle theft, 158
Multinomial regression, 116, 122, 126, 130
Multivariate analysis of variance
      (MANOVA), 160

Murder cases
   field study of, 76–77, 79, 158
   media coverage of, 100
   mock, 33
   pretrial publicity and, 5
   sentence length and coverage of, 83, 85, 86

N

Nagelkerke pseudo-R^2, 119, 122, 127, 129
Narrative, pretrial publicity and, 107, 108,
      112
National Intelligencer, 1
National news, 105
Natural delays, as remedy for pretrial public-
      ity, 89, 135, 137
Natural remedies, 10, 29
National Association for the Advancement of
      Colored People (NAACP)-spon-
      sored Legal Defense Fund, 144
Newspaper coverage
   in murder trials, 76–77
   readership, 105
   using Lexis/Nexis to assess, 79–80
New York City
   analysis of court cases in, 157–159
   crime coverage and crime rate in, 115
New York Civil Liberties Union, 104
Nolle prosequi, 82
Normative deviance, 101, *see also* Deviance
"Not guilty by reason of insanity," 82

O

Occupation, trial outcomes and juror, 143
Offenders, types of, 144, *see also* Defen-
      dant(s)
Outliers, 130–131, 152

P

PACER databases, *see* Public Access to Court
      Electronic Records databases
Parkman, George, 1
Partitioning-of-variance approach, 116
Path analysis, 51
Pearson's *r*, 114, 115, 160
Perception, attitude change and, 140–141
Peripheral cognitive processing, 109–110, 142
Perp walk, 104
Personal safety, concern for, 114, 117, 159,
      160–164

Persuasion, 140–142
Philadelphia, analysis of court cases in, 157–159
Phoenix, analysis of court cases in, 157–159
Plea bargaining
    access to legal resources and, 148
    crime rate, crime coverage, and, 119,
        120–121
    fear of crime, crime coverage and,
        119–120, 121, 128
    percentage of cases pleaded, 163, 164
    pretrial publicity and, 77–78, 84, 86,
        118–122
    rate of, 151–152
    sentence length and, 117–118, 122–126,
        152, 162, 163
Predeliberation verdicts, 62
Prejudice, determining, 6
Pretrial diversion, 82
Pretrial opinions, 150–151
Pretrial plea stage, 151
Pretrial publicity
    academic research on, 2–3
    access to legal resources and, 11–12
    amount of coverage, 87, 88
    antidefendant, 4, 50, 99, 103–105
    basic issues in, 3–5
    cultivation and, 108–111, 132–133
    cumulative remedy hypothesis, see Cu-
        mulative remedy hypothesis
    defense strategies and, 54–55
    economic-legal theory and, 139,
        143–150
    elimination of preexisting bias and, 63–64
    emotional, 37, 41, 43–45, 106
    evidence and, 34, 36, 64, 91, 137
    existence of effect of, 4–5, 19–29
    factual, 34–35, 37, 41, 43–45
    fear of crime and, 115, 119–120, 121,
        126, 131–132, 136
    field studies on, see Field studies
    gender effect and, 48
    history of, 1–2
    inadmissible evidence and, 50–51, 53
    indigent defendants and, 148–149
    jurors and, 17–18, 105–108, 136–137
    justice and, 149
    knowledge-guilt hypothesis and, see
        Knowledge-guilt hypothesis
    laboratory studies on, see Laboratory
        studies
    legal doctrine and, 5–7

    level of exposure to, 26–27
    measuring, 79–80, 82
    media theory and, 138–139
    newspaper, 76–77, 79–80, 105
    plea bargaining and, 77–78, 84, 86
    probative value of, 36, 37
    prodefendant coverage, 4, 31, 45, 50
    psychological perspective on, 138–143
    reinforcing existing beliefs, 106–108
    remedies for, see Remedies for pretrial
        publicity
    retention of, 87–88
    sensational, 59, 65, 136, 141
    sentence length and, 76–77, 78, 81–83,
        85, 86, 126
    social context and, 22
    stories of injustice, 32
    structural paradox hypothesis and, 17,
        138, 148–149
    subliminal persuasion and, 141
    trial complexity and, 37–38
    trial outcomes and, 3, 17, 81–83, 85, 92,
        134–136
    type of case and, 77, 154–155
    voir dire and, see Voir dire
    see also Media coverage of crime
Prior record, 144
Prison crowding, fear of crime and, 126
Probative information, in pretrial publicity,
    53, 75, 92, 107, 137, 153
Pro bono systems, 143, 146–147
Prodefendant publicity, 4, 31, 45, 50
Project for Excellence in Journalism, 105
Property offenders, 144
Prosecutors, plea-bargaining process and,
    121–122, 125
Psychological perspective on pretrial public-
    ity, 2, 138–143
Public Access to Court Electronic Records
    (PACER) databases, 79
Publication bias, 69–70

Q

Qualitative literature review, 67
Quantitative data, presentation in media,
    110–111

R

Race
    as defense strategy, 155

as factor in convictions, 54
    media crime coverage and, 101, 102
    trial outcomes and juror, 143
Radio coverage, 87
Ramsey, JonBenet, 100
Rape cases, 48, 59, 60, 63, 65, 136, 158
Rate data, 110–111
Reactance, 139
Reader's Digest, 31
Realist movement in law, 13–14, 15, 18, 139,
    143, 147–148
Regression approaches, 116
Relative salience, 100
Remedies for pretrial publicity effects, 18
    forging, 92–98
    interactions between, 10–11, 135, 137,
        151
    laboratory studies and, 9–10, 24, 28
    natural, 10, 29
    recommendations for, 150
    selecting, 138
    sentencing, 85
    see also Continuance; Cumulative
                remedy hypothesis; Defense
                strategies; Delays; Delibera-
                tion; Evidence; Jury instruc-
                tions; Voir dire
Reporters, law enforcement information re-
        sources and, 102, 103, 104, 112
Research
    design artifact, 62
    simulation, 73–74, *see also* Laboratory
                studies
Resonance, 111
Resource equity, access to legal services and,
        11–12, 15–16, 17, 148–149
Responsibility frame, 106
Retrial, 34
Reverse halo effect, 139
Robbery, 158
    bank, 78, 79, 83–84, 85, 86
Rorty, Richard, 15

S

Sacco-Vanzetti trial, 1
St. Louis, analysis of court cases in, 157–159
Sampling
    matched-case, 152
    sample selection, 78–79
    similarity, 23–24

theory, 23
San Francisco, analysis of court cases in,
        157–159
Science, 13
Scopes case, 1
Sealed sentences, 118
Seattle
    analysis of court cases in, 157–159
    relation between crime coverage and
                crime rate in, 115
Sensational publicity, 59, 65, 136, 141
Sentence length
    defendant socioeconomic status and,
                143–144
    fear of crime, pretrial publicity, and, 126
    pleaded sentence, 84, 86, 117–118,
                122–126, 162, 163
    pretrial publicity and, 76–77, 78, 81–83,
                85, 86
    tried sentence, 118, 128–131, 162, 163
    type of crime and, 83–84, 85
Sentences/sentencing, 151, 152
    death, 117, 132
    life, 117–118, 132
    remedies and, 85
    sealed, 118
Sequestered jury, 9
Sequestered voir dire, 138
Sexual harassment cases, 145
Shapiro, Robert, 104–105, 113
Shaver, Doug, 147
Sheppard v. Maxwell, 2, 5, 19, 75
Simpson (O. J.) trial, 2, 11, 38
Simulation research, 73–74, *see also* Labora-
                tory studies
Sixth Amendment, 4
Social context, pretrial publicity and, 22
Social science
    on defendant socioeconomic status, 143
    legal doctrine and, 6–7
    on pretrial publicity, 2, 7–12
    as theoretical base, 13
    treatment in law reviews, 14–15
Socioeconomic status, defendant, 143–148
Source discounting, 110
Spearman's rho rank-order correlation, 114,
        115, 160
Speck, Richard, 11
Statistical deviance, 101
Status, trial outcomes and juror, 143
Status deviance, 101, 102

Story placement, 30
Structural paradox hypothesis, 17, 138, 148–149
Student samples, 23–25
Subliminal perception, 140–142, 154
Supraliminal perception, 140–141, 143, 154
"Suspicion" condition, 54, 55

T

Television
    cultivation theory and, 108–109
    markets, 105
Television news, 87, 88
    local, 114
    national, 105
    racial attitudes and crime coverage,
        102–103
Theoretical orientation, 12–16, 138–139
Third-person effect, 31
Time interactions, significance of, 161–162
Toulmin-type system, 153
Trial(s), 151
    civil, 45–46
    conviction rate and length of, 37–38
    evidence, see Evidence
    fairness of, 85, 138
    judge, 118
    jury, 118
    media, 75, 92
    method, 118
    murder, 76–77, 78
    pretrial publicity and complexity of, 37–38
    pretrial publicity effect and type of, 90
    stages of, 131–132
    strategies, 155, see also Defense strategies
Trial outcomes
    amount of pretrial publicity and, 92
    deliberation and, 58
    evidence and, 25, 26, 35–37, 38, 43, 47,
        52–53, 57, 58
    Federal Judicial Center data on, 114
    knowledge-guilt hypothesis and, 16–17
    pretrial publicity and, 3, 8, 17, 81–83, 85,
        86, 126–128, 134–136
    socioeconomic status of defendant and,
        143–148
    types of, 82

variables in, 108
    see also Conviction rates; Verdicts
Tried sentence length, 118, 128–131
Type I error, 78, 151

U

Uncle Six experiment, 27, 106, 140
Unconscious messages, effect of, 139–142, 154
U.S. Supreme Court, Gideon v. Wainwright,
    147; Sheppard v. Maxwell, 2
Univariate ANOVA, 162

V

Variables, dependent, 151–152
    selecting, 116–117
Verdicts, 152
    individual, 54, 59
    predeliberation, 62
    pretrial publicity effect on, 81–82, 85, 86
    see also Conviction rates; Trial outcomes
Violent crime, fear of, 114, 117, 158–159,
    160–164
Violent offenders, 144
Voir dire
    individual, 14, 95, 138
    quiz for, 17, 96, 138
    as remedy for pretrial publicity, 8, 10,
        17, 35, 42–43, 49, 57, 93–96,
        111, 137, 138, 150
    sequestered, 138

W

Webster, John W., 1
White-collar crime, coverage of, 102–103
Wilson, Gregory, 146–147
Women
    interpretation of quantitative data, 111
    news coverage as victims of crime, 111
    see also Gender

Z

z-score tests, 153